PRAISE FOR
THE POWER OF VISION

"Insightful, engaging, and well-developed, The Power of Vision offers readers practical advice for making their lives and work extraordinary." -**WestBow Press Editorial**

"This eager treatise challenges readers to develop ambitious personal visions not just for personal gain but for the advancement of humanity." -**BookLife Review by Publishers Weekly**

"This book does not only tell you what a vision is and how to fulfil it but it carefully guides you through fulfilling it. It communicates high-level concepts in down-to-earth terms that anyone could follow."
-**Dr. Edem Ernest Edifor**, Metropolitan University, UK

"This is a well-written assessment of how to harness the power of vision to live an impactful, authentic life." -**Joseph Petrie,** Joseph Petrie Editorial Services

"Using empirical evidence drawn from historic data to demonstrate how clearly, extraordinary human beings (including leaders and inventors) have impacted the world is another interesting feature in the book." -**Mondiu Jaiyesimi,** Senior Consultant and AML and Forensics Expert

"The book provides motivation for readers to fulfill their God-given potential." -**Dr. Everod Edwards**, Rural and Suburban Mail Carrier, Canada Post

"This is a book to read, own, and share with everyone in and around our network. I don't think there's anyone who wouldn't benefit from reading this book." -**Ayodeji Aderibigbe**, PhD Candidate, Purdue University, USA

"You cannot but read The Power of Vision. It will take you from where you are to where you ought to be. It will take you from living a mediocre live to living an extraordinary life. It will cause you to journey from a meaningless existence to a life of worth and value.

This book will transform your life." -**Dr Samuel Ekundayo**, *The Purpose Preacher, Auckland, New Zealand*

"The writer of this book is on to something powerful. These words of wisdom challenges us not to succumb to mediocrity, and that we are more than ordinary, because we are extraordinary being. Loving the fact also that this book not only speaks to the young, but it speaks to everyone. The Power of Vison encourages, inspires, raises one's spirit and it is practical and realistic. It gets the attention that keeps you reading and wanting more. Thank you for this unselfish journey of revelation and hard work that will move people to achieve greatness. Thank you for the passion to see others move from ordinary to extraordinary." - ***Janet Williams-Edwards,*** *Revivaltime Tabernacle, Canada*

THE POWER
—— OF ——
VISION

PRINCIPLES AND PRACTICES TO HELP
YOU BECOME EXTRAORDINARY

OLUWASEUN OYENIRAN

THE POWER OF VISION
Copyright © 2020 Oluwaseun Oyeniran

All rights reserved. No part of this book may be used or reproduced by any means, graphic, electronic, or mechanical, including photocopying, recording, taping or by any information storage retrieval system without the written permission of the author except in the case of brief quotations embodied in critical articles and reviews. For details, write copyrights@oyeseducation.org

OyES Education titles may be purchased in bulk for educational, business, fundraising, or sales promotional use. For information, please email sales@oyeseducation.org.

ISBN 978-1-7774602-3-5 (hardcover)
ISBN 978-1-7774602-1-1 (paperback)
ISBN 978-1-7774602-2-8 (ebook)
ISBN 978-1-7774602-5-9 (Audiobook)

While the author has made every effort to provide accurate internet address at the time of publication, because of the dynamic nature of the internet, web addresses or links contained in this book may have changed since and may no longer be valid. The publisher and author does not have any control over and does not assume any responsibility for author or third-party websites or their content.

Cover Design: alphaplusdesigns.com
Interior Image and illustrations: © Oluwaseun Oyeniran
(unless otherwise stated)

To everyday people who recognize
that seeds of greatness reside within them

CONTENTS

Preface   IX

PART 1 - The Journey From Ordinary to Extraordinary   1

1 Vision: the distinguishing factor   2
2 Legends   15
3 The Process   19
4 Timeless Principles and Practices   28
5 Extraordinary Lives Backed by over a Hundred Years of Empirical Evidence   33

PART 2 - Private Labours   41

6 Principles of Personal Purpose and Passion   42
7 You Too Can Become Extraordinary   47
8 Vision Simplifies Your Life   53
9 Defining Vision   56
10 The Power of Paradigms   70
11 Disciplined Thoughts   81
12 The Core Is Grounded in Science   94
13 Dream Big; Have Big Hairy Audacious Goals (BHAGs)   106
14 Vision, Gifts, Talents, and Potential   122
15 The Three Circles of Extraordinary Individuals   140

PART 3 - Public Manifestations   150

16 Principles of Personal Management and Sustainable Growth   151
17 A Culture of Discipline   157
18 From Growth to Build-Up to Breakthrough to Extraordinary Life   168
19 Re-Vision   177

PART 4 - Practices of Vision That Make Ordinary Individuals Become Extraordinary [PRAXIS]   179

20 Plan and Take Action   180
21 Understanding the concept of time   185
22 Persistence and passion   187
23 The Genius of the "AND" versus the Tyranny of the "OR"   189

24 Character over Charisma	194
25 Triumphing despite Naysayers and Negative External Forces	201
26 Anticipate and Enjoy the Provision of Vision: Pro-Vision	204
27 Be, Do, Have	209
28 Level 7 Leadership	212
29 Corporate Vision and Corporate Destiny	224
30 A Note to Developing Economies	231

Appendices, Endnotes & Index — 236

Appendix 1: Summary of Research Findings	237
Appendix 2: Composite 3D and Phasal Nature of VisioN	242
Appendix 3: The Upward Spiral: Evolution of the Vision Flywheel	243
EndNotes	246
Index	259

PREFACE

Every single person on earth was born to be great. Each life was born to impact this world, with a unique purpose as distinct as each strand of DNA. Every individual, by design, was furnished with everything required to not only succeed but to multiply, to leave lasting legacies that will last for generations, centuries, and forever. Sadly, many live miserable lives without purpose, meaning, or impact. Overwhelmed by the challenges of survival, many succumb to mediocrity and just barely make it through each day.

But there are a few rare outliers. Very few people in history have made the league of people we can call extraordinary. Both in times past and present, there are limited number of men and women we'd term legends. In life, business, or ministry, their uncommon greatness is what everyone generally alludes to. They push the human race forward. And while some may see them as crazy, we see them as geniuses, because the people who are crazy enough to think they can change the world are the ones who actually do. They are the ones regarded as geniuses; their influences are transgenerational. It's obvious they did more than just set a goal; they achieved it. They were inspired and motivated to reach beyond what their physical eyes could see. The obstacles and challenges they faced became fuel for their creativity. Their wisdom exceeded whatever formal education or schooling they had. Their impact reached beyond their innate intellect, courage, and physical strength.

The simple question that inspired this book was, how do men and women become extraordinary in life? It is a befitting question because an extraordinary life requires more than mere success. Many people are successful today, but deep within, they know something is still missing. An extraordinary life is the one that is not only successful but significant. People who live extraordinary lives have an enduring legacy, so much so that years after they pass away, their impact and purpose continues.

The question of how ordinary people like you (and myself) can become extraordinary led me to over six years of research and findings. Applying a qualitative research methodology on secondary data, including review of biographies, articles, publications, speeches, and audiovisual recordings with data spanning over a hundred years, I was able to find the answer. The answer is vision.

Vision, a mental big picture of the future, propelled these men and women from mediocrity to superiority. It stirred them up from hopelessness to greatness. I became convinced that what distinguishes ordinary individuals from the extraordinary ones is the quality and clarity of their vision. People powered by vision are able to operate with a big-picture mindset that not only set a desired future in their hearts but also informed their daily actions towards creating that future.

Through this research, I was able to identify the process, principles, and practices of vision. Anyone—old, young, male or female—who carefully follows this process has a higher chance of becoming truly significant in life. These groundbreaking findings present what has often been seen as a complex subject in simple concepts and a framework that can be understood and applied by anyone. This book proves over and over that what our modern world prescribes to help you become great only leads to a loop of complexity, confusion, and doom. I found that people are not lazy; people dream about greatness, but they never fully reach the fulfilment of their dreams because they lack an understanding of the process, principles, and practices of vision.

The process of vision is like a flywheel that starts with the power of disciplined thoughts. Disciplined thoughts produce disciplined individuals. And disciplined individuals ultimately produce disciplined actions, or what I call extraordinary outcomes. It is disciplined thoughts and a focus mindset that results in specialisation and excellence that ordinary people only admire but never aspire to. Along with the process are various principles and practices of vision. The principles of vision include purpose, growth, personal management, focus, and passion. And the practices of vision include planning, perseverance, re-visions, discipline, build-up, break-through, and strength of character, all of which consolidates into a unique mix. As with any life-altering event, it all starts from the inside. In private, paradigmatic shifts ultimately bring about public manifestations. In the end, people who operate with vision create a desired future because their sense of true self informed a strong core belief system, which eventually allowed them to embrace change and stimulate sustainable progress.

I am excited for how this book will transform your life; it will do so counterintuitively, by not making you do anything more than you are doing (the growth industry includes hacks who bombard and overwhelm us with too many clichés and ideas that are not found on enduring principles. Indeed, you will find that all you need is first and foremost not an action but a shift in perspective: the ability to see with your mind's eye. Welcome to the realms of visionaries.

Oluwaseun Oyeniran
December 1, 2020

THE POWER
— OF —
VISION

PRINCIPLES AND PRACTICES TO HELP
YOU BECOME EXTRAORDINARY

PART 1

THE JOURNEY FROM ORDINARY TO EXTRAORDINARY

The journey to greatness starts with a mental process of seeing the big picture of what you could become as against what you have been or what you are right now. That mental process does not first and foremost require an action but a change in perception, a paradigm shift, the ability to *see* with your mind's eye. When you see a bigger, better picture, you can commit to a course and pathway in life that sets you apart for greatness. When you commit yourself to become more, you unlock certain unique gifts that have been strapped inside you. These various factors make your results more profound.

That mental process of seeing the big picture is called vision. And vision has a type of energy force field that propels you from mediocrity and stagnation into greatness. It is like a flywheel engine that is powered by disciplined thoughts. Disciplined thoughts produce disciplined individuals. And disciplined individuals ultimately produce disciplined actions and extraordinary outcomes.

Empirical evidence shows that what distinguishes ordinary individuals from the extraordinary ones is the quality and clarity of their vision.

Chapter 1
VISION: THE DISTINGUISHING FACTOR

Every single person on earth was born to be great. Each life was born to impact this world with a unique purpose, as distinct as their DNA. The beauty of human nature is such that all we require to not only succeed but to leave legacies that will last for centuries, generations, and forever, is already in us, like a seed. Despite possessing the seed of greatness, sadly, many live miserable lives without purpose, meaning, or impact. Overwhelmed by the challenges of survival, many succumb to mediocrity and just barely make it through each day.

But there are rare outliers. Our world has few people in life and history who made the league we can call extraordinary. Both in times past and present, there are limited number of men and women who we term as legends. In life, career, business, or ministry, people allude to their uncommon greatness. We are not only talking about greatness in terms of wealth or riches. We are talking about ordinary individuals who rose from obscurity to become uncommonly impactful and influential. Not just mere influence but trans-generational, long-lasting influence. They are the ones who push the human race forward and may be regarded at one point or another as crazy. Yet it is those who are crazy enough to think they can change the world who actually do change it.

> **Despite possessing the seed of greatness, sadly, many live miserable lives without purpose, meaning, or impact.**

These extraordinary individuals are regarded as geniuses. It is obvious they did more than just goal setting. They broke out of obscurity not by the usual external motivations. They appeared to have been inspired by something deep within them; something beyond what their physical eyes could see. Because of this unusual inspirational force, obstacles and challenges before them became fuel for their creativity and innovation. They became legends, wiser than whatever formal education or schooling they had. They had resounding impacts

– one that exceeded their innate intellect, courage, and physical strength.

Studying the greatness of these rare individuals made me acknowledge that it is possible for ordinary people to become extraordinary. So the question that followed was "how can ordinary people like myself and you become extraordinary?" The deeper thought was: "how do men and women become truly great in life?" It took me over six years extrapolating data as I looked through historical records and biography of people whose life depicted greatness. I looked back to over hundred years (for example Henry Ford's who was born in 1863). Data collection included articles, inaugural speeches, biographical report, almanacs and many other secondary sources. I subject extrapolated data to qualitative scientific research analysis. Then I finally found the answer to be vision.

> They are the ones that push the human race forward and have been regarded at one point or the other in their lives as crazy. Yet it is those who are crazy enough to think they can change the world that actually do change it.

I became quite convinced that what distinguishes ordinary individuals from the extraordinary ones is the quality and clarity of their vision. People powered by vision not only operate with a big-picture mindset that helps them create a desired future but their daily actions are purposeful, intentional, authentic, and remarkable. This is so because vision involves a mental, private process of deep, resolute convictions that results in public manifestations: progressive, extraordinary impacts, inspired by big dreams. The force of vision produces disciplined thoughts and a focus mindset that result in an excellence that ordinary people only admire but never aspire to. Extraordinary individuals applied the principles and practices of vision: passion, purpose, patience, persistence, perseverance, pro-vision, planning, re-visions, focus, discipline, build-up, breakthrough, and strength of character, which consolidate into a unique mix.

This book is not about myself; it is about a systematic study of enduring greatness. I must admit that I didn't invent the principles I share in this book, either. They have all been out there in the open, from long ago. It just so happens that my gift is in the area of finding things out. My passion for empirical truth, data, and finding missing links produced this work. As such, I am only presenting what I have found in over hundred years of historical records and scientific research. I believe strongly that if anyone follows the process this book carefully lays out, applying the principles and practicing the concepts, he or she can become extraordinary in life. This book is an attempt to decompose a relatively complex subject into simple and easy to understand concepts and frameworks. By so doing, this book presents enduring principles and practices that demystifies popular ideas in our world today; ideas that claim to make us more productive but are only making us more overwhelmed and confused. I am excited for how this book will counterintuitively transform your life by not making you do anything more than you are already doing. The growth hack industry is already getting many bombarded and overwhelmed with too many clichés and ideas that are not found on enduring principles. Indeed, you will find, as I discovered through research, that all you need is first and foremost not an action but a shift in perspective, a paradigm shift and the ability to see with your mind's eye.

> ...what distinguishes ordinary individuals from the extraordinary ones is the quality and clarity of their vision.

In a world filled with social images, consciousness techniques, quick fixes, and social Band-Aids that address acute problems (and sometimes even appear to solve them temporarily, but leave underlying chronic problems untouched to fester and resurface), it's a relief to find that we can achieve enduring greatness as an intricate component of our lives through integrity, humility, fidelity, temperance, courage, justice, patience, industry, simplicity, modesty, and the Golden Rule. This book is based on a journey to integrate life principles deep within—so that you can experience long-term significance and enduring greatness, as against the alternative: mere successes that are only short-lived.

A Personal Journey to Live a Life of Significance over Mere Success

I have four purposes in writing this book. First, it was out of a personal quest to find a way to live in the reality of my own purpose and reach the fullness of my potential. Like you, I too have pondered what I want my life to look like while I'm here and am also curious as to what legacy I will leave behind. But things have not always been that clear to me. On Wednesday, December 9, 2009, not knowing what exactly to make out of my life, I wrote the following lines in my journal while taking a personal reflection break as a student on the school farm:

Although I may not know tomorrow, I have hope that what is in me is greater and I will get illumination and clarity. I know I am born for more. What is behind me and what I see in front of me today cannot be compared to what is inside of me. I have a great destiny. I take courage that I am gifted and endowed and my purpose will shine forth as my gift brings me among great men.

What I wrote were just reflections of my heart. Life was difficult at that point. What I was experiencing at that point in my life is what has been referred to as "living in the culturescape."[1] I was basically allowing certain debilitating invisible, unwritten rules, beliefs and practices pre-imposed by culture and society saturate my life. Events leading up to that time in my life were not the greatest, just as that moment in my life wasn't the best. I struggled to gain admission into the university, and in 2004, when I eventually got in, I was offered a course I didn't primarily apply for.[2] It was like my destiny and purpose had been crushed. I spent the entire five years of school trying to sort my life out. Should I withdraw from school and start all over again? Should I surrender to fate? That year, 2009, was my final year in the university, and yet I had not figured out what life held for an ordinary Nigerian boy who lost his father eight years earlier. Although my home country returned back to democracy in the late 1990s, the impact of many years of military rule lingered. There was still a huge risk in the polity based on rising corruption among public officials, ethnic clashes, and insecurity. In short, there was little to no hope for me at that time. And I believe that situation is relatable to many of you reading this today.

Because there wasn't much to look forward to outside, I had to start looking within. Over the years, as I extensively studied the lives of extraordinary people, I came to the conclusion that despite all odds, I have what it takes to become truly great in life. I have always desired in my heart to do extraordinary things: impact other people's life positively, bring hope to many, and so on. I realised quickly, though, that becoming extraordinary precedes doing extraordinary things. Being preceded "Doing" and "Having" (Be, Do, Have). I realise that to have remarkable outcomes in my life, there had to be an identification of my true self (who I really am, deep down), my purpose, and the excellence of my gift. To record consistently great accomplishments requires not merely copying the lifestyles of extraordinary people but also understanding the enduring principles and practices that guide their lives and applying such to develop my own unique gifts.

So this project quickly became a knowledge exploration and academic adventure to probe into the minds, core operations, and intrinsic qualities of truly great people. Indeed, the power of vision was what I found to reside at the core of every great person. I hope you will find true purpose and meaning in life, just as I have, and that you will discover what you are born to do and thereby commit yourself to pursuing it with excellence.

> **I hope you will find true purpose and meaning in life, just as I have, and that you will discover what you are born to do and thereby commit yourself to pursuing it with excellence.**

The second inspiration for this book is to essentially help people break out of a cycle of mediocrity and poverty of the mind. During my research, I realised that being poor isn't just an inconvenience. It's a huge factor in how our lives—and our children's lives—turn out. It's like breathing in bad air; the more you're exposed to it, the more it hurts you. And this was what I found after carefully reviewing the US Department of Housing and Urban Development's Moving to Opportunity (MTO) experiment between 1994 and 1998.

With the objective of ending poverty, the MTO experiment was implemented by the government to determine whether providing low-income families with assistance by moving them to better neighbourhoods could improve their economic and health outcomes. As a result, approximately forty-six hundred families living in high-poverty public housing projects were randomly selected with opportunities to break out of poverty. The result? There was no impact of the MTO treatments on the earnings of adults and older youth.[3] This led researchers to an important conclusion that moving to new environments with an old mindset will not produce economic success. In particular, by looking at where kids grew up and where the kids' mothers grew up, MTO researchers were further able to identify roots of poverty.[4]

Evidence shows that a mother can mitigate effects of growing up in a poor neighbourhood. But if the mother also grew up in poverty, then she was also exposed to distress and trauma, and children whose mothers grew up in poverty perform below average on the IQ test. These findings show that you can move from a poor to a rich environment, but if you still have a poverty mentality, you'll remain poor and pass that poverty on to your children. In addition, adverse childhood experiences—like abuse, family dysfunction, violence, and neglect—can have long-term health effects, both physical and mental.[5]

Poverty is not a function of lack of opportunity; it primarily comes from not understanding one's life vision and purpose and misunderstanding the gifts, talents, and potential to fulfil that vision purpose. Once mentally locked in poverty, a problem arises where most people have no vision beyond their current reality. Discouraging situations passed on from birth can block one's mind's eye, resulting in loss of visions, dreams, and aspirations. Many people today are overwhelmed by life's challenges which causes them not to make progress or to live a life of significance.

I felt the urgent need to write this book in order to help people break out of their mental incarceration. I was encouraged to write a book to help people create a bigger plan for their lives, identify what gifts they carry, and ultimately break out of whatever poverty they are living in and that has been passed on to them from previous generations. The power of vision can help break generational curses. The power of vision creates a force that propels you out of obscurity and mediocrity into your greatness.

> **Poverty is not a function of lack of opportunity. Poverty primarily comes due to lack of understanding of one's life vision and purpose and a misunderstanding of the gifts, talents, and potential to fulfil that vision and purpose.**

The third push for this book came from a Business Insider September 8, 2018 report written by Thomas C. Corley. After spending five years studying hundreds of millionaires (including interviewing 233 wealthy individuals and 177 self-made millionaires)[6] and 128 poor individuals, Thomas, author of *Rich Habits: The Daily Success Habits of Wealthy Individuals*, found that there were three predominant paths rich people pursued in order to accumulate their wealth namely: "saver-investors," "virtuosos," and "dreamers." Thomas's study concluded that the dreamers were by far the wealthiest group. He found that dreamers pursued some big dream and were able to turn that dream into a reality. Their dreams eventually provided them with an enormous amount of income, profit, or gain, and they accumulated an average of $7.4 million in about twelve years. While my aim for this book is not only about money (as it appears great people featured on Nobel Peace Prize list than on Forbes list of the wealthy), evidence suggests that being vision oriented does truly pay. That's why getting your own unique vision should become a top priority. True, the discussion of wealth is important. What's more important, though, is how you too can capture your own dream and bring it to reality, together with all the benefits that it offers beyond material riches.

> True, the discussion of wealth is important. What's more important, though, is how you too can capture your own dream and bring it to reality, together with all the benefits that it offers beyond material riches.

The fourth and perhaps more pressing purpose for this book about the power of vision is that we are in a global health and economic crisis. This book will allow people pursue their vision as the world recovers from COVID-19. No other time is more appropriate to inspire us to dream again and become better. Everyday people can be reinvigorated back to life out of a global pandemic by the power of vision.

Overcoming Crises by the Power of Vision

As I write this in April 2020, we are in the middle of COVID-19, the novel Coronavirus outbreak. In human history, this is by far one of the most tragic health outbreaks. I am not exaggerating. Take a look at the numbers: as of April 16, 2020, the number of confirmed infected people was more than 2 million, with 135,662 deaths recorded in the United States. On April 14, 2020, the United States witnessed the highest single-day death toll of 2,129.[7] These are indeed unprecedented times.

The Coronavirus pandemic is clearly having a major social impact, marked by mass unemployment, separation of families, isolation, social distancing, and various other changes in how we live. Major psychological risks such as anxiety, depression, and self-harm are expected to increase. The global crisis has caused the world economy to crumble. Although cash flow concerns are high, what is more alarming is the productivity slump that has hit businesses, causing long-term impacts. According to a recent study, almost three in five (57%) leaders globally cited the negative impact on productivity as a top concern amidst the crisis.[8]

The coronavirus pandemic has brought great challenges to humanity, if not the greatest challenge of all time. It has caused problems in our personal lives, our families, our organisations, and all nations. These problems are not only of a new order of magnitude, they are altogether different.

While most are looking forward to the end of the crisis, many people have nothing to look forward to, as the pandemic appears to have carried away everything they had, including family, property, and money. Already at the brink of collapse, many are worried about their circumstances and what will become of their lives, finances, and future. Fear creeps in. People begin to doubt their potential and capabilities. As a result, they begin to experience emotional, mental, and physical exhaustion. The despair is palpable, and the mental struggle becomes real.

Worry follows, which depletes constructive emotions and has a sneaky way of stopping short of giving you all the facts. Fear and worry are trickery of mentally filtered negative facts, and they make bold declarations that tricks are facts. But facts are not the same as truth. Quite frankly, if you contemplate the total sum of recent pains and suffering long enough, it can drive you mad. But truth still prevails, and you can still thrive in spite of all that has happened. I want to reassure you; you will make it. In the course of my research, over and over again, I have seen how vision was the key that liberated many souls from the minefields of worry and disaster, out into the clear air of mental sunshine. In the face of a great pandemic or some other crisis confronting you, your vision can become your only source of hope because it holds the key to the future.

> **Worry...depletes constructive emotions and has a sneaky way of stopping short of giving you all the facts.**

The end of this crisis will definitely come; difficult situations such as this don't last forever. But few people are preparing for the new beginning that will emerge. The end of a crisis is the opportunity to begin again, to dream bigger, to do better, and to lead your life in a direction that creates deeper meaning not only for yourself but also for others around you.

Humans are endowed with the gift of creative visualisation and imagination, a unique ability to see things not only as they are but also how they should be. We have a special ability to use faith to evolve our facts and to establish new realities for ourselves. And this book will help you do just that as you read along.

The year 2020 has left an indelible impact on humanity. Whenever this book is being read, a recollection of 2020 draws on the pains of a global health crisis and a pandemic that has wreaked havoc on us. But it has also witnessed the best of humanity, as people rise in support of one another. As people recall terrible moments in history, we need to come into the full awareness of the residual effects of pandemic and position ourselves to be instruments of hope. In this time of long-range uncertainty, we must learn to dream again. We must face the facts of the day with unwavering faith and belief in our vision of a better future. Confronting facts with resolute faith and action can be a great combination for personal, professional, institutional and national progress. It's time to build ourselves individually and regain our confidence because the bedrock of economic and mental health is self-development. And at the core of any self-development effort is a mental big picture of a better future that surpasses the current reality.

Dreaming and beginning again requires the courage to start more intelligently and to use our gifts and talents innovatively to achieve better results. It is time to gain momentum and move forward towards destiny, with passion and power. Human beings have always figured out how to make things work. The lives of extraordinary people are marked with numerous challenges; as they overcame them, they kick-started a new era of innovation. Indeed, their triumph over difficult times transitioned them into greatness. Despite the growing challenges around them, great men and women developed the courage to participate in grand endeavours that changed the course of history. They brought new zeal to problems, and with daily hard work and the right attitude, they produced a better reality.

Vision Powered Them Out of Their Crises

Although it may not be perfectly comparable to a tsunami or a global pandemic, World War II wreaked major havoc on Japan between 1939 and 1945. The Japanese escalated the war in 1941 with a raid on the US naval base at Pearl Harbor. Japan eventually lost the war after a series of American aerial raids, including the only time an atomic bomb was used, on the Japanese cities of Hiroshima and Nagasaki. By the end of the war in 1945, hundreds of thousands of people had died, devastation disrupted millions of lives, and the country's economy collapsed.

In that same 1945, Masaru Ibuka did not have a specific idea of exactly what he wanted to do, other than a vague intention to create consumer products by applying technological advances. He went on to build what we know today as Sony out of the ruins of a defeated and devastated postwar Japan. Ibuka rented an abandoned telephone operator's room in the hollow remnants of a bombed-out old department store in downtown Tokyo. With seven employees and sixteen hundred dollars of personal savings, he began working. Ibuka's product development struggled, with a failed rice cooker and a failed tape recorder; he managed to stay alive selling crude heating pads and then a hodgepodge of products on contract for Japan Broadcasting Corp., such as voltmeters and studio control consoles. Then in 1955, the first hit, the breakthrough, a pocket radio developed with transistors.

> **Dreaming and beginning again requires the courage to start more intelligently and to use our gifts and talents innovatively to achieve better results.**

Long before the 1955 pocket radio hit, on May 7, 1946, shortly after moving to Tokyo, Ibuka created a prospectus where he documented the vision for his company; it included the following:[9]

> *If it were possible to establish conditions where persons could become united with a firm spirit of teamwork and exercise to their heart's desire their technological capacity ... then such an organisation could bring untold pleasure and tremendous results, regardless of the meagerness of its facilities or the limited number of employees. The end of the war brought us closer to realize this dream.*

To many, the pandemic and indeed year 2020 appear like a solitary confinement – we can't move or do all we desire to. Who was locked up for so long and still achieved great things in life? Nelson Mandela. He was imprisoned for twenty-seven years. In confinement in a dark room no bigger than a closet, his inner light bulb came on. It was in prison that his approach towards the struggle changed. Mandela who had initially favored armed struggle envisioned a more inclusive South Africa not divided by race or colour. It was in the dark moments of prison that he realised the armed struggle was not going to work, but a nonviolent approach would be more sustainable – even though the rest of his comrades would not favor his change of approach. After Mandela was finally released in 1994, rather than relieve the pains of prison time, his first speech about the future gave hope. He didn't seek revenge; rather, he sought reconciliation of all factions in South Africa. He preached peace, democracy, and freedom that both whites (who until then branded him as a terrorist) and blacks (who felt marginalised) started to believe in one South Africa.

The story of Joseph in the Old Testament is a popular one familiar to many. He held on to his dream despite being thrown into the pit, prison and Potiphar's house until he made it to the palace. Despite the challenges and obstacles he faced, Joseph continue to turn adversity to advantage working hard and refining his gifts until the golden opportunity came before the king. He knew all along that his breakthrough, the full manifestation and accomplishment of his vision would benefit many including those who hated him and sold him to slavery.

At one point in the course of my research for this book I couldn't stop but wonder how despite the huge challenges and obstacles these great men and women faced, they not only prevailed, they pioneered a new era. Could it be that an extraordinary life is marked by the ability to overcome challenges and difficulties? Could it therefore mean that the crises you are facing right now, if properly handled, can be a defining moment for yourself and potentially your generation and the entire human race?

In the face of crisis, in dark and precarious times, you can rise again, being propelled by your visions and dreams. As long as you can hold on to your vision, you have a higher probability of breaking out of obscurity and overcoming dejection. Crisis and difficult situations cause some people to break down, others to break through. Today, the call is on us to kick-start a new season of innovation and creativity. Embrace the new opportunities on the horizon.

It is a golden opportunity for us to start this new era together and

> Crisis and difficult situations cause some people to break down, others to break through.

to navigate towards our inner potential, as we create a new, innovative path. We must not waste it. It is time for us to build not just mere success but significance and legacy.

There is no better time to present a book that will give people an expectation of something more than current realities. In your hand is a tool to help you break out of whatever loss of hope and life you are experiencing.

The ability to live in the reality of your true vision is not just fantasy; it is indeed real life. For true visionaries, their dreamland is their real land. A powerful vision can help you create a desired destiny as well as propel you out of whatever physical or mental doldrums you're in. This is because vision opens your mind's eye to an exciting future ahead of you.

With the enlightenment that vision provides, you can foresee your glorious destiny. Starting with paradigmatic shifts, vision appropriately empowers you to take actions that will first and foremost align you with your purpose and eventually bring you into greatness by unravelling your gift or potential. Living in harmony with the principles and practices of vision brings focus, discipline, and strength of character, which are critical prerequisites for anyone who wants to thrive today. To revive your businesses, rekindle your passion, create new products and services, and keep moving forward requires an internal consistency that only comes when you live your unique purpose, powered by a distinct vision.

> The ability to live in the reality of your true vision is not just fantasy; it is indeed real life.

****

The power of vision transforms ordinary individuals into extraordinary ones, causing them to live beyond mere success towards significance and life-surpassing legacies. The power of vision helps you gain focus on what matters in life, even as it strengthens your certainty in the ability to make decisions confidently and quickly. The reason is because vision gives you values and principles that guide your life. The force of vision provides strength of character, the ability to live out your convictions, no matter what the crowd is doing. When you have strength of character, you can be gentle and humble because you can organise your thoughts and present them in a focused and consistent way. This book is relevant in our modern times due to the numerous alternative predispositions that can sway us from our true life's purpose. Never before in the history of humanity have there been so many distractions. The sad part is that many people who are honestly searching for true meaning in life have been snared in the "success hack" industry – the idea of cutting success journey short in a rather rough way, often without long-term aim or consideration for enduring greatness.

> **To revive your businesses, rekindle your passion, create new products and services, and keep moving forward requires an internal consistency that only comes when you live your unique purpose, powered by a distinct vision.**

Chapter 2
LEGENDS

Extraordinary individuals are in a different league of their own. Whether in times past or present, there is a limited number of men and women whose accomplishments and life influence put them in the category of people we term as legends. Whether in life, business, or ministry, they have an uncommon greatness.

I researched these legendary individuals while writing this book, and through data gathered on their lives, it was discovered that they not only had a distinct vision that powered them forward but they also had processes, principles, and practices that helped them accomplish great things. I highlight this process in Chapter 3, previewed the principles and practices in Chapter 4 and gave a brief overview of the legends in this book[10] in Chapter 5.

For example, if you hear the name Martin Luther King Jr., you know exactly who it is—the American civil rights activist whose oratory gifts still tingle the ear today.

If someone mentions Mother Teresa, what instantly comes to your mind is a person of charitable, selfless work who committed her life to helping poor people living in slums. She was a nun for most of her life, and she committed herself to a calling that many did not understand; she had the prospect of wealth yet chose to live like the poor people she devoted her life to serve.

What about Henry Ford? He's the American industrialist of the 20th century who revolutionised the automobile industry with the Model T. The transition from an agrarian to an industrial era can be attributed to Ford.

What about Masaru Ibuka? He's the man mentioned earlier, who started Sony in Japan in 1946, right after his country suffered a devastating defeat in World War II. He turned the company into Asia's best-known company and a symbol of Japan's economic and technical power.

Who doesn't know about Helen Keller? After being diagnosed with an unknown disease in 1882, Helen lost both her sight and hearing at nineteen months. With her world turned dark and having to endure unending silence, she became restive. With time and help, her inner eye began to open. She became a perfect model of what it means to live without physical sight but with vision. Helen learned how to communicate via sign language, and she could read and write in Braille, but she also became the first deaf/blind person to earn a bachelor's degree. By the time of her death in 1968, she had founded multiple organisations, written many books, gave lectures around the world, and won an Academy Award.

Joseph was an Old Testament character who at age seventeen was thrown into a pit and sold into slavery in Egypt, where he served Potiphar, Pharaoh's chief guard. He worked hard to earn Potiphar's trust and respect. Not willing to compromise his integrity, he was blackmailed and jailed for thirteen years. Again, working from who he truly was at the core—a man of integrity—he was soon released from prison and became the prime minister. The gift of translating dreams, which irritated his brothers so they sold him into slavery, was what eventually brought him before the king.

Nelson Mandela was locked in prison from 1962 to 1990[11] and eventually became South Africa's first black president. The same purpose that led him to prison was what set him free: the ideals of democracy and freedom for all. Mandela was widely regarded as an icon of social justice; he received more than 250 honors, including the Nobel Peace Prize. He is held in deep respect within South Africa, where he is referred to as the father of the nation.

Steve Jobs? You already know him. He was the cofounder of Apple computers, who created tools to amplify our creative and productive ability. He is the guru whose out-of-this-world thinking and marketing strategy made Apple one of the most valuable companies in the world. What was more fascinating was the fact that he did it in a highly competitive industry that already appeared saturated. He created a cult around the product simply because of his determination to amplify the human ability. Jobs ended up revolutionising at least six industries (personal computers, phones, animated movies, digital publishing, music, and tablet computing) by the time of his death on October 5, 2011.

Walt Disney was committed to making children happy. Using what he termed "Imagineering" (imagination and engineering),[12] he created animations, movies, cartoons, amusement parks, and resorts. Out of all nominees in the history of the Academy Awards, Disney won the most Oscars. He won twenty-six Oscars over the course of his career and was nominated a grand total of fifty-nine times, also a record. The interesting twist: Walt Disney was a below-average student and often fell asleep in class[13] underscoring one important message in this book that educational attainment or intelligent quotient (IQ) scores is not a requirement for greatness.

You can call them crazy, misfits, rebels, troublemakers, or round pegs in square holes, but they're the ones who see things differently. After reading about these people, you may imagine that they have a larger head or bigger body frame, but they are just ordinary people, like me and you. But they're not the type who are fond of rules, and they have no respect for the status quo. They challenge the norms, not because they are physically powerful. In fact, the opposite is the case because they are not in any way the mightiest or strongest. They are set apart by their capacity to act, their strength, and their ability to accomplish what they set out to do. You can quote them, disagree with them, glorify them, or vilify them, but the only thing you can't do is ignore them. They are world-changers. They propel humanity forward. And while some may see them as crazy, we see them as geniuses. The people who are crazy enough to think they can change the world are the ones who do.

I was on a quest to figure out how I, too, can serve my family, friends, community, and the world at large better, and my mind was drawn to these individuals. After six years of gathering qualitative data and research, I came to this conclusion: What distinguishes ordinary people from extraordinary ones is the power of their visions—the intrinsic quality and clarity of their visions.

> **They challenge the norms, not because they are physically powerful. In fact, the opposite is the case because they are not in any way the mightiest or strongest.**

You can call them visionaries or dreamers; they're the ones whose level of self-awareness, imagination, creative visualisation, and consciousness projects them into new frontiers. You can call what powered them visions or dreams, because visions and dreams are functionally the same. The only difference is that a dream is essentially a vision that continued to exist past the lifetime of the visionary (i.e., the final destination in the mind of the visionary includes many coming generations). Dr. Martin Luther King Jr.'s "I Have a Dream" speech is a model of distinguishing between visions and dreams. He was able to see the vision (or dream in this case), but the fullness of its manifestation occurred after he was assassinated.

In practice, visions and dreams are the same. Over the course of this book, I will use them interchangeably. Visions and dreams are distinct conceptualisations of the future inspired in your mind. They also come with a force or power that can propel you to uncommon, sustained greatness. And in the course of my research, I found that this intrinsic staying power made ordinary people truly legendary.

These individuals are extraordinary in the sense that they transformed our world and made an impact on the hearts of many. Their influences are transgenerational. It is obvious they did more than just set a goal. They were inspired and motivated to reach beyond what their physical eyes could see. The obstacles and challenges they faced became fuel for their creativity. Their wisdom was based on a specialised knowledge, and they knew more than what any school system could have taught them. Their impact reached beyond their innate intellect, courage, and physical strength.

Evidence shows that while having vision is a prime quality of extraordinary individuals, being able to dream and have visions is inherent in every human on earth. As you will find in the subsequent chapters, you don't need to have any special skills or personality attributes to become extraordinary. You don't have to do anything special or possess any special abilities. The technology we all rely on doesn't make us become extraordinary, either. You don't need any formal training or education. But one thing you need to understand is that an extraordinary life is not arrived at suddenly. Extraordinary individuals didn't just arrive at greatness overnight. Each of them followed a process.

> **Visions and dreams are distinct conceptualisations of the future inspired in your mind. They also come with a force or power that can propel you to uncommon, sustained greatness.**

Chapter 3
THE PROCESS

As I examined the lives of extraordinary individuals, I found that they took actions in situations where other people remained cerebral. They developed a rare intuitive ability coupled with a level of personal proactivity that allowed them to cause remarkable change. But their actions were not just ordinary actions; their actions yielded extraordinary accomplishments because they followed a specific process that transformed their lives.

The first event at the beginning of their journey to greatness (what I now call Vision Flywheel) was a paradigm shift. This paradigm shift begins to turn the flywheel of greatness. Paradigm shifts cause people to have a deep conviction about an event, situation, or cause. One character quality found consistently among extraordinary individuals was that they took actions that were backed by great convictions and deep beliefs. This overwhelming conviction compelled them to do the right thing; they knew they themselves were the answers. These paradigmatic shifts, which occur in the mind, can help you realign your life towards a more purposeful direction.

Extraordinary individuals, grounded in deep convictions, have a sense of personal purpose that emanated out of a clear understanding of who they truly are. Their lifestyle contradicted fads, trends, norms, and in some cases the physical law guiding the environment they operated in. Paradigm shifts and the consequent strengthening of one's core values and beliefs create the phenomenon of disciplined thoughts. In essence, disciplined thoughts produce deep beliefs, which usually start as inflection points or paradigm shifts, or what I call light-bulb moments.

> **Paradigm shifts cause people to have a deep conviction about an event, situation, or cause.**

With disciplined thoughts, we think deep truths that cannot be easily shaken off. With disciplined thoughts, individuals can align with natural (and supernatural) laws and principles, deep fundamental truths which are internalised and upon which unique habits and character emerge. As a result, the actions of these legends become powerful because of their level of discipline, conviction, and focus.

> **Extraordinary individuals, grounded in deep convictions, have a sense of personal purpose that emanated out of a clear understanding of who they truly are.**

Discipline is what make extraordinary people powerful, in whatever area they choose to build their strength. Discipline galvanised their energy and concentrated it. Discipline and focus breed excellence in the mastery of your inherent gifts. Discipline is the bridge between vision and its fulfilment.

The power of vision will make you become extraordinary because being great is not primarily a function of circumstances; being great is first and foremost a function of conscious choices and discipline. And vision provides you the distinct viewpoint to ensure that your choices and decisions align with your true self – your sincere desire to embody the values and achieve the goals you truly believe in. Being able to discipline your mind and channel your thought process (I refer to this process as Vision Attention Density, or VAD) is critical to being truly great in life. Moving from ordinary to extraordinary takes consistency and commitment, both of which are grounded in discipline.

Second, in the Vision Flywheel process, I found that extraordinary individuals are also disciplined in their lifestyle. The discipline of their thoughts clarified what they should and shouldn't do. A disciplined lifestyle follows disciplined thinking. They understood their passion and knew how to make the maximum contribution to others. With disciplined thoughts, they developed a better frame of reference about who they are as well as a precise estimation of their true self. Disciplined thoughts crystallise into a big-picture mentality in whatever you choose to focus on.

> **Discipline and focus breed excellence in the mastery of your inherent gifts.**

Focusing on who you are and what you can do allows you to discover your gift and develop

> **Discipline is the bridge between vision and its fulfilment.**

them from raw, latent stage to talents. In other words, disciplined individuals are those who through the power of disciplined thoughts and training strive to make unique contribution to others by ensuring their life activities fall within their gifts (potential) and core value system. Your gifts intersect with your passion and purpose to create what is referred to in this book as the Hedgehog Concept. Put simply, people become disciplined because they live their lives based on the Hedgehog Concept – a crystalline concept that flows from deep understanding of one's core values or the set of things one can do very well.

Finally, disciplined individuals produce through their disciplined thoughts disciplined, effective actions, characterised by powerful, extraordinary results and outcome. The disciplined actions of extraordinary individuals are what usually produce resounding impacts that continue to speak for generations and years even after they pass away. This trans-generational attribute is what make visionaries become truly extraordinary. I researched many legends and found that their purposeful works and actions continue to speak to us, even today. For many extraordinary people, their vision produced many future actions, many generations after they had passed away. The power of their vision was so strong that it gave many more people the opportunity to bring their own visions and dreams to life. Extraordinary people produced effective outcomes that last decades and centuries after they are gone.

In a nutshell, examining the lives of extraordinary individuals showed a consistent step-by-step process, which I now call the Vision Flywheel to greatness, shown in Figure 1. They all followed this process. As I noted earlier, these legends were not born with any special skills or abilities. What was different about them, however, was that they had vision. What many recognise as remarkable impacts, behind the scene, took months and years of private labour.

> **...being able to discipline your mind and channel your thought process (I refer to this process as Vision Attention Density, or VAD) is the most critical to being truly great in life.**

As an example of the Vision Flywheel process, let's take a quick glance at Dr. Martin Luther King Jr. As shown in Figure 1, his vision began as a gradual internal process after specific events in his life. These events resulted in a paradigm shift. Particular references were his childhood experiences of people in his neighbourhood who were victims of racial injustice during the Jim Crow days. Even though his parents, as Baptist ministers, lived in a relatively isolated parts of the neighbourhood, the reports of injustice still got to them. King began to develop disciplined thoughts, and with a paradigm shift, he came to a conclusion that informed a new way of life.

> **A disciplined lifestyle follows disciplined thinking.**

When he discovered the excellence of his oratory skills, he began to seek opportunities to develop his gifts and nurture his values, which were predicated on the stand that everyone deserves better treatment. As a disciplined individual, King concluded that the most effective way was through nonviolence, and so he sought training and knowledge, including traveling to India. This, then, finally led to disciplined actions. The antecedences of disciplined thoughts and disciplined lifestyle generated momentum over the years, as King continue to grow and mature. Then came the Montgomery Bus Boycott in December 1955, King's first major public manifestation that launched him to a national and international spotlight. But before the public manifestation of the bus boycott, in private, King's flywheel had already started gaining power and momentum.

Leading up to big performances are years of preparation and private labours, unknown to many. The private, personal, and sometimes painful processes that start with a new perspective and light-bulb experiences (undeniable truths that shifted his paradigms) allowed King to act with extraordinary tenacity and power. He came to the overwhelming conclusion that things needed to change; he was compellingly convinced that action had to be taken, and not just that but that he himself was the answer to the call. He had the firm belief that the status quo was the wrong approach and that a new, better reality needed to emerge. He began to take personal responsibility to bring about change. Little by little, he continued to build momentum and ultimately broke through into public manifestation. But it is not just any mere breakthrough; it was a sustainable breakthrough. It is not a doom loop because by following the process, King focused on intrinsic values that defined his habits; this allowed him to live an effective life and kept adding momentum to his personal progress.

Figure 1 presents a conceptualisation of the process I identified in my research findings. It is more of an evolutionary (rather than revolutionary), upward spiral process[14] that starts privately in the mind and later produces an impact that's visible to others.

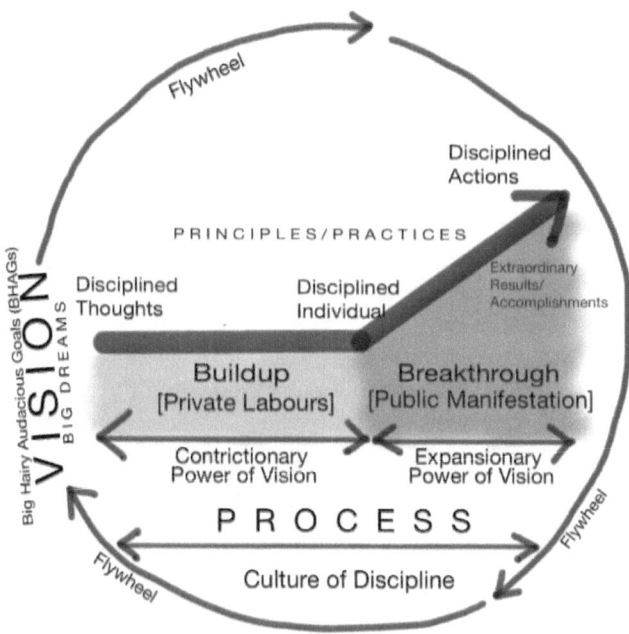

FIGURE 1: Vision Flywheel process[15]

People remain in mediocrity and barely experience greatness not only because they don't have vision but because they don't understand the process of vision as well as the corresponding principles and practices required to make a vision become a reality.

Despite being a relatively straightforward concept, vision appears to be a difficult subject to teach and understand. Apart from not understanding that visions take principles, processes, and practices, the uniqueness of each individual's vision, the invisible yet real nature of vision, and the faith-and-belief property of vision cause it to elude so many people. Visions and dreams as they appear are like clouds that look differently to different people at different times. Also, like clouds, visions can quickly fizzle away if the mind is not disciplined and trained to properly conceive, capture, and document its thoughts. Visions and dreams are not concrete until they come to pass. This reverse order of believing and working with something invisible, as though it were concrete, makes true vision divine and faith-driven.

The process that makes people who pursue vision become great stands in contrast to the popular ideas of our modern times. And this is what struck me after I conceptualised this Vision Flywheel process: Few people today, in trying to become great in life, take the time to explore or engage in what is so basic and fundamental. Few people take time to understand process, principles, or practices guiding a particular area of their lives. They say, "It's too difficult, complicated, and risky to follow my dreams." Others conclude with statements like, "I will fulfil my dreams when I get a little older." Yet another says with enthusiasm, "Vision is not for me; it's for leaders." Or this common assertion: "Vision is too abstract and futuristic; I want something that propels me to work right now."

> **People remain in mediocrity and barely experience greatness not only because they don't have vision but because they don't understand the process of vision as well as the corresponding principles and practices required to make a vision become a reality.**

It is these generally held ideas of our modern time that make people continue to try out various things, without accomplishing anything close to greatness. I realised that people genuinely want to pursue greatness. People are not lazy; they only lack clarity of vision. With vision, they will know how to live in the reality of their purpose and potential. All over the world, there are people who are incredibly gifted, yet they're not maximising their gifts. Raw gifts are latent; refined gifts become talents. The principles of vision provide the mental clarity to discover the unique gifts you were born with. Vision appropriately clarifies your original life pathway to navigate so that your raw gifts can be refined. Many talented people live without hope, fundamentally because they cannot apply their gifts for maximum results. The lack of vision is a serious universal issue that has caused

> **The process that makes people who pursue vision become great stands in contrast to the popular ideas of our modern times.**

many gifts, talents, and purposes to remain unfulfilled.

> **Vision appropriately clarifies the divine original pathway to navigate so your raw gifts can be refined.**

Today, a lot of people are living in poverty and frustration, not because they're not skilled but because their gifts have not made way for them. Mental Health America, in its 2017 Workplace Health Survey, reveals that 70 percent of American workers are not satisfied with their jobs.[16] But it is not just in America. Gallup's State of Global Workplace shows a similar worrying trend reporting that 85 percent of employees worldwide are not engaged or are actively disengaged in their job.[17] People all over the world get up in the morning and go to jobs they hate. People are losing hope about the future and are willing to give up just because they feel there is nothing more to look forward to. Even people who earn huge salaries often lack intrinsic satisfaction.

I travel around and give talks about vision, and it surprises many when I say this: The process of living with vision is not harder than the difficulty you are experiencing right now. It is not as complicated and complex as many assume. In fact, the opposite is the case; vision makes your life simple, more focused, and effective. Unlike the success and growth industry hacks who sell quick-fix materials and products that are high-level and high-handed (what I call wishy-washy strategies and ideas that don't last), a thorough process allows your life to align with fundamental principles and practices that have been proven and tested, time and time again, in life and history.

Vision is not about compounding what you are already doing. It is not about becoming overworked or overwhelmed with additional productive hacks. The power of vision is not about making you feel inadequate or pressured. It is about drawing you closer to the essence of your true self, closer to the original you at the core of your being. No matter your age or gender, vision is for you. You don't need to do more. Quite counterintuitively, you need to do less.

> **Many talented people live without hope, fundamentally because they cannot apply their gifts for maximum results.**

As I continue to give lectures around the world, presenting the findings in this book, I have come to see that people are interested in vision. However, I'm baffled that many have been misguided or incorrectly taught about vision. Instead of being taught vision in its conceptualisation process (as a matter of core, cognitive or mental conception), people are taught only the manifestation side of vision, or more precisely they are taught about results of extraordinary people who have been powered by their own vision. As a result, instead of conceiving and pursuing their own dreams, they try to copy certain qualities from those people. There's nothing bad about being inspired and motivated by the lives of extraordinary people; however, the issue is that most imitators appear fake in the end.

Copying is tantamount to borrowing strength. Borrowed strength or external force don't last because they don't come from your core source, so you can't own it, nurture it, or develop it in a sustainable way. You have to first become (being) before you can do. For example, I have seen several situations where people try their best to imitate the oratory gifts of Martin Luther King Jr., only to fill the room with the echo of their voices, void of content and power. Some people venture into charity and claim to be inspired by Mother Teresa, only to realise that the challenges of tending for the poor and needy transcends just fundraising and management. Greatness cannot be copied and pasted. There must be an internal driving force in order to become extraordinary.

The question then is, will getting my vision and following through with a defined process make me extraordinary? Since merely copying and pasting certain attributes doesn't seem to work, is there a specific way to truly become great in life, without appearing fake? More importantly, how do I leave a lasting, transgenerational legacy after I pass away? My desire is to not only succeed but to be significant and leave an enduring legacy here on earth. This may be your desire too. These are the questions and thoughts that plunged me into this research, analysis, and eventually this book.

> **Copying is tantamount to borrowed strength. Borrowed strength or external force don't last because they don't come from your core source, so you can't own it, nurture it, or develop it in a sustainable way.**

> **Greatness cannot be copied and pasted.**

It is a delight to decompose the phenomenon of greatness and unravel the foundational concept for living an extraordinary life. True greatness lies in having a clear big picture of what you are called to do here on earth. That big picture of your purpose and destiny is called vision. Vision is what gives your life direction and meaning. No matter where you are or what you have accomplished in life, the expansionary power of vision can help you reach a greater level of fulfilment. Our world today is filled with people who have eyes but lack vision. The most disoriented person in the world is someone who has sight but lacks vision. Conversely, even more frustrating are people who have vision (or some form of it) but lack the knowledge, tools, and resources on how to bring them to reality. So, it's one thing to know that vision follows a process, it is another thing to know how to navigate through the entire process. Therein lies principles and practices.

> **Our world today is filled with people who have eyes but lack vision.**

> **The most disoriented person in the world is someone who has sight but no vision. Conversely, even more frustrating are people who have vision (or some form of it) but lack the knowledge, tools, and resources on how to bring them to reality.**

Chapter 4
TIMELESS PRINCIPLES AND PRACTICES

My research also made me discover that the process of vision conception (private labour and build-up) to manifestation (public breakthrough) is built on fundamental principles. An extraordinary life is based on timeless, self-evident principles which I found to be common among truly great people throughout history, yet it can easily elude many who are overwhelmed by the hustling and bustling of life.

A key step to achieving your highest aspirations and overcoming your greatest challenges is to find the principle or spiritual law that governs your life. Of course, how you apply a principle will vary greatly and will be determined by your unique strengths, talents, and creativity, but ultimately, being extraordinary in life will always come from applying fundamental principles that govern life itself.

> **A key step to achieving your highest aspirations and overcoming your greatest challenges is to find the principle or spiritual law that governs your life.**

It is true that the world is changing and will continue to change as we move forward in time. But that does not mean we should stop our search for timeless principles. Think of it this way: While the practice of bottling water evolves and changes, the chemistry of water remains fixed; it is and will always be in the proportion of two atoms of hydrogen and one of oxygen: H_2O. This is why I liken this book as a search for timeless principles, the enduring chemistry of extraordinary individuals that will remain true and relevant, no matter how the world changes around us. Yes, the specific application will vary and change from individual to individual (the bottling), but certain immutable power of vision (the chemistry) will endure.

There is an unending search for new stuff in our generation, and as a result, the discussion of timeless principles and concepts are relegated to the bottom and tagged "for older folks." But truth be told, there is nothing we can claim to be new in our modern economy. Great visionaries who invented the automobile in the 1880s, faced the abolition of segregation in 1950s, created coloured televisions in 1960s: Did they feel it was any less of a modern era? And in each rendition of the new economy, visionaries adhered to certain basic principles, using rigor and discipline. As we imbibe these principles in our lives today, it does not conform to old ideas or thoughts. As it worked in the nineteenth and twentieth century, so can it work for us in the twenty-first century and for centuries to come.

> As we imbibe these principles in our lives today, it does not conform to old ideas or thoughts. As it worked in the nineteenth and twentieth century, so can it work for us in the twenty-first century and for centuries to come.

Some people will point out that the scale and pace of change is greater today than in the past, and as a result, ideas from centuries ago are not applicable today and won't be a hundred years from now. Perhaps. But one thing to keep in mind is that some of the visionaries discussed in this book faced challenges and changes comparable to what we face today. For example, Martin Luther King Jr. faced similar resistance seen by many of today's freedom fighters; Henry Ford lost court cases trying to protect his company. Ibuka built Sony during a crisis, despite many failed attempts and almost being bankrupt experimenting with different ideas. Yet, applying principles shared in this book, they emerged through the turbulence of their time. What was more fascinating is that they not only engaged in the modern events of their time, they pioneered them. Many of you reading this book will not only challenge the status quo of your time, you will pioneer a new era with the power of your vision.

As you immerse yourself in the coming chapters, keep one key point in mind: This book is not just about being futuristic and predicting the future. It is not even about the individuals you're reading about, per se. It is ultimately about one thing: the timeless principles and practices of vision that can make anyone become truly great. It's about how ordinary individuals can become extraordinary by activating the power of their

> ...processes create the groundwork that allows you to imbibe enduring principles and values into your life.

unique vision.

It's important to be able to recognise, embrace, and follow through time-tested principles. Following a defined process creates the groundwork that allows you to imbibe enduring principles and values into your life. And it was such a relief to find that no matter what profession or career individuals take, anyone can become great in life. Greatness is not associated with any industry, country, or geographical location. Every single one of us was born to be great. As it was in this research, so also it is today, that legends do come from all walks of life. The power of their vision distinguishes them.

People need to break the cycle of mediocrity. If we succeed in cracking the code of how vision can make ordinary individuals become extraordinary, I believe it will be of tremendous value to everyone around the world. An ordinary teacher can become extraordinary. An ordinary singer can become extraordinary. An ordinary preacher can become extraordinary. An ordinary worker can become extraordinary. And so on.

Every generation needs men and women who will redeem time by living with a vision of the things that are to be. Like these legends paved the way for others and pioneered a new era, we too can activate the power of vision, follow through the process, apply principles and practices, do the work that is truly required, and in the end become legends ourselves.

The first step towards creating an improved future is developing the ability to envision it. Vision will ignite the fire of passion that fuels our commitment to do whatever it takes to achieve excellence. Only vision allows us to transform dreams of greatness into the reality of achievement through human action. Vision has no boundaries and knows no limit. Our vision is what we become in life.

> **Every generation needs men and women who will redeem time by living with a vision of the things that are to**

So I want to invite you on a journey to greatness in this book, where I document the very principles and practices that make ordinary people become extraordinary. All I ask of you is that you open your mind's eyes to see.

I'd like to point out before closing this section that, above all, this book is primarily for individuals, not institutions or corporations. I believe strongly that people are the bedrock of institutions and that what gives rise to a strong corporation are collections of extraordinary, vision-oriented individuals. I also strongly believe that by starting with vision from an individual point of view, we can raise people who truly understand who they are and where they are going. The principles and practice of vision bring about the discipline, direction, focus, and excellence that is indicative of true personal greatness. Vision makes people become the right "who" and have a clear grasp of their "what" to do in life.[18] Institutions and corporations will benefit by having vision-oriented individuals on their teams.

> The first step towards creating an improved future is developing the ability to envision it.

A lot has been written by other authors about the "why": why you exist, start with your why, why your institution exists, and so on. But I believe fundamentally that to know who you truly are is the first, right thing to start with. And only vision can provide that mental clarity.

Institutions today require disciplined, exceptional individuals who produce outstanding contributions to the larger organisation. Yet to produce those outstanding individuals requires the teaching of vision beyond corporate circles.

Most books that discuss the topic of vision focus on the organisation or attempt to look at the topic from a corporate point of view. The implication was that people saw vision as a top-bottom concept reserved for a special group of people. While making it motivational and exciting, authors who wrote about vision in the past only painted the results and manifestations of vision. The few who wrote about the principles excluded the actual processes and practices

> Vision has been made to appear like an outside-in concept, when in reality, it is an inside-out concept that originates from your core.

of vision. As a result, vision has been made to appear like an outside-in concept, when in reality, it is an inside-out concept that originates from your core.

It is my hope that this book will help change the narrative and confirm that vision is indeed for everyone. As long as you have a mind, and you can think, you can dream. This book can help individuals become great through the power of their unique vision. Organisations can use it in building their employees to become extraordinary individuals, the right "whos," to help move their institutions forward into new frontiers of innovation and growth. Needless to say, truly great companies are visionary in nature primarily because they are led by visionary individuals who understand the principles of shared vision.

> **As long as you have a mind, and you can think, you can dream.**

Chapter 5
EXTRAORDINARY LIVES BACKED BY OVER A HUNDRED YEARS OF EMPIRICAL EVIDENCE

People powered by their unique vision become extraordinary. And this book is an account of how true this statement is. The visionaries (or if you like to call them legends) discussed in this book were selected after extensive preliminary research, including first finding out areas where a person's life was followed by an enduring legacy or remarkable impact. A larger list was drawn and then a gradual narrowing down followed. Data was gathered from as far back as the 1860s. Here is the final list of individuals selected for research:

Martin Luther King Jr.
Nelson Mandela
Mother Teresa
Helen Keller
Joseph in the Old Testament

Henry Ford
Walt Disney
Masaru Ibuka
Steve Jobs

Based on the large volume of data gathered, I was first tending towards coding the data and running various quantitative analysis – a method an award winning econometrics researcher like myself would have naturally gravitated to. But empirical analysis doesn't only have to be quantitative.[19] Indeed, empirical research methods derive from the application of observation and experience to a research question rather than being grounded in theory alone.[20] And although I don't think qualitative methods are uniquely positioned to answer truths or deliver generalizations, they can provide insight into patterns, behaviours, contexts, relationships. Using real-world evidence in investigating various assumptions and assertions is what qualitative empirical research method is all about[21] and is what, in my opinion was the right one for this study. Under qualitative research design, empirical studies evolves to test conventional concepts of evidence and truth while still observing the fundamental principles of recognizing the subjects beings studied as empirical.[22]

The information extrapolated from data on these extraordinary individuals (summarised in Appendix 1) was the basis for determining what it means to be truly visionary. It became overwhelmingly clear that what distinguishes a visionary is not just wealth or success but long-term success, an enduringly great and significant legacy, which has positive impact on a large number of people around the world.

They were normal everyday people with nothing special about them. They were not born with any special abilities per se, yet they became extraordinary.

Indeed, I researched other individuals who exhibited qualities of a visionary. Legends are around us too. Anywhere you find people exhibiting disciplined thinking, disciplined lifestyle, and disciplined actions, who live based on principles rather than fads, trends, or clichés, you will most likely find an extraordinary individual powered by vision. You can find people who fit into the Vision Flywheel framework, so you are right to expand this list by making your own. I chose to report on these based on publicly available data and how much they fit the model of enduring greatness, especially after they passed away. The data also provided enough spread to cover various works of life and gender. It is important to also note that the focus of this research was to identify core principles and a world view that applies to any religion, occupation, or career. Irrespective of what these individuals represent, important aspects of their lives demonstrate timeless principles—universal, natural, and spiritual laws—that govern vision and reflect enduring greatness.

A number of things jumped out of my preliminary analysis which was worthy of note and counterintuitive to what I expected. Interestingly, these findings appear to be the very root of what made these individuals sustainably great. A full documentation of interesting findings from this research is included in various bonus materials accompanying this book. But here is a highlight: First is that most of these visionaries are humble, as opposed to the egocentric bravados we would have expected them to be. In public, they had a larger-than-life appearance, but they are truly humble and focused people. In addition, it doesn't matter whether you have charisma or not; you're still qualified to become great, as data shows that being great does not require you to please other people or for them to love you. It's more about serving people with the value and excellence of your gift. In the process, you may not necessarily be liked by everyone. Furthermore, while visionaries do become wealthy, money is not usually their motivation. They were purely driven by their vision and the passion that comes with bringing it to pass. They were not after material things, either. They were focused on destiny, the glorious future inspired in their hearts. Legends used money and material resources to accomplish their vision, but money was never the driving force. I'll add one more interesting finding: being great is much more than having high education grades, IQ scores or being "smart"

Let me introduce you to nine extraordinary individuals I found to be powered by their vision. A summary table[23] of my research is found in Appendix 1.

Martin Luther King
Martin Luther King Jr., the middle child of Martin Luther King Sr. and Alberta Williams King, was born on January 15, 1929. Who would have thought that on the shoulders of this ordinary boy from Alabama rested monumental civil rights accomplishments, influential decisions, profound actions, and the steadfast progression of humanitarian rights that had far-reaching implications for equality and social justice?

Nelson Mandela
On July 18, 1918, when Nelson Mandela was born in the tiny village of Mvezo, near the banks of the Mbashe River in Transkei, South Africa, nobody would have been able to predict that he would lead South Africa out of apartheid after being incarcerated for more than twenty-seven years. Nelson Mandela, whose birth name Rolihlahla in the Xhosa language commonly translates as "troublemaker," withdrew from making trouble after his release from prison but focused on reconciliation, which led the nation into a united government with his captors. Who would have thought Mandela would become the first black president of South Africa, elected after time in prison for his anti-apartheid work? Who would imagine a troublemaker would win the Nobel Peace Prize in 1993?

Mother Teresa
When she was born on August 26, 1910, in Skopje (the current capital of the Republic of Macedonia), telling people that little Agnes Gonxha Bojaxhiu, who took the name Sister Mary Teresa, would become one of the greatest humanitarians of the twentieth century would most

likely fall on deaf hears. But with the power of her vision, she impacted the world in a most profound way. Combining profound empathy and a fervent commitment to her work, Agnes became Mother Teresa and spent the later part of her life in the slums of Calcutta, India, aiding the city's poorest and sickest people. Not long after, her work spread internationally, as she carried on with incredible organisational and managerial skills. She developed a vast and effective organisation of missionaries to help impoverished citizens all across the globe. In 1982, during the siege of Beirut, Lebanon, Mother Teresa travelled through a war zone to evacuate orphaned children with her bare hands. In December 1988, when a massive earthquake hit the republics of Armenia and Georgia, Mother Teresa was there to help. She was awarded the Nobel Peace Prize for her work in 1979, donating the $192,000 prize to the poor in India. By 1986, Mother Teresa operated 517 missions in more than a hundred countries. Her commitment to serve the poor and those in need has been described as "magical, miraculous."[24]

Helen Keller

Helen Keller was born on June 27, 1880, in Tuscumbia, Alabama, and became deaf and blind nineteen months later as a result of an unknown illness, perhaps meningitis or scarlet fever. My early search about vision started with some of her famous quotes: "The most miserable person in life is not the one without sight but the one without vision," and "The only thing worse than being blind is having sight but no vision."

I was fascinated to study her life and discover her accomplishments. In those days, people who were deaf and blind were usually banished. They were like fugitives in their own land. Struggling to accept that her world had gone dark as she lost her sight, and lacking the ability to hear anything, young Helen became restive and aggressive. Her parents were advised to take her to an institution for handicapped people, but they were determined to give it their best. With the help of a medical doctor's recommendation, in 1887, they hired a trained teacher, Anne Sullivan. Sullivan became Helen's teacher and lifelong companion. Sullivan soon taught Helen to read and spell in Braille. Helen grew in leaps and bounds, advancing way beyond children her age with no disability.

Helen became the first deaf-and-blind person to earn an undergraduate degree; she achieved that grand accomplishment while writing her first memoir, The Story of My Life, which was published in 1903. That became one of the many accomplishments of Helen as she became more distinguished over the years. She wrote articles in popular magazines and also wrote many books and gave lectures. She travelled to many countries, giving speeches and empowering young people with disabilities. Not only that, she helped pioneer many national programs that attend to the needs of deaf and blind people. She became a political activist and the first deaf-and-blind person to earn a bachelor of arts degree. She inspired others by being a powerful example that physical eyesight was not required to live an extraordinary life.

Joseph of the Old Testament

Joseph, a character from the Old Testament, was part of the fundamental fabric of the Judeo-Christian tradition. His life was typical of someone who was powered by vision. He was a perfect case study, and I was able to identify with his struggle. These Ps summarise his life: From his Parents' house, he was kidnapped by his own brothers and thrown in a Pit. From the Pit to slavery in Potiphar's house. From Potiphar's house to Prison, and from Prison to the Palace. Studying Joseph's life taught me many things, including the reality that other people may be jealous and envious of our dreams. Joseph's life was also a perfect depiction of what I called the constrictionary[25] and expansionary power of vision. He dealt with blackmail in Potiphar's house, but all through the obstacles, he kept his focus and discipline. Joseph demonstrated many important points we will discuss in the chapters to follow. Starting out as a rather arrogant young man, "Daddy's favourite," who had to go through experiences that strengthened his character. He became a forgiving, loving, and caring family man. Yes, he was gifted, but gift without character will inadvertently lead to disaster. Eventually, we saw how his gift made him stand among great men. Although the gift he had was to interpret dreams, his purpose was to be a leader and a deliverer of his people.

Henry Ford

Henry Ford was born on July 30, 1863, on his family's farm in Wayne County, near Dearborn, Michigan. On his fifteenth birthday, Ford received a pocket watch from his father and proceeded to take it apart and reassemble it. It was clear that he was destined for bigger things. Unsatisfied with farm work, when he was sixteen, he walked to Detroit to find work in a machine shop. He worked as an apprentice at a shipbuilding company, before joining the Edison Illuminating Co., where he worked under famed inventor Thomas Edison. He learnt many skills along the way that eventually helped him to design and produce his first engine-powered vehicle. When young Ford left his father's farm for Detroit, only two out of eight Americans lived in cities; when he died in 1947 at age eighty-three, the proportion was five out of eight. Ford's Model T automobile played a tremendous role in bringing about this urbanisation. Ford, then, is an apt symbol of the transition from an agricultural to an industrial America. He revolutionised vehicle manufacturing and brought the car to the mass market, selling over one million vehicles in 1920. In the twenty years it was produced, Ford sold more than 15 million Model Ts. The Ford Model T was named the most influential car of the 20th century in the 1999 Car of the Century competition, ahead of the BMC Mini, Citroën DS, and Volkswagen Beetle.[26]

While the Model T wasn't the first car, as there were other auto manufacturers at that time, his vision of a refined production line made it possible for him to produce cars faster and cheaper. As a result, the Model T was the first car the average person could afford. The company continued to improve, and within a decade, Ford produced half of all the cars made in the United States. Their employees were among the first to receive standard forty-hour weeks, two-day weekends, and $5 wages, which helped to increase efficiency, driving the cost of a Ford car from its launch price of $825 to $360 by 1918.

Walter Elias Disney
Walt Disney (born in Chicago on December 5, 1901) was the fourth son of Elias Disney, a peripatetic carpenter, farmer, and building contractor, and his wife, Flora Call, who had been a public schoolteacher. When Walt was an infant, the family moved to a farm near Marceline, Missouri, a typical small Midwestern town. Who would have believed that Walt Disney, a boy who was a below-average student, would become an American motion-picture and television producer and showman, famous as a pioneer of animated films and as the creator of such cartoon characters as Mickey Mouse and Donald Duck? He became a man whose imaginative leaps allowed him to vault ahead. A true visionary whose passion was fueled by purpose and determination. He also planned and built Disneyland, a huge amusement park that opened near Los Angeles in 1955, and before his death, he had begun building a second such park, Walt Disney World, near Orlando, Florida. The Disney Company he founded has become one of the world's largest entertainment conglomerates.

Masaru Ibuka

Masaru Ibuka was born in Japan on April 11, 1908. Called a "genius inventor," Ibuka could well be the person who turned Japan's electronics industry into what it is today. The visionary powered a tiny recording company that grew into the giant Sony Corporation, from the ruins of a defeated and devastated postwar Japan. Sony's first product, an electric rice cooker, was a flop, but his development of the tape recorder, transistor radio, Walkman, PlayStation, and many other products put Sony at the forefront of technological innovation. For more than three decades, it has been the world's most successful and recognised electronics company.

Steve Jobs

Steven Paul Jobs was born on February 24, 1955, in San Francisco. His biological parents were two University of Wisconsin graduate students who gave him up for adoption. Steve's adopted father tried to pass along his love for mechanics and cars. Although Steve showed little interest in mechanics, he later admitted his early life with his dad showed him the fundamentals of good design. Through cars, his father gave Steve his first exposure to electronics. Recognisably smart but directionless, he dropped out of college and experimented with different pursuits before co-founding Apple in 1972. Starting with an experimental device called a Blue Box, which allowed electronics hobbyists to make free telephone calls, Apple went on to create it first breakthrough device in 1976, a computer called the Apple-1. Over time, Apple came up with the iPod, iPhone, iTunes, Macintosh, and many other products that revolutionised the mobile phone, personal computing, and electronics industry. In 2018, Apple officially became the first US company with $1 trillion market capitalisation. Using what many coworkers referred to as a reality distortion field, Steve Jobs successfully revolutionised at least six different industries before he passed in 2011. It was interesting to find that Steve Jobs had a high school GPA of 2.65 and was a college dropout.[27]

****

In the bonus materials and resources accompanying this book (see Appendix 3 for the list), I went deeper into additional important, rather fascinating findings from the power of vision research. It is worth going deeper into these materials, as they appear to provide new information you'd never expect. One of the additional resources included twelve myths about vision that was demystified. Another resource details seven extraordinary habits about visionaries discussed in this book. One of such habit is that they never fell into the trap of a great idea. Other interesting findings include the fact that more visionaries appear on the list of Noble Peace Prize than on the Forbes list of wealthy people. This goes to point out that true visionaries' focus is not first to chase money or riches; those came along as added benefits of vision. This research also shows that you don't need to be liked by everybody to become extraordinary in life. Some of the more interesting finds include bragging versus humility and the overwhelming obstacles that litter the road to greatness, as contrary to the idea that everything becomes easy once you find your vision.

PART 2
PRIVATE LABOURS

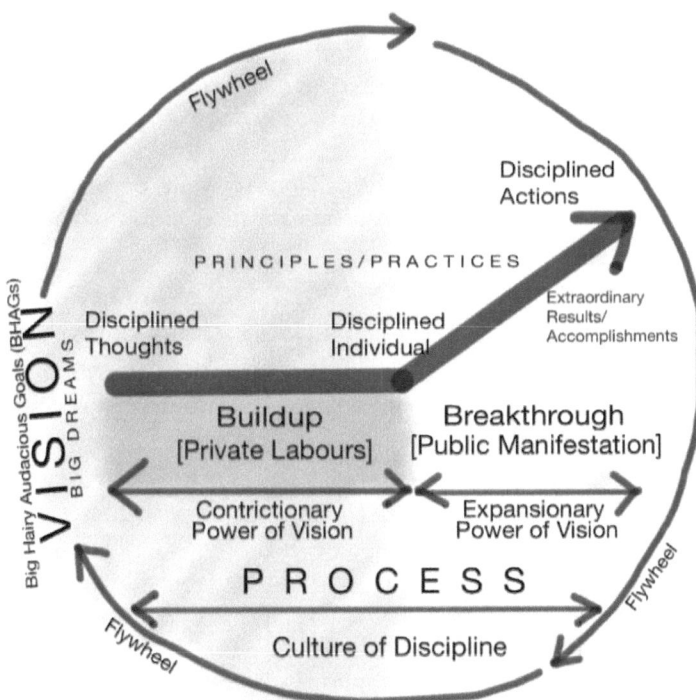

Chapter 6
PRINCIPLES OF PERSONAL PURPOSE AND PASSION

The principles of personal purpose and passion are essentially that every human on earth exists for a reason. But purpose itself is transient. To be effective in life requires that you find out your true purpose and meaning, discover what you are born to do, and commit yourself to pursuing it with excellence.

Your vision serves to clarify and qualify your purpose. Vision provides clarity of purpose because in practice, vision is your life's purpose, revealed to your heart.

Reaching the fulness of your potential and living a life of passion requires a clear vision. A lack of vision ultimately results in a lack of a clear purpose or what you are truly passionate about because vision and passion both originate from the heart.

> **Vision provides clarity of purpose because in practice, vision is your life's purpose, revealed to your heart.**

The world is filled with people who are busy but not ultimately effective or satisfied. They do a lot, expending time and energy, but accomplish little of value. There is an obvious lack of purpose and vision. Consequently, they spend their lives toiling day after day but never make any headway.

One of the dilemmas of contemporary society seems to be a lack of meaning in everyday life. Some people are aware that their potential is being underutilised. They dread Mondays and live for the weekends because they hate their job as Gallup's 2013 State of the American Workplace Report shows that just 30 percent of employees are engaged and inspired at work.[28] Their calendars are filled with to-do lists without actually getting any purposeful work done. Many are caught in the thick of thin things.

A few are content with their lives, but they also have a vague sense that the life they are experiencing should have more significance. Still others live on a surface level, pursuing a series of emotional highs that leave them empty and constantly searching for the next thrill to satisfy them. If they are short in accomplishing their targets, they apply extrinsic force or external power. There is an obvious lack of direction and vision; there is no plan for sustainable growth.

None of these people realise that hidden within them is the key to living a more fulfilling life than they could imagine. Few people understand that what's required for a truly impactful life is intrinsic. Already inside of each of us is the seed of greatness, the potential to become extraordinary. You only need to be disciplined enough to focus your thoughts, concentrate your energy, and fan the flame of what is already within you. Our hearts of understanding must be enlightened to see beyond the surface. With the mind's eye opened, the powerful forces of vision can propel you forward, even in the face of tragedy, as you come into the revelatory experience of the greatness that lies within and ahead of you.

> **With the mind's eye opened, the powerful forces of vision can propel you forward, even in the face of tragedy, as you come into the revelatory experience of the greatness that lies within and ahead of you.**

Intrinsic versus extrinsic motivation

Take the case of Daniel Vassallo, who left his $500K job at Amazon in February 2019. Daniel gave up the promotions, perks, benefits, and future prospects at Amazon; he knew there was more to life. He realised that his motivation to go to work each morning was decreasing—almost in an inverse trend to his career and income growth. He summarised it in the reward-versus-motivation chart shown in Figure 3 below.

Daniel concluded that he needed "intrinsic" and not "extrinsic" motivators. He realised that extrinsic motivations are not sustainable and don't last. Daniel stated, "I would be delusional to think that earning $1M or $10M would suddenly make it different. And I feel the same with every other extrinsic reward or material possession. Getting them feels good for a while, but this wears off quickly. The things that don't wear off are those that I've been doing since I was a kid, when nothing was forcing me to do them.... I know my strengths, and I know what motivates me, so why not do this all the time?"[29]

FIGURE 3: Reward versus Motivation
(Source: Daniel Vassallo)

What we learn from Daniel's story is that there are lots of people out there who are living well but not living their best. There is a need to shift from extrinsic motivations to intrinsic motivation.

Most of what you require is intrinsic and already inside of you. You only need to be mentally disciplined enough to see what lies within you and to fan your intrinsic abilities into a flame. In every case I studied, people who turned out to become extraordinary, by human standards, showed little promise for greatness and little hope of being able to change the lives of others around the world. But after having captured their life's vision, these people lived with power and energy that undeniably transcended their natural capacities, with an intensity of commitment that far exceeds anything they had previously demonstrated in their lives. The results of their efforts further show us how powerful the force of vision can be in transforming ordinary individuals into extraordinary people.

> ...there are lots of people out there who are living well but not living their best.

Do you have a sense of personal purpose? Do you know who you truly are at the core? Do you know why you were born? Does your purpose give you a passion for living?

Life is intended to have meaning. If all you can point to after years of working for other people is a gold ring, silver watch or a pension, then your life is a tragedy in the making. Understand that there is more to your life. Make the effort to know why you exist. And in the light of that knowledge, take steps towards experiencing a remarkable life.

Your life doesn't have to be aimless, repetitive exercises, because you were not designed to simply ride a rocking horse. You were meant to be going somewhere, to be headed towards a destination. You were born to be distinct and to fulfil a unique purpose. People who don't understand their unique purpose often engage in mindless copying of others or unhealthy competition with them.

You are inherently original and designed to be exceptional and special. Because your DNA is unlike any other person's, you are born to stand out and not blend in or to be normal or average. At first glance, it is common to assume that we are all born to be and do the same thing and for us to blend in. You are not born to blend in; you are born to be outstanding. Every human being has a special purpose for which they were created. No one else can accomplish what you have been born to do in the world.

And that is why you have a special vision, distinct as your DNA. Pursuing and fulfilling your vision is what gives your life purpose, meaning, and value. Until you conceive your vision and pursue it with passion and purpose, you are not really living.

Have you taken time to figure out what you are wired for? Have you taken a moment to examine your life? Are you on the right pathway of purpose and destiny? Irrespective of what has happened in your past, are you ready to dream again and commit yourself to your purpose from today and going forward? It is only when you seek a deeper understanding and see what doesn't necessarily appear to the physical eyes that your life begins to fulfil purpose and make an impact.

> **You are not born to blend in; you are born to be outstanding.**

Many are alive, but inside, they have no real purpose for living. It's a deeply depressing reality that while many open their physical eyes, their minds eye has become shut, and they cannot see the unique vision for their lives. As a result, their dreams have been buried within, together with their potential and purpose.

Imagine a world without Martin Luther King Jr., Nelson Mandela, Mother Teresa, Helen Keller, Joseph in the Old Testament, Walt Disney, Masaru Ibuka, and Steve Jobs. Without Helen Keller, we wouldn't have the American Civil Liberties Union, an organisation she cofounded, and through her activism and advocacy work, many policies relating to deaf and blind people were revamped, including removing the disabled from asylums and organising commissions for the blind in thirty states by 1937. How could we have lived in this world without the joy that Mickey Mouse gave us? I did a number of edits of this work on my iPhone, and of course, the iPhone wouldn't have existed without Steve Jobs. What about our approach to charities, particularly how we care for people living in slums? Without Mother Teresa's brave efforts, many would probably still be languishing in destitution. Without Ibuka, Sony wouldn't exist, and so we could not enjoy the PlayStation and Walkman and many other products that defined moments in consumer history.

> **It's a deeply depressing reality that while many open their physical eyes, their mind's eye has become shut, and they cannot see the unique vision for their lives.**

Chapter 7
YOU TOO CAN BECOME EXTRAORDINARY

In leading discussions about vision, one constant theme I observed is what I call the illusion of time. Young people have the illusion of time and feel that discussions about vision are for older people. Older people too fall into the illusion of time and conclude with statements like, "I could have pursued my dream when I was younger." What I gather among young people is the feeling that they have time and can later come to the idea of vision when the time is right.

It cannot be overemphasised that the power of vision can work for all ages. So no matter your age, old or young, or your gender, male or female, you can operate with the power of vision and position your life on a pathway that culminates in the extraordinary.

The power of vision can work for all ages

You may claim that you are young, and age is still on your side. You create the impression that you can enjoy now and work later, and as a result, you catch every trend or fad as you run back and forth, with no clear life vision or grand object that drives you towards excellence and greatness.

You sound tired of trying to please your friends or fit into the clique. To a large extent, you don't even know who you are or what your life is all about. Neither do your so-called friends.

Perhaps you identified some gifts that have already made you popular, but due to your lack of vision and discipline, those gifts remain latent and unrefined. Refined gifts become talents and potential. You need vision, focus, and discipline to help you discover, develop, and distinguish your gifts from a virtual (mental) location to a real location.

Perhaps you are claiming you are responding to peer pressure when, in reality, what you are doing is a manifestation of a lack of personal purpose. This lack of personal vision and purpose makes you react instead of respond. Reacting is indicative of spontaneous actions, without any depth of thought or insight. Responding involves some level of mental consciousness and cognition. Truly great people are not reactionaries. They are visionaries, grounded in core values and beliefs. They are empowered and not fazed by peer pressure. Their vision help them respond effectively.

Perhaps you're a little older, in your forties. You're known as the procrastination master as you continue to drift from pillar to post, without working towards any set destiny inspired by your vision. You have attended many conferences, seminars, and strategy retreats, yet you're still stagnant. Perhaps you feel depressed because you have been on the same spot for many years.

Every time you celebrate someone else's promotion, you end up jealous and envious. "That should have been me" becomes your common statement.

And it's not that you don't have a set of goals or a destiny in mind. The problem is that you lack an understanding of the process of how vision works. It is not the job you are doing that has held of you down; it is your lack of a bigger picture and the steps required to fulfil your life's vision.

> **Truly great people are not reactionaries. They are visionaries, grounded in core values and beliefs. They are empowered and not fazed by peer pressure.**

There's yet another misconception that visions are for older entrepreneurs or people who lead large organisations. As I mentioned earlier, this book is not about institutions; it's not even about the individuals discussed, per se. It is about principles and practices that individuals of all types and all ages can apply to their own lives. The power of vision will work for you, as long you can breathe, as long as you have a mind that can think, as long as you are alive and can think, that is all you need because vision is primarily a conception in the mind.

> **It is not the job you are doing that has held of you down; it is your lack of a bigger picture and the steps required to fulfil your life's vision.**

And you can start today. Understand that life is about change and transformation. You must be willing to accept positive change. You cannot do what you are doing the same way you are doing it and expect a different result. You cannot become better by thinking old thoughts. You have to renew your mind and thoughts.

You have to think better thoughts, dream bigger dreams, and elevate your game plan. Visions demand a better you and, as such, are transformative in nature.

> ...dreaming alone is not sufficient to bring your vision to pass. You have to do more than just set goals.

You need a vision, a bigger picture that is clear enough to guide your steps daily yet big enough to take a lifetime to accomplish. And it is by following simple, daily steps that you engage in activities that culminate in greatness.

You too can become great by dreaming big and setting big hairy audacious goals (BHAGs). But dreaming alone is not sufficient to bring your vision to pass. You have to do more than just set goals. Dreams require energy, enthusiasm, and strength that must be put to work in order to propel you forward. You too can become extraordinary by proactively pursuing your vision, taking targeted actions that cumulatively make you become a formidable force in your world.

And this force is what will help you triumph in difficult situations. Those who attempt to do something no one has ever done before—simply because they were powered by their vision—face many obstacles and challenges. Inevitably, there will be resistance, opposition, and difficulties, but your vision will propel you forward.

To get to the fullness of your purpose as great people do requires being diligent in pursuing your vision, despite all odds. While encouragers appear along the way (people referred to in this book as positive external value forces – P-EVFs), you must always remember that the primary motivation to pursue your vision must come from within.

Your vision will make your life meaningful because vision is the juice of life. Vision is the primary motivator of human action, and therefore, everything you do should be driven by your vision, the clear big picture of the future in your mind. Your vision will influence the way you conduct your entire life. It will dictate how you spend your time, money, and resources, and how you prioritise your to-do list.

> Your vision will make your life meaningful because vision is the juice of life.

You too can become extraordinary by the power of vision because it gives your life direction. Purpose cannot be accomplished without direction. Vision provides direction. Vision is established on the pillars and signposts of principles and values, which themselves become clearer as your life becomes powered by vision. Principles make sense when you have a sense of personal purpose and vision.

> **Principles make sense when you have a sense of personal purpose and vision.**

You too can become extraordinary by the power of vision because it gives you the foresight to see the end of something, even before it begins. With vision, you develop the special capability: beginning something with the end in mind, a process of creatively envisioning the end of something before you even start it. This special ability helps you to streamline your endeavours, keeps your focus on your purpose, and points you towards your destiny.

The question to ask yourself is, what do I want my life to be like in the end? You can ask yourself this at any point in your life. Imagine what you want your obituary to say when your life is all done.

Take a minute to reflect on this, and you will immediately realise that certain things you are doing now don't amount to meaningful, purposeful work. You have to learn to take personal responsibility to redirect your life in the direction that is a reflection of your true self.

Beginning with the end in mind makes you become proactive and responsible; you're able to respond to events of your life rather than react to them. It enables you to take charge of your choices and make decisions that help you lead your life based on your intrinsic values and beliefs.

Beginning with the end in mind activates your private constrictionary discipline, which in the end leads to public relevance and an expanded power of vision.

Beginning with the end in mind is living with a mindset that clearly considers how we want things to end, even while we're just at the starting point.

****

The stories of the people I highlight in this book depict typical, everyday people who became extraordinary by the power of their vision. They are people just like you and me. So there is hope for you today. Take Mother Teresa, for example. She was born in Armenia. Her story follows that she became a nun and went to India, where she served as a schoolteacher. It is possible that she was on track with a purposeful life. Just like many of us, what we appear to be doing may look important until a new experience, encounter, challenge, or situation comes to shift our paradigm. This was the case with Mother Teresa; while on the public bus on her regular day, it was impressed upon her heart to go help the people living in the slums of Calcutta. She later formed a charity called Missionaries of Charity, but having a name for it wasn't as urgent as the action that needed to be taken to help those in the slums.

A report mentioned how urgently she wanted this to start; when she reported to her superiors, she couldn't wait for them to answer her. She retorted at one point what appear to sound like this: "I am ready to start immediately." She didn't ask for money; she just wanted to work. In August 1948, donning the blue-and-white sari that she would wear in public for the rest of her life, she left the Loreto Convent and wandered out into the city. After six months of basic medical training, she voyaged for the first time into Calcutta's slums, with no more specific a goal than to aid the less privileged and those in need.

Let's take another example from my research: Henry Ford. Ford was a farm boy who had less than a sixth grade schooling. He wasn't born into a wealthy family and never had any influential friends, yet he rose to great heights. While carriage with horses were the norm in his time, he had a dream of a horseless carriage. Ford understood and applied the principles of vision and went to work with the tools available to him. He didn't wait for everything to fall into place. Today, we can all witness to the power of his dreams and vision. Ford's Model T, introduced on October 1, 1908, spawned mass automobility, altering living patterns, leisure activities, landscape, even the atmosphere. He became the greatest automobile manufacturer of all time, laying the foundation of the twentieth century more than anyone else.

For Mother Teresa, notice that she technically wanted to start another branch of work out of what she was originally called to do. She must have faced a lot of opposition and obstacles. Yet she stood with her conviction. Starting with nothing, she built one of the world's largest charities; this is the power of vision in full display.

Henry Ford had no formal school training and was a mere farm boy, but he pioneered the way of living in the twentieth century; his legacy endures today.

The principles of personal purpose are intractably embedded in discipline. Discipline derives from the idea of being a disciple to a philosophy, disciple to a set of principles and an overriding purpose, to a superordinate goal (or a person who represents that goal). The drive to fulfil your life vision must come from a place of personal discipline that comes from within, a function of your independent will. Your purpose become established as you discipline your mind to focus on your deep values, your convictions, and their sources.

> **The principles of personal purpose are intractably embedded in discipline.**

You must understand, develop and be strengthened in your personal purpose in order to fulfil your life's vision.

Keep in mind that the activities that will drive your vision are not going to be easy or convenient. But you'll say yes to them because they give sense of direction and value deep inside you, which also make it possible for you to say no to other things. It is not responding to impulse but a function of independent willpower, the power to act with integrity to your true self, who you truly are at the core.

In the end, irrespective of your socioeconomic background or education, you can apply the same timeless principles found in the life of great people and live a life of meaning, direction, purpose, and passion. You too can become extraordinary.

> **You too can become extraordinary.**

Chapter 8
VISION SIMPLIFIES YOUR LIFE

This book is about people of all ages and from all walks of life who discovered who they truly were at the core. It describes how ordinary people can maximise the power of vision and impact their world and bring to life the big picture of their purpose and potential.

As you read this book, keep in mind that the focus is to build you as an individual so you can develop intrinsic strategies and innovative approaches. No matter your age or gender, through simple, daily effort, you can position yourself for extraordinary accomplishments in life.

The key idea is that you grab on to the core, first and foremost, so you stop wasting your precious energy and resources on irrelevant things. For the young, being able to focus your attention on the essential ingredients of being extraordinary sets you on a strong footing along the path of significance and destiny. For older readers, once you are able to apply the principles shared, you can fulfil your life's purpose. You will truly appreciate how to focus your mind's eye on the right things in a world of information overload. You will learn the rudiments of vision and time, and appreciate the fact that you're never too old to dream again.

> **No matter your age or gender, through simple, daily effort, you can position yourself for extraordinary accomplishments in life.**

You will be able to live a simple, clean, straightforward, and elegant life, with lots and lots of fun. You will find that once you tap into the three-dimensional, constrictionary, and expansionary power of vision, you will see remarkable results in your life. Indeed, you will come to realise that everything has been working together to bring you to this vantage point and into your destiny. Needless to say that visionaries usually become leaders. This is because vision imposes a certain discipline and focus that crystallises in the excellence we all admire. Show me a person of vision, and I will show you someone destined for greatness.

I am not suggesting that exercising the power of vision is going to be easy, and as a matter of fact, not everyone will fully understand it (as some are just okay living in mind-numbing mediocrity). But you have the opportunity to learn the underlying principles that make ordinary individuals become extraordinary; why wouldn't you take advantage of it? Yes, becoming extraordinary requires work, but the momentum of the power of vision returns more energy to you than it expends, as you advance on your divine pathway. Conversely, staying ordinary inherently leads to a depressing process that drains more energy than it puts back in.

> **The key idea is that you grab on to the core, first and foremost, so you stop wasting your precious energy and resources on irrelevant things.**

You too can become extraordinary, just like the people you will read about in this book. Helping you become extraordinary is truly at the heart of this entire project.

It is okay to not be okay with being average. You are called for more. You should not leave this earth without leaving a lasting legacy. You must be committed to ensuring that you maximise your gifts, talents, and potential so that the world will remember you for good, even after you are gone.

****

I am talking about the desire to be more than just merely successful. In your ordinary life, you probably are already successful. But a truly extraordinary life contributes more significantly to the lives of others. People who had extraordinary lives die empty, knowing fully well that they gave everything they had. An extraordinary life is what causes you to leave an enduring legacy behind. When we recall the various individuals in this book, something is triggered in us; we connect with the energy force field that continues to radiate through their spirit. Their vision

> **...vision imposes a certain discipline and focus that crystallises in the excellence we all admire.**

powered them to live an extraordinary life of purpose. For example, you cannot listen to a Martin Luther King speech or visit Disneyland and not be filled with awe. That is the power of vision at work. Your life can be the same too, no matter who you are, how old you are, or what gender you are.

Chapter 9
DEFINING VISION

Vision is one of the most misconstrued subjects. People use the word vision to conjure up all kinds of images. We all know vision is important, but few have fully grasped what vision truly entails. Vision is not formed by just being futuristic, as many assume. The main essence of vision is to create the future, but it also includes specific strategies and actions aimed at bringing that new future to reality. Being overly futuristic without any core foundational precedence is similar to making wishy-washy declarations, as many people do today. So to avoid falling into the trap of ignorance, it is important to understand what vision is all about.[30]

In its most basic form, vision can be defined as a clear mental image of a preferable future. It is a big picture of your future inspired in your mind. Vision is a mental picture of your destiny. Vision is a future-focused big picture specific enough to shape decision-making and broad enough to allow innovative strategies for realising the vision. Vision involves the application of one's internal intuition, inner wisdom, or Wise Advocate to imagine, discern, visualise, and conceptualise immaterial, invisible things until they effectively manifest into reality.

> **Vision is not formed by just being futuristic, as many assume.**

Vision involves the utilisation of our imagination: the ability to see the potential, to create with our minds what we cannot at present see with our eyes; and our conscience: the ability to detect our own uniqueness and the personal, moral, and ethical guidelines we follow. It's the deep contact with our basic paradigms and values, and the revelation of what we can become.

These definitions of vision connote a number of common elements, which I will attempt to describe.

A mental process: The mind and the mind's eye. Vision is a phenomenon that takes place in the mind. In essence, it originates from your core—inside of you—and is derived from your core values and beliefs. It paints a visual reality, a portrait of conditions that do not exist currently. This picture is internalised and personal. It is not somebody else's view of the future but one that uniquely belongs to you. The clearer this mental picture, the more powerful. A fuzzy and vague perspective is just an idea and not a concrete vision. It also involves the use of the brain, or more precisely the subconscious mind, or what I call the sixth sense, to detect the invisible or unseen realms.

Future-focused big picture: Using the power of creative visualisation and the ability to focus the mind ahead, rather than dwelling on or seeking to replicate the past. Vision presupposes that the present is not enough and that something different, better, is required. Vision is not about maintaining the status quo. Vision is about stretching reality to extend beyond the existing state. Vision is not about recapturing the good old days. Vision is about the desire to create the days that have not yet come into existence. Vision presupposes that there are two perspectives: the perspectives of how things are (a past or current state) and the perspective of how things should be (a future state). It doesn't just bring these perspectives to mind; vision shows you the better states and informs you what precise action to take. This forward-looking property of vision initiates change. To get to the future state, you have to go to a new location.

One of the greatest gifts to humanity is the gift of creative visualisation. If you visualise the wrong thing, you'll produce the wrong thing. Top performers and athletes often utilise the power of creative visualisation. Most world-class athletes and peak performers are visualisers. They see it; they feel it; they experience it before they actually do it. To become truly outstanding in life requires the use of creative visualisation, to see it, feel it, and experience it before it actually becomes a reality.

At the most basic form, vision is actually pieces of information that the mind decodes and forms into something concrete. As you will see in subsequent sections, your vision is based on thoughts and deeply held values. So while vision is forward focused and futuristic in nature, the pieces of information that inform your vision are not always in the future. In fact, vision is a special ability to collect data from the past and present, and to project something really great ahead of you. While a large portion of your vision is primarily a future-state scenario, it's important to be able to understand, acknowledge, and appreciate your past and present.

> **One of the greatest gifts to humanity is the gift of creative visualisation.**

This ability to see where you are coming from and where you are now (the current paradigm, assumption, or reality) and the ability to project into the future (a new paradigm, assumption, or reality) at the same time, and on top of that, having the willpower to take action towards the desired future is what I term the 3D of vision.

Your Life Purpose in 3D

Vision is your life's purpose, revealed to you in three dimensions. Truly great people have been found to use the power of 3D vision to propel themselves forward. Contrary to wishes, sweet-talking, and vague desires, vision is made up of information from the past, it provides actionable details for today, and it has a sufficient purview of the future. This unique three-dimensional viewpoint is what makes visionaries extraordinary.

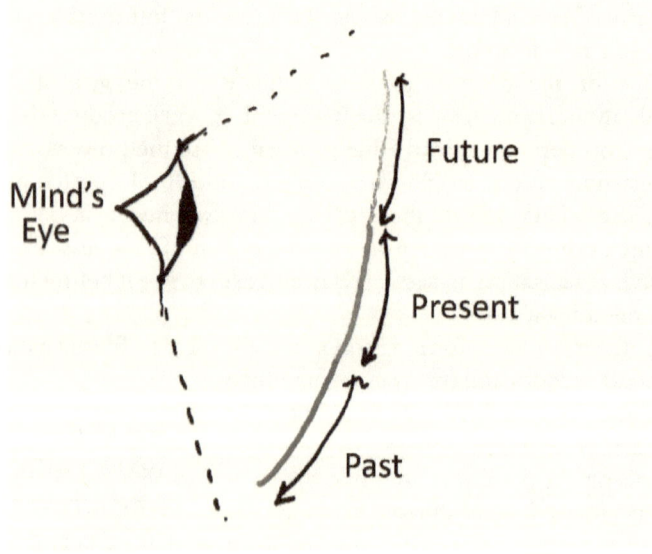

FIGURE 4: The 3D of Vision

People who have always complained about their past experiences can change their destinies for the better by simply getting a vision for their lives. Without the three-dimensional capability, you could potentially miss important information that would help your vision. Yet without a clear 3D vision, you may have regrets when you recall memories of the past. Unless you understand this three-dimensional nature of vision, you may not fully grasp your purpose. Not understanding how events of the past and present become the basis of a better future could result in the possibility for you to relive the pains of the past together with its rhetoric.

I always like to use this illustration to explain the 3D of vision: Assume that you were incredibly poor when you were growing up, and your parents struggled to make ends meet. Then you got the opportunity to break out of that cycle of poverty. Assume that your purpose now became to help everyone you find in poverty to also break out of it. You own this unique purpose because you had a real, undeniable, and life-transforming experience. It is an event that was major in your life, information or knowledge that you specially possess because of life circumstances.

The time of poverty was in your past. As bad as it was, ignoring it or wishing it didn't exist wouldn't change it. And you needed that information in order to learn how to break out of poverty. Your hindsight (the ability to see the past, as bad as it may seem), the insight you gain from it in your present, and the development of foresight from both your past and present, all inform your three-dimensional power of vision. This simply means that the 3D of vision is foresight, with insight, based on hindsight. These revelatory three dimensions are powerful and can instantly lead to a light-bulb moment for anyone who has been struggling with a terrible past, not understanding why they went through such difficult times.

> The 3D of vision emphasises the significance of possessing a keen awareness of past and current circumstances and possibilities, and notes the value of learning from and building on the past.

You can apply this illustration to any part of your life that you wished never existed. With vision, you can rewrite a better end, no matter how bad the past and present may have been. You can use the future-focused power of vision to create a new reality. Rather than wish it away, use it. It can become the unique knowledge that only you possess and a critical prerequisite for the formation of your vision.

Conversely, a good experience in the past can be the point of inflection. Whether good or bad, recognise that it was for a purpose; by facing the future, you can use these experiences to your advantage.

The 3D of vision emphasises the significance of possessing a keen awareness of past and current circumstances and possibilities, and notes the value of learning from and building on the past. The three-dimensional nature of vision also brings about the depth, meaning, persuasion, passion, and strength of that particular vision. Appendix 2 shows a conceptual composite evolution of the 3D of vision and the phasal nature of vision.

3D Times 3D

People who capture the three-dimensional nature of vision also apply three more Ds to bring their vision to life: discover, develop, and distinguish. They tend to discover themselves and their God-given gifts and abilities. They also develop these gifts through continuous training and application. Those who get to the peak of their development also gain the strength of character that sustains their gifts. The final stage is how vision ultimately help in distinguishing them from the multitude. The discipline of self and the mastery of inherent gifts and potential sets certain individuals apart from the crowd and places them among great people in life.

The Power of Vision

In physics, power is energy that is produced by mechanical, electrical, or other means and used to operate a device. In social or psychological constructs, power is the ability to do something or act in a particular way. The human ability to do something, to exert our will, is one of the most mysterious social forces in our existence. We can obtain power through our closeness to or relationship with people in positions of influence. However, a more sustainable way to become powerful is by having special information. The power of vision comes with having a peculiar knowledge because of your exposure to unique pieces of information (or what I call revelation). This knowledge-power is the type that comes after new information causes a change in your perspective and paradigms. That type of power comes with aha! moments of deep insight and compels us to operate with renewed understanding. This power that appears to be a conception in the mind is what makes vision a powerful concept.

Vision is the capacity to see beyond what your mere eyes can see, seeing with your empowered, disciplined, and transformed mind, into your destiny and fullness of your purpose. Vision is having a clear grasp of your individual divine pathway uniquely created for you to navigate. And this is the beauty of vision: it can lead to radical simplicity of your life while increasing your personal effectiveness and productivity. It brings so much peace when one is clear—about what is essential and eliminating the non-essentials in one's life. The power simply comes from knowledge. Knowledge is the key. Being able to conceptualise and process information from the past (good or bad past experiences) while being effective today (present relevance) as you advance into your future (future, forward-looking orientation) is a visionary paradox that I will shed more light on later in this book.

Vision is not just a vague idea of what you will do one day. Vision is what will take you out from wishing that things will get better (wishland) to making concrete resolutions and taking specific actions (realland). When it is well conceived, vision can become a very powerful force that originates from within; it doesn't require any other person or external force motivating you to take action. Vision comes with a special type of power: the capacity to act, the strength to accomplish something. Vision produces the vital energy to make choices and decisions based on one's inner guidance, intuition, and intrinsic values. Vision, a set of distinct codes or information, comes with the capacity to overcome deeply embedded habits and to cultivate higher, more effective ones. One of the greatest forces in life is the force of vision. Clear vision gives us passion that keeps us continually moving forward in life.

> ...this is the beauty of vision: it can lead to radical simplicity of your life while increasing your personal effectiveness and productivity.

The power of vision propels you from ground state to the mountaintop

The power of vision can be illustrated like this: Let's assume the top of a mountain is your future state; if that's what you describe as your destiny, it means that by the time you get to the top of the mountain, you have accomplished your vision. At the top, there's no more need for power to be exerted. However, before you get to the top, right from the bottom (in the ordinary, current state), there's need for power to get to the mountaintop. The travails of climbing require exerting energy and strength.

Therein lies the purpose of this book. The power of vision lies in its ability to propel you forward. The power of vision lies not only in its ability to show you the big picture future but also how to activate and harness the energy force field that propels you towards your purpose and destiny. Along the way, you become equipped with the tools and resources to make that vision come to pass, as you learn the processes, principles, and practices that will make your life extraordinary. Unlike other books that show only the results of their vision (their own mountaintop), motivating you to live yours, this book takes you deeper, step-by-step, into the how vision is formed in your mind. Through the proprietary Vision Flywheel framework developed in this book, you will learn how you can start from where you are and with what you have to become truly extraordinary in life.

> **The power of vision lies not only in its ability to show you the big picture future but also how to activate and harness the energy force field that propels you towards your purpose and destiny.**

Vision in its true form must be value-based, purposeful, and relevant to time and context. For true visionaries, the imaginary world of their visions is more real to them than the concrete reality around them. In fact, the visions of visionaries are their reality. Even more, vision is what gives you a special type of power that makes you distort reality, so that even in the face of what appear to be a dead end, you can create a road. In essence, vision gives you the power to manifest in what I call a "reality distortion field" (RDF): the ability to refuse to accept limitations that stand in the way of your ideas and to have the conviction that you can overcome any difficulty. RDF is the phenomenon of being able to bend reality – the conviction that reality is malleable. This field (or more precisely the positive force field emanating from your core) is what enables you to convince others that they, too, can achieve the impossible.

Sight is not the same as vision. You can lose your sight once it gets dark, but that is not the case for vision. Whether during the day, at noon, or in the nighttime, you can have vision. Sight is a function of the eyes, but vision is a function of the mind. It is possible to have sight but no vision. One of the greatest hindrances to vision is sight. This is because what you are seeing physically (including the current or past successes in front of you) can become a hindrance to the vision you see with your mind's eye. Ordinary people get overwhelmed by their sight, but extraordinary people create a new, better reality with their vision. Sight can cause you to lose focus due to distractions; vision provides clarity and focus despite the distractions.

> **Sight is not the same as vision.**

> **One of the greatest hindrances to vision is sight.**

Well-articulated vision should stir up your passion and invite you (and others) to greatness. Vision represents a future beyond what is possible today or what we think possible tomorrow. Vision is an invitation to a tomorrow or destination of greatness. It forms the highest-level objective that challenge us every single day. Vision helps us to see into a future better than today, thereby elevating our hopes and aspirations. Vision is crucial in our lives as individuals or in our institutions (in which it becomes corporate vision). The power of vision is a prerequisite to get to your mountaintop.

> **Sight can cause you to lose focus due to distractions; vision provides clarity and focus despite the distractions.**

You have the power, use it for good.

Despite how powerful each of us can be, evidence shows that individuals don't always use their power effectively. Researcher Ron Carucci and his firm commissioned a ten-year longitudinal study of more than twenty-seven hundred people and found, contrary to generally held assumptions, that indeed the greatest misuse of power wasn't for self-interest.[31] Many people are powerful but don't acknowledge it, merely for fear of being judged or a fear of making a mistake. For some, abandoning power just seemed easier and safer.

And the saddest part in the waste of power is that the good it could do to change the world goes unrealised. Don't forfeit all the great things you could do in this world simply because you didn't use your power. You are so much more powerful than you realise. Instead of shirking or shunning your power, embrace it. Resolve today to use it for the greater good and live a life that shows it.

While the power of vision can become a remarkable force for impacting our world for the better, there have been instances where it has been misused for personal gain or immoral reasons.

The Vision of Hitler

Sometimes, what we call vision is not what vision is truly all about. I found the story of Adolf Hitler to be a prime example of how vision can be ill-conceived. Hitler, the German political leader who lived from 1889 to 1945, has generally been known in history as the man whose hands are stained with the blood of millions killed in the devastation of the Second World War and the horror of the Holocaust. But Hitler was not born a brutal tyrant; he became one. He led the Germans into one of the most brutal wars ever known to humanity, leading to the death of millions of people. It was startling to find that he attributed his terrible actions and motives to a vision. Indeed, Hitler's vision was documented in Mein Kampf, his autobiography.

> **It was startling to find that Adolf Hitler attributed his terrible actions and motives to a vision.**

Hitler's vision included the desire to restore German lands to their greatest historical extent, real or imagined. To that extent, he declared the superiority of white Aryan race, with particular vitriol reserved for the Jews he viewed as "parasites." Their elimination, he said, "must necessarily be a bloody process." Hitler's vision as documented in Mein Kampf outlined the central tenets of a Germany under Nazi control: military expansion, elimination of impure races, and dictatorial authoritarianism.

I point out Hitler's vision to show that vision can go wrong. The objective of a true vision is to produce a future better and brighter than today. While the effort to conceive and bring your vision to life is private, its manifestation is for public benefit and to bring greater good to humanity.

Through Hitler, we understand that one can misuse the power of focus. If you focus your thought-mind on the negative, you will activate a negative power of vision. Because what you focus on becomes your vision and destiny. It's a self-fulfilling prophesy: The negative mental image you hold will eventually come to pass. In its private form, your focus or what I call vision attention density (VAD) must be in line with your Wise Advocate, your attentive mind that seeks your overall best interest in the long term. In its public manifestation, it must focus on the wellbeing of others and love and serve a larger audience for their benefit. There are so many "Hitlers" out there who use the power of vision to lure people to themselves for selfish and self-centered purposes. If your vision is only leading to personal benefit, it is not a true vision and ill-conceived. If you find that your vision has any of Hitler's characteristics, is time to dream again. It is time to carry out what I call re-vision. And for a number of people reading this, what you call vision could actually be a re-vision.

Re-vision is a process of fine-tuning our original vision as we grow in knowledge and gain new perspectives that expose us to more relevant information.

Constrictionary and Expansionary Power of Vision (Private Labours That Benefit the Masses)

Vision will first constrict you (in private) and then expand you (public manifestation). It so happens because vision primarily clarifies and qualifies purpose and gives us direction in life. When you have a vision for your life, there is a tendency to move in a direction that will make the vision clearer and achievable. This so happens because people with vision (visionaries) tend to attract the right resources (human and material) while at the same time repelling the wrong resources. Vision therefore comes with constrictionary and expansionary properties. This constrictionary property, as it turns out, is the personal effort and labour you put into working out your vision and purpose. With time, the constrictionary power of vision causes your flywheel to turn and produce tangible results that keeps building momentum. With more momentum, private successes becomes of public benefit to many other people. In essence, constrictionary power of vision occurs in private and ultimately leads to the expansionary power of vision and public manifestations.

It is critical to note that vision will first constrict you. The constrictionary power of vision is such that it forces you to break out of your comfort zone. Things that are not in line to help your vision become a reality become irrelevant and fizzle away. Vision comes with focus and discipline. It tends to narrow down your capabilities into purposeful, result-oriented actions. The implication of this is that you tend to lose connection with things that are not in line with your purpose. This sometimes includes former friends, relations, or associates who have no role to play in your future and cannot help you get to the next phase in your growth and overall purpose. The mental orientation that vision gives your thinking may make some people around you uncomfortable.

The constrictionary power of vision manifests itself in your community, by virtue of the new, special information or revelation that you have, and you appear to be ahead of them. Being separate from your community is usually first seen as betrayal. But as you will come to learn, being ahead of your community because of your vision should actually be seen as leadership.

You could also become a threat to people around you, especially those who are comfortable with the status quo or who benefit from the ignorance or mediocrity of others. Keep in mind that true vision comes with the responsibility to use the power of special information to challenge existing norms, not for the sake of destroying them but to engage them with the aim of creating a better culture.

> ...being ahead of your community because of your vision should actually be seen as leadership.

As a result, vision takes conscious and consistent effort. It doesn't just happen by chance or accident. There's no shortcut to the process; otherwise, you risk the possibility of not fulfilling your destiny. Vision requires hard, rigorous, lonely, inglorious work in order for it to come to pass. This is because the conception of vision is usually personal and private. But the application and manifestation of vision is public. Your vision will launch you into a new reality that causes you to be noticed. This is another paradox of vision, such that the private labour and suffering of one person's vision is for the collective enjoyment of the public and indeed the global benefit to humanity. And the benefits often happen to be enjoyed by people who first rejected you and your vision. It is interesting that they become the chief beneficiaries. This is exactly the case with Joseph.

It therefore becomes obvious that since vision requires such discipline, practice, focus, character, and a culture of excellence, it sets the visionary apart from the multitude. Being separated for excellence and being particularly known for doing what others aspire to do makes visionaries become influential. Such visionaries usually become leaders.

Vision makes you humble because through the specialisation capabilities that come with it (e.g., being able to recognise your niche in life and fulfil your destiny), visionaries operate within their areas of specialisation. While many people today are afraid of specialisation because it creates the impression that you might become obsolete, visionaries specialise and are able to impact many lives and fulfil their purpose. It is based on the discipline, focus, and depth of vision that allow the visionary to have a unique niche while at the same time having global influence. Humility has both constrictionary and expansionary properties.

The private labours and constrictionary power of vision is what allows talents, gifts, and potential locked up within to find expression and manifestation. In private, small flames can be developed. Your unique gifts and talents can be discovered and developed to become excellent. As a result, you gradually get the opportunity to apply your unique gifts to solve special problems only you can solve. But it all starts by having a distinct vision for your life. You must know what you are in this world for.

> **Vision requires hard, rigorous, lonely, inglorious work in order for it to come to pass.**

While true visionaries are specialists in their area of calling, they don't find it difficult to work with other visionaries in reaching a bigger mandate. Contrary to what is generally assumed, visionaries anticipate collaboration and support because they are fully aware of what they can and can't do. And it is this passion, commitment, and humility to serve the world with their unique gift that eventually enlarges the reach of the visionary and results in the expansionary power of vision.

The expansionary power of vision is such that it allows you to see, operate, and live beyond your physical assets, launching you into a realm where you can access the invisible, intangible things supernaturally secured for you. The expansionary power of vision is what makes it appropriate for your vision and the future you desire to be bigger than you and your current circumstances. In effect, vision has the capacity to attract human, natural, and supernatural resources towards the fulfilment of a bigger, better future. It directly follows natural and spiritual law that what you focus on you become; anything you water germinates and grows.

Vision Makes Your Life Beautiful

Because of its ability to keep you focused, vision eliminates conflict and rivalry in your life. You don't need to seek attention; people just know you for your gift because you exhibit direction and excellence in what you do. True visionaries are humble, knowing fully well what their gifts are and the unique contribution they can make within their niche (I expand more on this in subsequent chapters).

> The expansionary power of vision is such that it allows you to see, operate, and live beyond your physical assets, launching you into a realm where you can access the invisible, intangible things supernaturally secured for you.

The expansionary power of vision reaches its peak as other people derive their own vision, life, and purpose through the manifestation of your distinct vision. As each visionary specialises in one area or another, multiple visionaries can work together without envy, jealousy, or struggle. The coming together of two or more visionaries leads to a corporate vision. Visionaries sharing a similar vision (corporate vision) that inspires them to want to arrive at a similar destiny results in what I call corporate destiny. Co-visionaries (two or more people who understand the power of vision and as a result have disciplined their thoughts and actions) can become destiny partners. Destiny partners, an important component of the expansionary power of vision, are important in the life of a visionary. Co-visionaries and destiny partners are the bedrock of institutions that are built to last. Identifying a co-visionary is a major life decision that can lead to expansion if done right.

What is more fascinating about vision is that it makes you become what I call a Level 7 leader. There has been a lot written about levels of leadership, and some authors rank leadership from Level 1 to Level 6. None of those leadership levels captures what a true visionary depicts, hence the reason I created another level in this book. The beauty of vision is that it makes you outstanding and great, not for the purpose of any organisation or institution (as Level 6 leaders appear to do) but for the primary purpose of fulfilling a higher, usually deeply personal purpose (Level 7 leadership). True visionary leaders attribute their driving force to God or an unseen supernatural force; they give glory to this force for the huge blessings they bring to humanity, not the money, fame, recognition, or popularity.

Just simple, graceful, and amazing life as found in one form or another in the lives of extraordinary individuals, such as Martin Luther King Jr., Nelson Mandela, and Mother Teresa.

That is what the power of vision can make your life become.

Chapter 10
THE POWER OF PARADIGMS

Our perceptions eventually become our convictions. Perception governs not only the way we see but also how we behave. Our perceptions are deeply embedded. Our perceptions become the lens through which we see the world and also shape how we interpret the world. Our vision is fundamentally shaped by perceptions and paradigms.

The Flaws of Modern-Day Perceptions

In my research and travel, I have come across many notable and significant people who did amazing things but could not be categorised as extraordinary. This is because they erred towards the negative. Their fame swells like a balloon, only to get deflated by their personality flaws. Instead of sustained greatness and legacy that inspires others for many years to come, we find it difficult to identify any good thing they stand for. These self-acclaimed public figures are great in their own eyes, but for the wrong reasons. Sadly, they are defined by many people as their role model or hero.

Many of these so-called role models are only superficial. They are image-conscious celebrities who exploit social media constructs to create an impression in people. They cover up their personal flaws with Band-Aids and quick fixes, leaving their underlying chronic problems untouched. While they show some level of human emotions and good will, their ultimate focus is self-fulfillment and personal ego. Then one day, these flaws surface, and we begin to wonder why we never saw those personality defects before. They operate with the power of vision to an extent, but it is ill-conceived like that of Adolf Hitler discussed earlier.

No one is perfect; the issue is being true to who you truly are. The problem is that by showing one face in public and having a different persona in private, you demonstrate a lack of character and integrity. Some appear one way in public, knowing they are not who they claim to be. You cannot fake enduring greatness. Becoming extraordinary in life is not about covering up personal flaws but about aiming for your true self. When who you are—your values and core beliefs—matches what you do, your outcomes are bound to be genuine, true, and resounding.

I studied truly great people and saw that our modern world desires greatness but keeps moving further from it. I became aware of a phenomenon called confirmation bias, where one knows something to be fundamentally wrong but which the society accepts to be okay and as a result make one feel that it is okay too. We lack the patience to understand principles that govern how things run. Seeing how widespread confirmation bias is showed me that our modern time has gone far beyond the foundational life principles that were handed to us.

You cannot fake enduring greatness.

Years ago, our parents taught us about things that created a deeper sense of value. Today, those values appear to be at variance with modern ideologies. For example, we were taught the Golden Rule: to do unto others what you'd have them do to you, and the basic rule: to love your neighbour as yourself, not less than yourself. But what we see in society today is the desire for personal ego over community; service and commitments are replaced by a selfish and self-centred agenda.

When who you are—your values and core beliefs—matches what you do, your outcomes are bound to be genuine, true, and resounding.

We want to be great, but we don't want to look within to identify what sustains true greatness. Our generation appears to be churning out new ideas after ideas, strategies after strategies. We are on an endless quest for innovative techniques of human effectiveness; yet, the very foundational pillars that hold our lives seem to be eroding over time. We earn degrees that make us look smarter, we have business ideas, we employ tactics that expand our influence and make people do what we want. We seal our public appearances with a smile in order to gain more social capital. Yet our idea of enduring greatness pales due to a lack of integrity and the habits that sustain it.

Our issues originate from what can be described as the biased perception phenomenon.

Biased Perception

Each of us grew up with two mental maps: the map of the way things are (current realities) and the map of the way things should be (potential realities). The latter represents a future state which is informed primarily by our beliefs and values. We interpret everything we experience through these mental maps. We seldom question their accuracy; we're usually even unaware that we have them. We simply assume that the way we see things is the way they really are. And our attitudes and behaviors grow out of those assumptions. The way we see things is the source of the way we think and the way we act.

> We are on an endless quest for innovative techniques of human effectiveness; yet, the very foundational pillars that hold our lives seem to be eroding over time.

Getting a clear mental picture and a clear vision as an extraordinary individual, you need to understand your own inherent biases.

Let me indulge you in an intellectual exercise. Take a look at Image 5 for a few seconds (if you've come across this exercise before, you can move on to the next section below titled: "Light-Bulb Experiences").

Now look at Image 5 again and carefully describe what you see. Do you see a woman? How old would you say she is? What does she look like? Describe what she's wearing. What kind of roles do you see her in?[32]

Now, look at the Image 6. Can you describe the lady you see? You might call her young, lovely, rather fashionable, with a petite nose and demure presence. She might be a dating partner for a single man; a clothes designer might hire her as a fashion model.

But what if I were to tell you that you're wrong? What if I said this picture is of a sad-looking woman in her seventies who has a huge nose and certainly is no model. She's someone you probably would help cross the street.

Who's right? Look at the picture again. Can you see the old woman?

If you can't, keep trying.

Look at the other picture again. Can you see her big hook nose? Her chin?

If we were having an in-person meeting, a one-to-one, I could point out clues to you as we discussed the picture in detail. You could describe what you see to me, and I could talk to you about what I see. We could continue to communicate until you clearly showed me what you see in the picture and I clearly showed you what I see.

Because we can't do that, look at Image 7 and study the picture there and then look at Image 6 again. Can you see the old woman now? It's important that you see her before you continue reading. Keep trying until you see it.

IMAGE 5

IMAGE 6

When I first did this exercise, I didn't see the old lady in the picture; if you didn't, either, you should have experienced what I call a light-bulb moment or aha! experience as the scales gradually fall off your eyes and you begin to see the old lady. For those who have done this exercise before, recall the feeling you had when you had the light-bulb experience.

This exercise yields some insight about personal perception. It shows, first and foremost, how powerful preconditioning affects our perspectives. Taking the first look at Image 5 was the preconditioning that only made you see one side to the next picture. The question is, if less than ten seconds can have such an impact on the way we see things, what about the conditioning of a lifetime? The influences in our lives—friends, family, school, church, work, and all other social constructs around us—all have an impact on us but in a rather subtle, unconscious way. They shape our frame of reference.

This frame of reference formed the perception of the people who were involved in the MTO experiment we discussed earlier; despite being moved to a wealthy neighbourhood, with the provision of financial tokens, they could not take advantage of the opportunity because of mental poverty. They could not break out of the mental captivity that their perceptions created.

The biased perception exercise also shows how our attitudes and behaviours originate from our perceptions. Perceptions are the basis for integrity in our lives. We cannot live effectively, in the reality of our true purpose and potential, if what we see is different from the way we talk and walk. Both our attitudes and behaviours have to be congruent with what we see in our mind.

> The influences in our lives—friends, family, school, church, work, and all other social constructs around us—all have an impact on us but in a rather subtle, unconscious way.

This brings to the surface the very reason why many people remain stagnant. Stagnancy (or, more precisely, unstained movement) is the attempt to make artificial changes in attitudes and behaviours without internal alignment. I have seen so many people adhere to strict routines and course corrections, including those who never miss Bible study and never skip church, who end up failing in the long run simply because they had the wrong perception of who they truly are.

> Stagnancy (or, more precisely, unstained movement) is the attempt to make artificial changes in attitudes and behaviours without internal alignment.

We need to become aware of ourselves, including our potential; awareness helps us acknowledge our own shortcomings as we begin to see people differently, from a better point of view. The more understanding we have of the original image in the biased perception experiment, the more clearly we can see that it contained both the old woman and the young lady.

For many, fundamental biases in perception have carried on for long. We all think we are seeing clearly (from our own point of view), as objectively as it can ever be, only to find out that we had perception biases.

IMAGE 7

Our point of view might not be all that there is to the picture of our lives. There could potentially be a better viewpoint. Our fundamental perception creates our world view as we see things not as they are, but as we are, or as we have been conditioned to see things.

The effort therefore becomes to find out the truth of what the true state is, or to clear our lens of every obstruction to our vision, so we can behold our true state. The more aware we are of our basic perceptions or the assumptions that subconsciously guide our lives, and the extent to which we allow life experiences to shape our perspective, the more we can take responsibility for those underlying assumptions and subject them to examination. By doing this, we can

> **Our fundamental perception creates our world view as we see things not as they are, but as we are, or as we have been conditioned to see things.**

better identify the subconscious influences over our lives and effectively appreciate what determines our vision.

As you continue to read, I ask that you attempt to review your reality, your current map of how things are, and remain open to the new knowledge or positive external influences (value forces) that carry fundamental truth, a new information of how things should be.

Light-Bulb Experiences and the Need for New Perspectives and Paradigms

If you just did the bias perception exercise for the first time, I can imagine the light bulbs still springing up in your mind. This light-bulb moment came when you saw the composite picture in another way. The more you were bound by the first picture, the greater the light bulb when the new perspective emerged in the second picture.

These light-bulb experiences or aha! moments have preceded almost every significant breakthrough in human history. It is the threshold where we break away from tradition, the status quo, and the old way of thinking and doing things. It is the point of awakening – the tipping point that launches us towards embracing new knowledge and understanding.

Those experiences become paradigmatic moments where we examine our frames of reference, theories, and assumptions. These light-bulb moments became points of inflections for the extraordinary individuals profiled in this book. It was that moment when they saw their world, not in terms of physical sight but in terms of depth, meaning, and understanding. It was the foundation for their conception of a new vision for life, or a review of an existing vision, to make it better (the review of an existing vision is a process I call re-vision).

> ...light-bulb experiences or aha! moments have preceded almost every significant breakthrough in human history.

This new, better perspective emerged within Martin Luther King Jr. as he observed the mistreatment of African Americans because of the colour of their skin. What followed was a call to a lifetime of action against injustice. Gradually, the mild-mannered, inquisitive child who eventually rebelled against segregation turned into a dedicated young minister who continually questioned the depths of his faith and the limits of his wisdom; the loving husband and father who sought to balance his family's needs with those of a growing, nationwide movement.

Depending on how strong a light-bulb moment is, it can paradigmatically shift your life to a new horizon. The revelations that come through light-bulb moments become critical components for visions; they propel ordinary people to become extraordinary. In such a reflective moment, Martin Luther King Jr. got fired up by a vision of equality for people everywhere.

Steve Jobs had a similar light-bulb moment, a paradigmatic shift, in 1965, which later gave rise to Apple in 1976. In 1965, he watched as students of the University of California, Berkeley clashed with police and the National Guard in protest against America's involvement in the Vietnam War. Northern California became a hotbed as footage of clashes and riots in Berkeley and Oakland was beamed around the globe, fueling sympathetic movements. Feeling helpless, people like Jobs took the protest to another level. In 1976, he decided to make a big impact by challenging an authoritarian regime, not with stones or arms, but using computers. He took the battlefield to the business world.

It was a call inside of another call, a light-bulb moment on September 10, 1946, that caused Mother Teresa to resign her teaching call and moved into the slums in Calcutta, India. That moment in 1946 would forever transform her life. With just some basic medical training, she voyaged for the first time into Calcutta's slums with no more specific a goal than to care for the underprivileged. The actions following that turning point in her life had never been experienced before. Her work brought hope and life to the destitute, the deserted, and their families, and it quickly spread around the world as support poured in. Mother Teresa's organisation, Missionaries of Charity, subsequently spread around the world. From her base in India, she had a presence throughout the globe, including the slums in New York. Mother Teresa was considered one of the twentieth century's greatest humanitarians.

In Nelson Mandela's case, he had multiple light-bulb experiences. In the struggle for freedom in apartheid South Africa, Mandela was part of the ANC, and in the 1950s, they launched a non-violent operation of strikes and protests called the Defiance Campaign against the unjust laws of apartheid. By 1953, Mandela concluded that the non-violent approach wasn't working and came up with a new plan for political struggle. Although he supported non-violence as a principle not a tactic, the Sharpeville massacre in 1960, when South African police killed sixty-nine protesters, became the last straw for Mandela. That light-bulb moment resulted in the creation of ANC's underground military wing, Umkhonto we Sizwe, or Spear of the Nation, in mid-1961. After Umkhonto we Sizwe launched military actions in 1961, Mandela was arrested in 1962. In 1964, Mandela and some of the others tried with him were convicted and jailed for life. While in prison, Mandela was offered freedom several times on various conditions, including renouncing violence, but he refused.

It took a long time before a new perspective came for Mandela. It is possible that the solitude of prison allowed him to connect with his inner, true self. He experienced another light-bulb moment, a paradigmatic shift, and just as he had embraced violence without the permission of ANC leaders, he wrote to leaders of the white supremacist government in 1985, initiating peace talks. Umkhonto we Sizwe abandoned its policy of violence in 1990 as negotiations to dismantle apartheid and set up of free elections continued. Mandela's rhetoric had changed from the sharp, angry words of a young revolutionary to the considered, dignified wisdom of a beloved elder.

He later recounts what he wrote in 1979, which was published in his last book, a collection of notes and writings, *Conversations with Myself*. Here is an excerpt:[33]

> *Habits die hard and they leave their unmistakable marks, the invisible scars that are engraved in our bones and that flow in our blood, that do havoc to the principal actors beyond repair. ... Such scars portray people as they are and bring out into the full glare of public scrutiny the embarrassing contradictions in which individuals live out their lives.*

A crisis like the coronavirus, a life-threatening illness, or any other life-altering event can cause a fundamental shift in our priorities. It can make us suddenly take on new roles that we never knew we could handle and be able to lead efficiently because they emerge out of a great conviction and change in perception.

Whether it's an instant light-bulb experience like the bias perception exercise, or the slow and gradual ones that took years to come to Mandela in prison, we must recognise that these light-bulb moments move us from one world view to another. And this change in world view brings about powerful changes in our attitudes and behavior; it ultimately becomes the basis of our relationship with others and the universe.

THE POWER OF VISION

To make a lasting impact, as extraordinary people do, is to see differently, think differently, feel differently, and behave differently. Thinking different thoughts is what precedes doing great things. By operating from the core, we can expose ourselves to new, deeper knowledge about our potential and capabilities and in turn align our attitudes, actions, and behaviours accordingly. Instead of trimming the leaves and branches, we can go to the core, the roots of the tree, and nourish it so it produces better fruit. For your life to take a new turn and have new meaning, you need a new perspective, a light-bulb moment that forms at the core of your being.

> **To make a lasting impact, as extraordinary people do, is to see differently, think differently, feel differently, and behave differently.**

New perspectives are required because we cannot become what we ought to be if all we can see is what we currently are. There has to be a clearer vision emerging from new perspectives, which are hinged on individual habits or character. What we become is a product of what we see. To become extraordinary is to change what we see. What we see is highly interrelated to who we are. We can't go very far to changing our seeing without simultaneously changing our being at the core, and vice versa. Paradigm shifts or light-bulb moments are the foundation for vision because they create the lens through which we see the world.

> **Paradigm shifts or light-bulb moments are the foundation for vision because they create the lens through which we see the world.**

Chapter 11
DISCIPLINED THOUGHTS

The principle and practice of focus is embedded in the assertion that whatever you focus on grows, what you think about expands, and what you dwell upon determines your destiny. What this means in literal terms is that, the quality of your thoughts determines the quality of your life.

Generally speaking, positive personal changes are seen as discoveries. What this means is that they are not seen as change at all, but as revealing what was always hidden deep inside.[34] The concept of vision derive its revelatory backing from this. And since vision originates from and is conceived in the mind, disciplined thoughts as a mental process that takes place within us, plays an important role in vision formation, conception and revelation. But we are able to actually understand this mental process and mind mapping through a process of solitude and self-awareness.

In our world today, it's so easy to get caught up in the thick of thin things in life. As we work to keep our schedule full of items and agendas and to-do lists, it is highly possible for what truly matters most to get buried under layers of pressing problems, immediate concerns, and outward behaviors. While many strive to use their imagination and creative abilities, they end up living in their memory and past experiences. As a result, instead of enjoying limitless potential, they strive to escape their limiting past. In the end, whatever so preoccupies our mind is what dominates our attention. Whatever we hold in our mind determines what we see. But through solitude (or what some call reflection) and introspection, we can reset the defaults, take charge of what we dwell on, and position our lives on the path towards greatness.

The Power of Solitude and Self-Awareness

Solitude is when we are quiet and still enough to allow self-awareness to take place. Solitude doesn't have to involve travelling away or isolating oneself (although that may happen). Self-isolation that results in paralysis of thought and disorientation is not the same as solitude, either. People whose lifestyles are built on consistent reflection and introspection can experience solitude and self-awareness, even when their life is busy. Solitude allows us to pause momentarily and experience inner tranquility. It allows us to process information in the slow cooker of our minds and allows for organic truth to germinate. In moments of solitude, we allow information to precipitate so we can identify vital components and see how they add up to what we already know or else discard them completely. It is the power of solitude that allows your vision to stay sharp and in focus. Visionaries, as I found, have moments of solitude where they regurgitate information and reflect, meditate, and examine them. The end product of effective solitude is a stronger sense of self-awareness or a more ponderous term used by some psychologist called metacognition.[35]

> In the end, whatever so preoccupies our mind is what dominates our attention.

Solitude and self-awareness afford humanity one of its greatest gifts: the ability to think about what we're thinking about. Self-awareness, the ability to recognize our feelings as it happens, activates our imaginative abilities and sensitises what scientists have referred to as Wise Advocate.[36] Our Wise Advocate is our inner guide, our conscience or our attentive mind, which can see the bigger picture, including our inherent worth, our capabilities, and our accomplishments. Through the mental process of imagination, we can visualise the potential, uncreated worlds within us. With conscience, we connect with our true self, who we truly are, based on our sincere desire to embody the values and achieve the goals we truly believe in. With self-awareness, our minds can come in contact with universal laws and principles. As a result, self-awareness helps us to identify our own singular talents and avenues of contribution, and using the personal guidelines within, we can effectively develop them. Combined with self-awareness, imagination and conscience empower us to rewire our minds and bring them to a higher level of functioning and power.

> The end product of effective solitude is a stronger sense of self-awareness.

Self-awareness can be a nonreactive, nonjudgemental attention to inner states. But this sensibility also can be less equanimous; typical thoughts bespeaking emotional self-awareness include "I shouldn't feel this way," "I'm thinking good things to cheer up," and for a more restricted self-awareness, the fleeting thoughts "Don't think about it" in reaction to something highly upsetting.[37]

Self-awareness also has an emotional intelligence component to it. Emotions are impulses to act, the instant plans for handling life that has been encoded in our genes. The very root of the word emotion is motere, the Latin verb "to move", plus the prefix "e-" to connote "move away," suggesting that a tendency to act is implicit in every emotion. But self-awareness gives us the ability to manage our emotions increasing our capacity to soothe ourselves, to shake off rampant anxiety, gloom, or irritability and the consequences of failure. We can therefore be able to motivate ourselves, have genuine empathy for others (fundamental "people skill") and altruism (being attuned to what others need or want).

> Through the mental process of imagination, we can visualise the potential, uncreated worlds within us.

Self-awareness is about mindfulness,[38] being fully knowledgeable that you're living in the reality of your true purpose, intent, and desire. The peak of self-awareness is that it enables you to recognise the many things competing for your attention and empowers you to be able to focus—by choice—on the ones that are in line with your core values, discarding the ones that are nonessential.

Although, there is a logical distinction between being aware of feelings and acting to change them, University of New Hampshire psychologist, John Mayer, finds that for all practical purposes the two go hand-in-hand: to recognize a foul mood is to want to get out of it.[39] What follows awareness therefore is the power to rewire our minds.

Rewiring Your Mind

By default, our brain automatically forms a mental picture and also shapes our current realities out of what we have been exposed to. Like a sponge, our brain takes in external (sometimes negative) information, or what I call value forces. From a young age, these forces have shaped our lives, up to and including this moment in time. With the power of solitude, self-awareness, and the resulting mindfulness, we can reset what has already been preformed in our minds—negative, self-imposed limiting habits and character—through a process of rewiring. The process of rewiring involves choosing to focus on truths: who we truly are, the big picture. This rewiring process has sometimes been referred to as consciousness engineering[40] because it involves making conscious choices of what to accept or reject in the mind. Rewiring helps us to remove the limitations that keep us from manifesting our true self, as well as our gifts and potential.

The mind is not the same as the brain. Our brain only receives inputs and generates the passive side of experiences. It is our mind (or what some call our heart) that is active in focusing our attention and in making decisions. It is important to make this distinction because the discussion about vision is less about using your brain as it is about using your mind. Vision is about constructively focusing your attention with your mind. Your mind is where the real thinking occurs. Your mind is where vision is conceived or inspired.

> **Vision is about constructively focusing your attention with your mind.**

Being able to focus your mind in positive, beneficial ways will help you rewire your brain; with support, you can take corrective actions and form habits that makes you become extraordinary.

In effect, your mind gives you the power to determine your actions, decide what is important (and what is not), and reassess the value or meaning of situations, people, yourself, and events.

The brain receives information from the environment, including images, verbal communication from others, emotional reactions, bodily sensations, and so on, and then processes that information in an automatic and rote way. No thought or awareness is involved (at least initially). Once it processes these inputs, the brain presents the information to our conscious awareness.

This is where the mind comes in. At this point of information processing, the mind has the ability to determine whether it wants to focus on that information coming from the brain or on something else. In comparison to the mind, then, the brain is passive; it does not take a long-term, value-based approach to actions. In order words, the brain does not incorporate your true self or Wise Advocate into its process but merely reacts to its environment in habitual, automatic ways.

Everyone was born complete with creativity and the ability to do really great things in life. It is like the hardware is already there. But it is through bad wiring or what some people call wrong scripting that we become victims of circumstances and our true self and destiny are derailed.

Everyone was born with a unique purpose and potential. Each one of us is a divine original, a special creation; there are no duplicates. There is no other person like you in the whole universe. Take a moment to let that sink in. You are a divine original. That there is no other person like you, out of the over 8 billion people all over the world, should make you feel excited, humble, privileged, and responsible at the same time; you want to fulfil all that you were born for and that which is inside of you. Renowned fingerprint pioneer Sir Francis Galton calculated the probability of two whole fingerprints matching and found the result to be somewhere around one in 64 billion (1.562513%)—making your fingerprints uniquely yours. Your iris (eyes), tongue, gait, and ears are also unique. Don't let anyone think of you as ordinary. Even though you may appear like you are heading nowhere in the beginning, with the power of vision that emerges from a renewed thought, you can become empowered. Your accomplishments have no limit; the only limitation comes from not recognising who you truly are at the core.

> While self-awareness brings about the knowledge of our current reality, it is through focus that we are able to direct our attention.

No matter who you are, irrespective of your age or your current personal challenges, to live in the reality of your vision, you must recognise yourself as a divine original. You are a unique brand, an original at the core. Your life cannot be a waste; it cannot be useless. In fact, the opposite is the case. You are inherently designed to not just succeed but to have a long-lasting impact. There is no other version of you. You have been specifically created to fulfil a purpose here on earth.

> You are inherently designed to not just succeed but to have a long-lasting impact. There is no other version of you.

Understanding this is fundamental to a life that's fruitful, fulfilled, purposeful, and truly significant beyond mere success.

And this is why a rewiring process is essential. It brings us into alignment with our inherent identity: who we truly are. Who you are is primarily your core beliefs and values, as well as what you do or create with those beliefs. I refer to what you do or create based on your identity as your purposeful life's work. Your thoughts represent fractional units of what you believe. And as you continue to read this, if you have not already done so, I want you to find a quiet place to assimilate the following sections, as they are key points in the rest of the book.

Operating from the Core

Human beings of all ages share the fundamental intuition that hidden deep inside each of us is the ability to improve. As a result, positive personal changes are seen more as discoveries and revelation of what has been inside of us all along. The theory of operating from the core is founded on the idea of living based on your inside, or interior. Operations at the core and living a life free of negative outside influences is what author Caroline McHugh calls "interiority."[41] As we become more self-aware, many of us discover ineffective wirings or deeply embedded habits that are totally unworthy of us, totally incongruent with the things we really value in life. We all know deep inside when our integrity is at stake, when our life and actions are in conflict with our core values. We don't have to live with those wrong wirings. The first step is to use our imagination and creativity to rewire our lives so we are more congruent with our deepest values and with the principles that give our values meaning and bring our vision to life. We will discuss more about this rewiring process in the subsequent chapter.

For now, the task is to recognise our faulty social mirrors and correct those wrong perspectives in our lives – perceptions we have carried for so long. This awareness of wrong wiring is what kicked off a transformational process for the extraordinary individuals I researched. They reached a level of overwhelming conviction in their lives, where their perspective changed and their paradigm shifted. This rewiring stage is where the power, the energy, of vision is brewed. Visionaries live based on principles of integrity, truth, and intrinsic alignment. This internal re-writing and intrinsic

> **Your thoughts represent fractional units of what you believe.**

alignment marked the point where their lives efforts became effective and their actions became impactful and widespread because they are in alignment with who they truly are. In short, that is why they became great.

Being able to access a situation intuitively is one of the many benefits of self-awareness. By gaining deeper understanding into the working of the soul's wisdom and guidance, we are able to effectively envision, conceptualise, articulate, and unravel our true self in its full potential and power.

I theorize our core to be the epicenter of our lives, composing of our basic beliefs and assumptions; it serves as the lens through which we see and interact with the world. It forms the basis of our worldview.

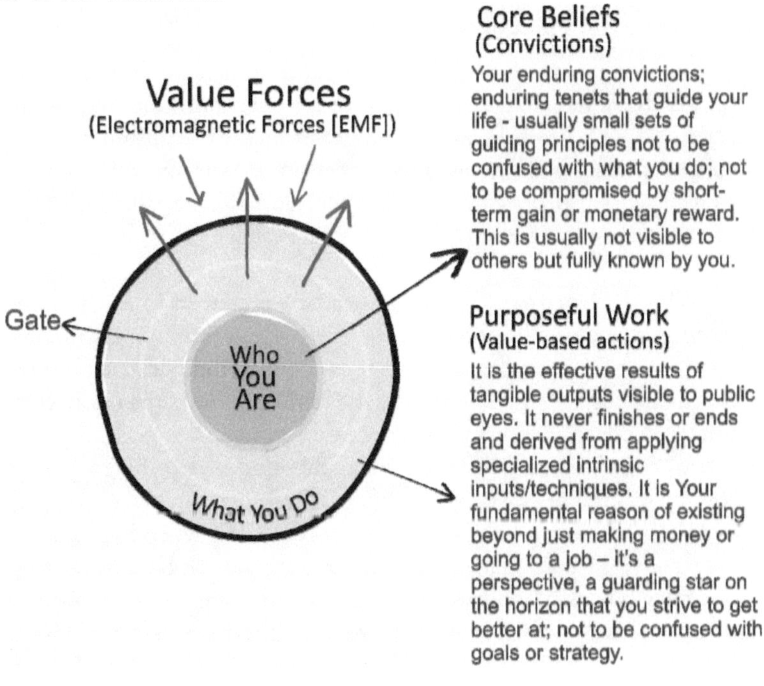

> **By gaining deeper understanding into the working of the soul's wisdom and guidance, we are able to effectively envision, conceptualise, articulate, and unravel our true self in its full potential and power.**

Value Forces
(Electromagnetic Forces [EMF])

Gate

Who You Are

What You Do

Core Beliefs
(Convictions)
Your enduring convictions; enduring tenets that guide your life - usually small sets of guiding principles not to be confused with what you do; not to be compromised by short-term gain or monetary reward. This is usually not visible to others but fully known by you.

Purposeful Work
(Value-based actions)
It is the effective results of tangible outputs visible to public eyes. It never finishes or ends and derived from applying specialized intrinsic inputs/techniques. It is Your fundamental reason of existing beyond just making money or going to a job – it's a perspective, a guarding star on the horizon that you strive to get better at; not to be confused with goals or strategy.

FIGURE 8: Operating from The Core

As shown in Figure 8, this is where we conceive our vision. I developed Figure 8 to describe how we can rewire our mind and intuitively tap into the power of vision. It starts with your thoughts. But there is more to The Core.

The framework in Figure 8 shows who we are at the core. It shows us how we can use our endowment of self-awareness to examine our mental maps. The framework also helps, if we value the correct principles of purpose, to make certain that our mental maps accurately describe our true territory, and that our paradigms are based on principles and true reality. It is here that we use our endowment of a Wise Advocate as a compass for our conscience in helping us detect our own unique talents and areas of contribution in the universe. It is this mental, neuronal activities at the core that allows us to use our imaginative abilities to mentally create the end we desire, as big and audacious as it can be. The entire workings of our core effectively use self-awareness, inner wisdom, and imagination, which ultimately gives direction and purpose to our beginnings and provides the substance of inner personal coherence. It is also here at the core that our focused efforts achieve the greatest results.

As it appears, the idea of the core touches on the fields of psychology, neuroscience, quantum physics and the mathematical scientists who work to explain the relevance of quantum theory (the science dealing with matter and light at the atomic and subatomic scale as well as their properties including electromagnetic radiations) on our mental states, self-identity, beliefs and free will

What I theorize as The Core has been referred to as the mind in various literatures. In particular, an array of research in classical physics have sought to address the mind-brain connection because no physical mechanism is able to explain how the brain generates the unobservable, inner psychological world of conscious experiences and how in turn those conscious experiences steer the underlying brain processes toward desired behavior and actions. In essence, the operations at our very core exude an imaginary value force that science have sought to ascertain.[42] Thanks to modern quantum physics we can now affirm the interplay between two types of physical entities in space: unobservable quantum states, which are vectors describing what exists in the physical world, and quantum observables, which are operators describing what can be observed in quantum measurements.[43] With the biological feasibility of identifying mind states with quantum states, brain science has given us the ability to elaborate on what we have always known which is this: our true self, our beliefs and will power emanate from our core – from within.

Further evidence from research by the Institute of Heartmath confirmed that electromagnetic fields (EMFs) or energy fields radiate from deep within each individual and can be detected by other people and indeed the environment around them.[44] As shown in Figure 8, this unseen energetic system flows through you to others and creates your sphere of influence. Magnetic fields attract us to, or repel us from, other force fields, people, and circumstances of life which are in harmony or dissonance with the nature of our dominating thoughts. What I have found to ultimately distinguish extraordinary individuals is how much they get done with this power within them and those within their sphere of influence. In essence, the purposeful work of visionaries is a direct reflection of who they are at the core, which is directly proportional to the amount of their electromagnetic energy. That is why the names of Martin Luther King Jr., Nelson Mandela, Steve Jobs, and other extraordinary individuals carry power and a level of influence whenever they are recalled.

> **The entire workings of our core effectively use self-awareness, inner wisdom, and imagination, which ultimately gives direction and purpose to our beginnings and provides the substance of inner personal coherence.**

If quantum physics sounded too complex for your comprehension, to put the entire operating from the core idea into a more concrete perspective, this is what you need to remember: Before any great accomplishment can be reached, we must magnetise our minds with the intense vision of what we desire to become.

Your core beliefs create a driving force that ultimately creates room for your gifts, what you can do exceptionally well, to find expression. In essence, you connect with your gifts and talents at the core. This helps you do meaningful, purposeful work. At your core, the epicenter of who you are, your moral compass gives you direction and allows you to successfully navigate the many challenges in life. Who you truly are at the core is the undeniable you, the only you that you're truly aware of. Your core houses your beliefs, which motivate all your actions. Core beliefs must come before personal goals and practices. Before any great action or result comes great conviction.

Yesterday, when I listened to Martin Luther King Jr.'s "I Have a Dream" speech, I could feel the force field radiating from his heart. Test it yourself; pick any of his speeches and listen to it, and notice how you feel. It doesn't matter how many times you listen or where and when you listen to it. The energy that radiates is a function of the power of vision, the clarity and quality of his world view, the integrity of his personality, and the power of his belief. It is not necessarily because of you and me listening to those speeches, it is the fact that Martin Luther King Jr. operated from The Core. Through the power of vision that originated from his core, he identified and lived his purpose. You too can do the same. Even though King was assassinated when he was thirty-nine, the enduring legacy and power of what he did within his lifetime still speaks to us today.

Positive and Negative External Forces

While positive external forces become undeniable truths that cause paradigmatic shifts, negative external forces tend to suppress our self-discovery and growth by imposing their own suggestion of who we ought to be. Negative external value forces (N – EVFs) usually tend to erect the mental barriers that shield us from the truth of who we are, the blessed one at the core. Positive external value forces (P – EVFs), on the other hand, tend to confirm our divine originality by calling forth the seed of greatness from within and helping us align with who we are originally meant to be.

Both positive and negative external forces come from outside, without. Unlike negative external value forces, positive external value forces usually connect and agree with our Wise Advocate. Positive external value forces also stimulate the manifestation of our unique vision. Positive value forces are like the watering that provides the nutrients and nourishment for the seed and gifts in us to germinate. These could include positive, growth-stimulating role models, mentors, teachers, friends, and indeed anyone who helps us along the value-adding loop.

The growth environment these positive forces create allows the seed of greatness in us to find full expression. Those who find such an environment should make an effort to sustain it. It is important to encourage this type of vision and growth environment to thrive (or to create one if it doesn't already exist). Become a force of goodness. Take responsibility for creating an environment where dreams becomes reality. Ensure you're relevant in the vision of others by creating an environment that models and encourages the manifestation of corporate vision.

Suppress negative voices. The only thing to gain from negative forces is to either suppress them or use them to help you know what to avoid. Be proactive in guarding your core by using the imaginary gates shown in Figure 9. The **Become a force of goodness.** power of deep insight coming from inside allows you act in accordance with passion and purpose. The power of vision lets you act according to your own values instead of being acted upon by other people and circumstances.

The Gates and the Power of the Sixth Sense

The idea of the gates also brings about a phenomenon that I call the sixth sense. All human beings have five sense organs: eyes for seeing, skin for feeling, nose for smelling, ear for hearing, and tongue for tasting. But there is a sixth sense that people who operate from the core possess. It is a deeper, spiritual sensitivity that allows them to operate in a realm beyond just the five sense organs. Calling the sixth sense intuition will not do it justice because the sixth sense magnifies the capabilities of the other sense organs. The sixth sense brings about a deeper understanding of external value forces and shows how to identify whether they are negative or positive. Extraordinary individuals have developed the special ability to balance which value force to allow in by using this imaginary gate. A strong, mature, and well-trained sixth sense can be a powerful resource in the toolkit of visionaries to the extent that their interior, subconscious, and inner core can be shielded from external influences that can block their unique vision from coming to pass.

This allows them to maintain alignment on the continuum, the resulting degree of their integration, harmony, and balance, and their positive impact on every aspect of their lives. Extraordinary individuals operate from the core, inside-out. They become truly great because the basic beliefs and perspectives they hold at the very core of their being are congruent with their actions.

Your Core Must Be as Distinct as Your DNA

When developing your own vision, avoid copying other people's vision. As great as the vision of the extraordinary individuals discussed in the book appear, I encourage you to not fall into the trap of copying and pasting their vision as yours. Core beliefs do not come from mimicking the values of others. This tragic trap results in many people remaining in perpetual mediocrity. The reason is because it ends up coming from outside and at most only becomes an intellectual stimulation where you are calculating what you should believe and estimating what is popular. It is a mistake to base your life on opinion rather than core beliefs and values.

When forming your core beliefs, the most important step is to capture what you authentically believe, not what the world thinks about you or what other individuals believe or what external (especially negative) values are being imposed on you by other people.

Your core belief is intrinsic and does not depend on the external environment.

As a visionary, the operations at your core do not require external rationality or justification. Your core beliefs serve as your anchor and hold you steadfast, irrespective of current circumstances, trends, or fads.

Your core holds the ideals of your true self and your full potential that you always work towards, providing you with guidance, inspiration, and motivation. It must be bone deep and is to be preserved at all cost and followed consistently in life. Core values shape your character, your behaviour, and what you are like. They hold strong, no matter what, especially in times of stress and temptation. Core values help you make decisions that you will hold true to your most inner self.

What You Do (Purposeful Work)

Purposeful work is something you continuously pursue but never fully complete. It is an action triggered by your mind at the epicenter, which is based on your core value system. Walt Disney captured the never-complete nature of purposeful work when he commented,

"Disneyland will never be completed as long as there is imagination left in this world."[45]

The purposeful work of Martin Luther King Jr. will continue to speak whenever discussions of race and civil right are mentioned. Talk of helping people living in slums, and your reference will be Mother Teresa.

The cumulation of your purposeful work becomes your legacy.

Mother Teresa showed us how core values (who you are) and purposeful work (what you do) combine to produce your impactful whole being. She raises millions of dollars for those affected by the Chernobyl nuclear disaster,[46] directly helped those affected by the Armenian earthquake, traveled to war-torn Lebanon to carry dozens of children to safety with her bare hands (purposeful work), and never outgrew the fundamental belief she had that she was called to help the poor and needy (core values and beliefs).

Building out of a core belief, Masaru Ibuka started Sony with rice cookers, heating pads, and other products that failed until Sony became a world-renowned electronics giant, which has now ventured into the entertainment and movie industry as well as electric cars. Ibuka's Sony evolved from tape recorders and transistor radios to colour TVs, VCRs, and Walkmans to PlayStations and electric cars; it still pursues its core purpose of experiencing the sheer joy of applied technological innovations that bring about "untold pleasure and untold beliefs and the elevation of the Japanese culture."[47]

Steve Jobs moved Apple from mere personal computing to the iPod era, then to iPads and iPhones, all meaningful and purposeful works that come out of an enduring core belief of "amplifying human ability."[48]

Chapter 12
THE CORE IS GROUNDED IN SCIENCE

We as human beings are called the Crown of Creation because of our brain.[49] Austrian-born American neurobiologist and Nobel Prize laureate Eric R. Kandle had a career studying the brain and tells us that we direct our brain with "the most complex set of processes in the universe," the mind.[50] Eric also identified the emergence of a new biological science which has just started to yield its deepest secrets to biological analysis. Starting from the revolutionary work of James D. Watson and Francis H.C. Crick in 1953 when they discovered the DNA, we were given an intellectual framework for understanding how information from the genes controls the functioning of the cell.

Until recently, we haven't had a sort of the owner's manual for our brain that could identify the mental processes that switch our brain to full power. But we have it now. In the last 15 years new research has identified the mindset or mental attitude that literally changes your brain to change your life. In addition, this shift in attitude stimulates the growth of new connections that expand high order brain function to enable you to reach even greater heights. And this is where the power of vision, the ability to mentally *see* bigger and better, derives its roots from. Neuroplasticity, the term used for the process of reprogramming your brain, requires a conscious decision and a specific practice. This entire process form the scientific basis of vision formation which I believe is largely missing in literature. Thanks to recent works in the field of psychology and neuroscience, coding a better picture of ourselves into our subconscious is now simpler than many might imagine and its results can radically transform your life.

The ability to constructively focus your attention with your mind is what many psychologists, psychiatrist and neuroplasticity expert have focused on in the past two decades and more. Among them are Dr. Jeffrey Schwartz and Dr. Rebecca Gladding who focused their 2011 book, *You Are Not Your Brain* on the subject. A number of researchers have also delved into the topic. Evidence shows that the brain is capable of sending out false, deceptive messages in an unrelenting fashion. Their findings join a large body of research that highlights the functions of the brain and explains how our perspectives, beliefs, and habits are formed with particular emphasis on the power of the mind. Their research shows that what we eventually *see*, our vision, is based on function of the brain and how it processes information and how the mind can be used to reset the brain. It is important to pay close attention to the rest of this chapter, as what I share below is central to this entire book. It is lack of understanding of the following that cause some religious people to not breakthrough because using high sounding ideas and spirituality without knowledge results in repeated cycle of stagnancy.

Findings from medical research mirrors what happens at The Core, as described in the previous chapter. I put The Core framework beside a representation of the brain in Figure 9. This brings my findings about extraordinary individuals powered by vision into perspective so that you can see that you can become one too. Don't only take what I present in this book at face value; it is an empirical truth that you can apply to your own life, with guaranteed results.

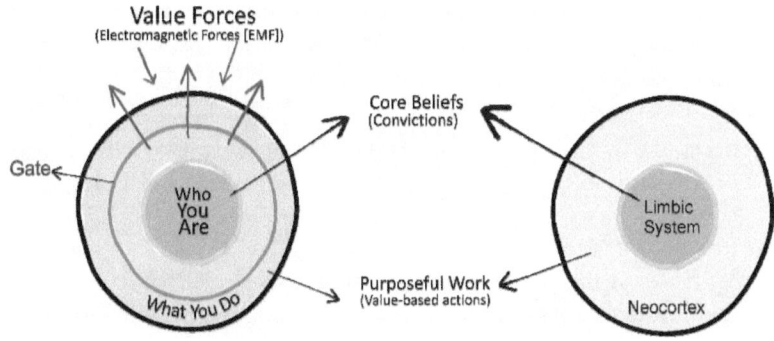

FIGURE 9: The Core – Grounded in Science

Scientific research has shown that the neocortex (what some researchers call the left brain) corresponds with what you do. The neocortex is responsible for rational and analytical thought and language. The limbic brain, on the other hand, is referred to as the right brain and corresponds to who you are. The limbic brain is responsible for all our feelings, such as trust and loyalty. It is also responsible for all human behavior and all our decision-making, but it cannot communicate.

The brain puts things into our consciousness, but it is the active mind that makes choices about whether to listen and decides how to listen. In the process of making those deliberate decisions and choices, you rewire your brain.

Although people use both sides of the brain, one side or the other generally tends to be dominant. Of course, the ideal would be to develop the ability to cross over between both sides of the brain so that a person could first sense what the situation called for and then use the appropriate side to deal with it. But people tend to stay in the comfort zone of their dominant hemisphere and process situations according to either a right- or left-brain preference. Both sides of the brain are important for visionaries on their journey to greatness.

The Science of Rewiring Your Mind to See Vision

The brain does its job, and it does it well, by presenting to us both true and deceptive messages. A lot of the messages the brain receives are deceptive because a lot of what has been wired into our brain was imbued when we didn't have adequate insight, knowledge, or understanding; we lacked the ability to process the meaning of those messages. Deceptive brain messages are false ideas, inaccurate thoughts, or unhelpful impulses, urges, or desires that take you away from your true goals and intention, your true self in life. These deceptive messages are influenced by family dynamics or the dynamics of the larger community. Who we are, the habits we develop, and the core beliefs we hold about ourselves (good or bad) are essentially functions of the right brain.

If we use the brain dominance theory as a model, it becomes evident that the quality of our first creation (who we are by default, before being rewired) is significantly impacted by our ability to use our creative right brain. The more we are able to draw upon our right-brain capacity, the more fully we will be able to visualise, to synthesise, to transcend time and present circumstances, to project a holistic picture of what we want to do and to be in life.

Rewiring Your Mind to See the Big Picture of Your True Self and Destiny

Dr. Jeffrey Schwartz's work also touched on the theory of true self, which was described as:

> "*living according to your true self ... seeing yourself for who you really are based on your sincere striving to embody the values and achieve the goals you truly believe in. It includes approaching yourself, your true emotions and needs, from a loving, caring, nurturing perspective that is consistent with how your loving inner guise (Wise Advocate or Inner Voice) sees you.*"[51]

Other scientific findings on the true self report that the true self is perceived as positive and moral and that this tendency is actor-observer invariant and cross-culturally stable.[52] The true self is also closely related to the theory of self-actualisation in that both are based on the idea of leveraging one's abilities to reach one's full creative, intellectual, and social potential through *internal* drive.[53]

Your Wise Advocate, which works with your true self, is the aspect of your attentive mind:

> *that knows what you are thinking, can see the deceptive brain messages for what they are, knows where they came from, understands how you feel (physically and emotionally), and is aware of how destructive and unhealthy your patterned, automatic responses have been for you.*[54]

The Wise Advocate wants the best for you; it loves and cares for you, so it encourages you to value your true self and make decisions in a rational way based on what is in your overall long-term interest. Dr. Schwartz concluded by recognising the Wise Advocate as a cognitive construct or a higher spiritual capacity. The spiritual capacity appears to be a more sacred phenomenon that occurs within you at the core and gives your true self context. All people have the Wise Advocate working in them at multidimensional levels, and it is a universal beneficial truth that we are all given by grace.

It therefore means that your life vision is inherently illuminated by your Wise Advocate. With the help of our Wise Advocate, personal vision is often a catalyst for wise decisions. Our inability to become fully self-aware due to the shutting down of our imaginative ability and consciousness has led many to continue living by their wrong wiring; as a result, they remain in perpetual mediocrity.

But each of us can rewire our brain by the power of focus. We are who we are because of what our right (limbic) brain has stored and from where our neocortex responds to outside stimuli. We can use this powerful right-brain capacity to rewire and store the image of our true self that fits our life's purpose and destiny. Rewiring the mind has everything to with focus.

The Power of Focus

The power is in the focus. Changing your life starts with changing your beliefs. Changing your beliefs starts one thought at a time. Our old thoughts have gotten us here; it will take new, better thoughts to show us our destiny. Step-by-step, we can refocus our mind on our true self, using the Wise Advocate, to establish new realities. We can change our paradigm with the power of what we choose to focus on.

We can reconfigure our entire belief system and radically redefine who we are through focus, one thought at a time. It has been scientifically proven using Hebb's law, which states:

"Neurons that fire together, wire together."

This means that when groups of nerve cells (or brain regions) are repeatedly activated at the same time, they form a circuit and are essentially locked in together.

When nerve cells in your brain are repeatedly activated in the same pattern, they eventually form a brain circuit. Once the circuit is established, the brain areas involved in the circuit automatically respond in the same way every time a similar situation arises. This causes the circuit to become stronger, which is how habits are created and maintained. This is what is referred to as **Hebb's law**.

The image below explains Hebb's law using a simple demonstration.[55]

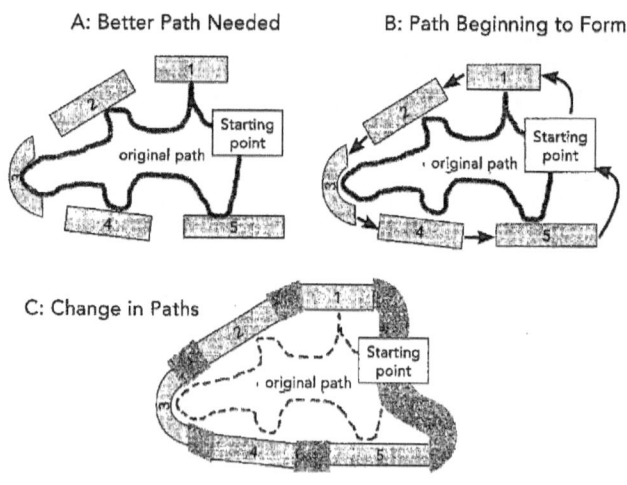

FIGURE 10: Hebb's Law[56]

> New neural pathways in the brain as a result of the rewiring process.
> **A** represents the original path and the fledgling little patches, **B** represents the new path beginning to form, and **C** represents the new path becoming preferred, while the original path withers. Note: Hebb's law is represented by the linkage or connections formed between the little patches, not the entire circuit (or path).
> A: The individual realises that he/she has something greater and can become more and begins to *see* better. B: New mental pathways begin to form in the limbic right brain though exposure to a true divine original self-image, and destiny begins to form in the mind. C: Old, ordinary neural pathways begin to wither as the better, preferred, and true you begins to emerge. Visionaries constantly carry out this process by seeking truth and finding out what models maximises their gifts and potential.

But Hebb's law only fires the neurons together; it doesn't guarantee that they will stay together. For your true-life vision to come in scope, and to indeed form a new perspective that becomes a life principle, the neurons carrying the new messages need to consistently fire together and stay as so; otherwise, the old wrong way of thinking will creep back in.

Building on what I describe as The Core, the brain-mind-physics nexus have been explored by scientist providing neuroscientists and psychologists with better conceptual framework for describing neural processes. Quantum mechanics got a natural place for consciousness.[57] But it was Dr. Jeffrey M. Schwartz and a few other researchers that provided a clear neurophysical model of the mind-brain interaction using quantum physics.[58] Their work gave rise to the phenomenon called the **Quantum Zeno effect (QZE).** Put simply QZE postulates that:

> *Focused attention holds together and stabilises brain circuits so they can wire together as in Hebb's law. Once they are wired together, the brain will respond to similar situations in a reliable, hardwired way.*

QZE allows the brain to stay activated long enough so that Hebb's law can take effect. Focused attention holds together and stabilises brain circuits so they can be wired together. Once they are wired together, the brain will respond to similar situations in a similar way.

The main thing to keep in mind at this point is that focused attention is the key ingredient. The cornerstone of the power of vision lies in your ability to focus your mind on your true self and the purpose you were born for. Through the power of focus, you can recruit your mind to focus your attention and as a result rewire your brain to operate in tune with your true self.

Repeatedly focusing your attention on fulfilling your purpose and constantly aiming to live in the reality of your maximised potential is what I refer to as Vision Attention Density (VAD).[59] In essence, the more you sustain your focus of attention on something (i.e., the denser your attention is), the more likely your life actions and habits become wired into your brain. Vision attention density is the first and most important step in creating a clear, strong, enduring big-picture mentality. Vision attention density makes the quantum Zeno effect kick in and causes focused attention to have powerful effects on the brain by activating Hebb's law.

VAD is a process of recruiting your mind to focus your attention on your big picture and as a result reconfigure your brain to operate in tune with your true self and ultimately bring the vision to pass. VAD starts with a paradigm shifts, is precipitated in solitude, is consolidated through self-awareness, and produces a stronger core.

> **It is your VAD that makes you see beyond what is and appropriately positions you to experience and bring to pass what should be.**

When VAD is low, you may focus on details of your vision in unconstructive ways; habits that take you away from your vision and purpose get wired into your brain. However, if you actively choose to focus your attention and repeatedly apply it to a wholesome, constructive activity that pertains to your vision, you will rewire your brain in healthy ways that are consistent with your true self. In the end, you become what you focus on. Your vision materialises.

It is your VAD that makes you see beyond what is and appropriately positions you to experience and bring to pass what should be. Simply put, you can distort reality and current events. You can gain the power to create a new reality and an end result that aligns with your true self: better outcomes that favour you. Strong VAD allows you to see the invisible things that the eyes of other cannot see. With time, the strength of your VAD ultimately makes you act and do more than others. What this means conclusively is that strong VAD produces a reality distortion field.

You may wonder why we went through all the various terms, concepts, and scientific processes. What does Hebb's law, QZE, and VAD have to do with vision, you ask? The answer is quite apparent. This scientific discussion is the breakdown of vision as a mental conception that ultimately produces sustainable powerful actions and outcomes. In this way, vision attention density is crucial for what is called self-directed neuroplasticity. By making deliberate choices to focus our attention and responses, we mould our brain to form in a way that allows us to operate in the reality of our true purpose and potential. We can apply new functions to our brain that were previously used for something else. We become more aware, more present, more powerful. And there lies the power of vision.

> By making deliberate choices to focus our attention and responses, we mould our brain to form in a way that allows us to operate in the reality of our true purpose and potential.

Self-Directed Neuroplasticity

As the word sounds, in this process, neurons form new paths, like a plastic, and become hardwired. Neuroplasticity can be automatic or self-directed. Auto plasticity is the first wiring of the brain based on defaults (as a result of external, mostly negative EMF) in which case only if the first wiring matches our true self at the core that a rewiring process might not be required. Self-directed neuroplasticity is the process of forming a new mindset by executing a rewiring process that matches your true self (increasing your influence through EMF). The power of focused attention, along with the ability to apply commitment, hard work, and dedication to direct your choices and actions, requires your brain to work for you and with your true self. This is the state when your limbic brain and neocortex are in sync. This is the state when who you are is the same as what you do; there's no misalignment or lack of integrity. You are who you say you are and how others see you. You become more in control of circumstances and events around you as shown in Figure 11. Instead of becoming a reactionary by following default setup, you can become a visionary, doing what defines you intrinsically.

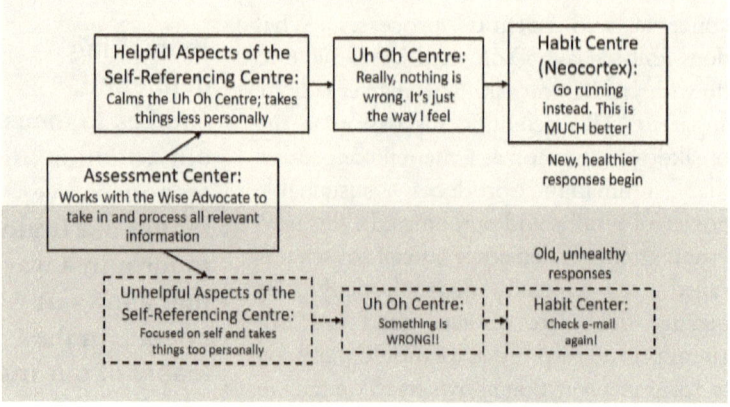

Figure 11: Wise Advocate, strengthened and in control[60]

We can teach our core to function in extraordinary ways by actively focusing our attention on healthy circuits, which are most effective in bringing about a behavior, action, and attitude that fit our destiny. This is what makes vision powerful. And self-directed neuroplasticity is the source of hope and motivation that people, in practical terms, can take charge of their future and destiny, irrespective of what the present looks like.

From Change in Perspective to Being Powered by Vision

Let's recap what we've covered in this section. It is all about thoughts, perceptions, and paradigm shifts. A sudden event of life, like a pandemic or some other life occurrence (both significantly good or bad, painful or sweet) can cause a shift in our perspective, or what we focus our mind's eye on. Your vision of a better, extraordinary you can then be formed and brought to reality in practical terms. With self-directed neuroplasticity, we can automatically focus our mind's eye on a preferred future.

A new perspective emerges in life. You can change from individual Z (Figure 12) to individual A (Figure 13). Individual Z lacks direction and meaning; it's life is dominated by external value forces. Individual Z is not living a balanced life and is not living a principled life because it's reactionary in nature, aiming for only short-term gains. As a result, these individuals, who most likely appear intelligent, are less stable because they take all sorts of education and training with the hope that their socioeconomic status will change.

Individual A, however, operates with the power of vision and is able to have long-term orientation, irrespective of education and socioeconomic background. The reason is because they operate based on principle, driven by inner commitment to their personal purpose and passion, rather than being guided by external value forces. Individual A lives a value-based life. This is a life of equanimity, meaning, satisfaction, and productivity, derived because decisions and actions are guided by rational thinking and mental composure. You can now see better and do what may have scared you before. Before, your normal response would have been irrational, but now, you can apply more rational thinking. You begin to think, I can see myself handling the situation with all the love, the power, the self-control that now defines who I truly am. Indeed, you can rewire your brain, reset your life, and become more empowered.

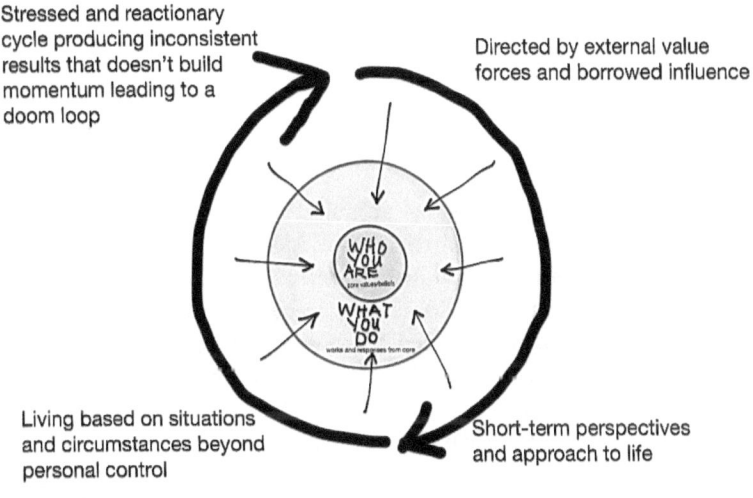

FIGURE 12: Individual Z: Distressed life with no power of vision

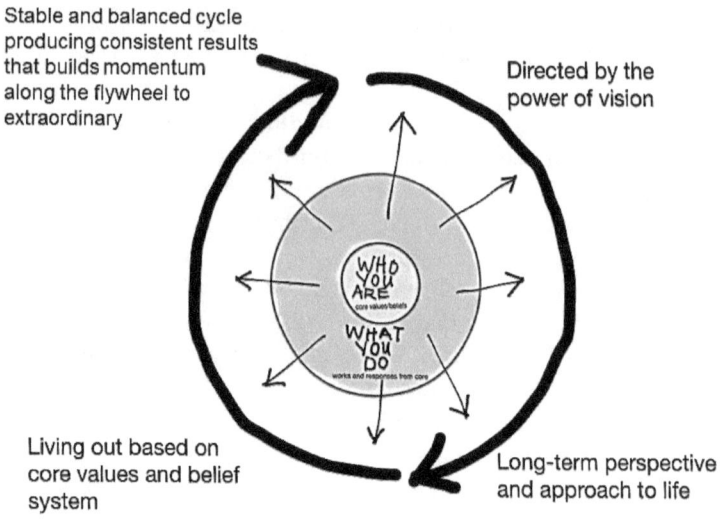

FIGURE 13: Individual A: Principled and balanced life powered by vision

If you follow this model, day after day, your behavior will change. You don't have to live out of old wiring, the wiring the world handed you, involving negative external value forces, including those from your parents or by society or by genetics or by your environment; you can reconfigure your life by rewiring your mind to conform with a better script that aligns with your value system.

***

In summary our personal appraisal of every personal encounters and our responses to them are shaped not just by our rational judgement or our personal history, but also by our distant and central past. This leaves us with sometimes tragic propensities and automatic reactions to act without deep reasoning or true awareness. But with awareness, we develop the ability to stop automatic reaction that have become etched in our nervous system. This is one of the essence of the power of focus and disciplined thinking.

An extraordinary life is one that is disciplined and focused on its vision. Focus comes through discipline, and discipline brings about focus. Using the power of thoughts, you can change you life by changing what you think. Vision Attention Density (VAD) a process of consistently focusing on paradigmatically better, true thoughts aligns you with your true self, your intrinsic beliefs, and your values. A disciplined life is the product of a disciplined mind. A disciplined life produces great accomplishments. A disciplined mind is a mind that thinks disciplined thoughts.

Chapter 13
DREAM BIG; HAVE BIG HAIRY AUDACIOUS GOALS (BHAGS)

Put yourself in the shoes of Martin Luther King Jr. You were born at a degrading time when Jim Crow lynching was commonplace. Restaurants display signs saying either "Whites only" or "Coloured here." Restrooms, water fountains, buses, and other public places have the same racial labels. While you were never a victim directly, you can no longer turn a blind eye to the stories and accounts of your neighbours, who were victimised as a result of racial segregation and injustice.

Your career as a Baptist pastor didn't directly involve you on the front line of Civil Right movement. But your doctorate degree in theology was combined with your oratory gift, which was becoming undeniably polished with each sermon you preached. At age twenty-five, the Montgomery Improvement Association (MIA) was formed, and some older folks came to ask you to lead the group; after your election as president of the association, your first major task was to organise and lead a major protest, the first of its type for the African-American Civil Rights movement: the Montgomery Bus Boycott. Your first task involved a boycott of the local bus system, inspired by Rosa Parks, who refused to sit in the back of a public bus.

What would you do?

Onlookers during that time could have said, "King appears cool and young, but does he have the street credibility this job requires? He's a family man with too many commitments; how could he respond quickly to the association's urgent requests? The struggle for the movement will involve potential prison time; this Baptist preacher doesn't look like he wants to go to prison."

In Atlanta, a group of family friends convened by King's father invited him over and attempted to dissuade him from returning to Montgomery.

Perhaps you're thinking that he was elected president of MIA, got his PhD at twenty-five, and became a successful Baptist pastor. "Martin Luther King Jr. might have just been lucky. He looks smart in retrospect, but it could just as easily have been a fluke."

Good point. And I would be inclined to agree with you, except for one thing: King had a long and consistent history of committing himself to big, audacious challenges. Looking as far back as 1951, we see this bold commitment behavior by King: In 1951, he was valedictorian of his class at Crozer Theological Seminary and was elected president of the student body, which was composed almost exclusively of white students. He not only led the student body as the first black president, his speeches and presence already indicated someone who would be extraordinary. In 1955, King earned his PhD in theology from Boston University.

In 1959, he travelled to India to discuss the Gandhian concepts of peaceful noncompliance (satyagraha) with Gandhi's followers. King became increasingly convinced that non-violent resistance was the most potent weapon available to oppressed people in their struggle for freedom. He was a rising minister who wasn't shy to speak truth to power, even at his very young age.

In one of the boldest moves of his life, in 1963, he helped organise a march on Washington, where over two hundred thousand people gathered outside the Lincoln Memorial to hear his stirring "I Have a Dream" speech.

His rising tide of civil disobedience had a strong impact on national opinion and resulted in the passage of the Civil Rights Act of 1964.

That eventful year was climaxed in December, when King was awarded the Nobel Peace Prize. In his acceptance speech in Oslo, King emphasised his faith in the future of humankind and his belief that we are able to shape our eternal future. At that time, he was the youngest person to ever earn a Nobel Peace prize (until Malala Yousafzai, who was seventeen when she won in 2014). This and many other attributes have shown the inherent pedigree of Martin Luther King Jr.

In the face of obstacles, he became irreversibly committed to the Civil Rights movement physically, psychologically, publicly. It became a matter of "I was born to do this."

By the time of his assassination in 1968, he had helped implement the Civil Rights Act of 1964 and the Voting Rights Act of 1965.

History records today that compared to his relatively small frame,

Martin Luther King Jr.'s accomplishments transcend the Civil Rights movement, which outlawed segregation, promoted voting rights for blacks, and more. King had audacious goals, including economic freedom for all.

These were no mean accomplishments. They were extraordinary. They were big, hairy, audacious goals (BHAGs), a concept developed by Jim Collins and Jerry Porras in their book Built to Last.[61] According to Jim and Jerry, BHAGs are challenging, audacious—and often risky—goals and projects towards which a visionary entity channels its efforts (stimulates progress).

We can adapt personal BHAGs from Jim and Jerry's framework as a powerful mechanism to stimulate personal progress. BHAGs are fundamentally big dreams that serve as a powerful mechanism to propel you to greatness.

What follows a deep conviction is a realisation of who you truly are at the core. You develop your ability to dream big (or set BHAGs). You also develop the ability to take bold, disciplined actions that produce outstanding results. Both the dream and actions are neatly embedded in what vision is all about.

In the beginning, it will all appear like baby steps, but it will come out of a deep awareness of yourself and a consciousness or clear grasp of the context or situation. Depending on how powerful the light-bulb experience or paradigm shift is and depending on the strength of your VAD, all of which continue to grow as more new knowledge accumulates through continuous focus, you can operate from the core and set big, almost unbelievable goals. These goals usually stimulate growth and progress and make people blast off in comparison to others. This is how ordinary individuals become extraordinary.

> **BHAGs are fundamentally big dreams that serve as a powerful mechanism to propel you to greatness.**

Visionaries may appear straitlaced and conservative on the outside, but they're not afraid to commit themselves to big, hairy, audacious goals. They can move from selling transistor radios and Walkmans to building electric cars, like Masaru Ibuka's Sony, or from fighting segregation in Alabama to fighting for human rights of all people, like Martin Luther King Jr. A visionary can start as a schoolteacher and end up running one of the largest charities in the world, like Mother Teresa did. They can start as errand boy and become a prime minister in a foreign country, like Joseph. They can be orphaned and end up creating revolutions in multiple industries, like Steve Jobs. A BHAG may be daunting and risky, but the adventure, excitement, and challenge get the juices of extraordinary individuals flowing, creating immense forward momentum.

> Visionaries may appear straitlaced and conservative on the outside, but they're not afraid to commit themselves to big, hairy, audacious goals.

Dream big. Don't sell yourself short. Commit yourself to challenging, audacious—and even risky—goals and projects, towards which you can channel your efforts and stimulate your growth and personal progress. Most people do things because they have to. Wouldn't you like to do things because you want to, based on your purpose? You must choose to be on the offensive rather than the defensive when it comes to taking responsibility for your destiny. Become proactive in pursuing your vision.

Always remember that you are here to accomplish what nobody else can do. You're a divine original. Never expect anything less than the highest thing you can go after. Always expect more than what you have because your vision holds the expansionary keys to your life. Always be in the flow of doing more than what you are currently doing, but make sure that your actions originate from disciplined thoughts, as discussed earlier. Dream big. Somewhere inside, you have the ability to dream. No matter how challenging it gets, don't give up, because your vision is the key to fulfilling your life's purpose.

> A BHAG engages people; it reaches out and grabs them in the gut. It is tangible, energising, highly focused. People get it right away; it takes little or no explanation.

You don't need to spend hours wordsmithing your goal into a verbose, meaningless, impossible-to-remember vision statement. No, the goal itself—say, for example, you want to climb a mountain—is so easy to grasp, so compelling in its own right, that it could be said one hundred different ways, yet easily understood by everyone: "I am going to climb Mountain Everest." When an expedition sets out to climb that peak, it doesn't need a three-page, convoluted vision statement to explain what Mount Everest is.

Think about your own life. Do you have verbose statements floating around, yet no bold goals with the clarity of climbing Mount Everest? Do you have your personal BHAGs? If you tell people you're going to climb Mount Everest, they will know what Mount Everest is (the tallest mountain in the world) and become aware of the daunting task required to climb it.

Some people spend so much time creating personal statements or brand statements, when the pragmatism of vision is what can truly define a person. Some personal statements I have seen do little to provoke forward movement (although some do reflect and preserve the core). For example, a personal statement like "I want to serve the poor" is indicative of a value proposition targeted towards helping those in need, but it lacks the purposeful venture or the audaciousness of a big dream. To stimulate progress, I encourage you to think beyond the traditional corporate statement and consider the powerful mechanisms of bold dreams and BHAGs.

Your vision must be big and bold enough to the point of falling in the gray area where reason and prudence might say, "This is unreasonable," but the drive for progress says, "I believe we can do it nonetheless." Again, these aren't just goals; these are big, hairy, audacious goals.

Let's take a look at more examples from the visionaries profiled in this book.

In 1907, Henry Ford, a forty-three-year-old businessman, promoted his company by announcing an astounding BHAG: "to democratise the automobile." Ford proclaimed his plan to:

> build a motor car for the great multitude.... It will be so low in price that no man making a good salary will be unable to own one—and enjoy with his family the blessing of hours of pleasure in God's great open spaces ... everybody will be able to afford one, and everyone will have one. The horse will have disappeared from our highways, the automobile will be taken for granted.[62]

At the time of this BHAG, Ford was just another businessman; more than thirty companies clamoring for a slice of the emerging automobile market. As Daniel J. Boorstin mentioned in the book The Americans: The Democratic Experience, in a search for novelty, social inventors appear to have lots of solutions and seek problems they can solve. Yet, no company had established itself as a clear leader in the chaos of the young industry; Ford had only about 15 percent of the market by that time. This outrageous ambition to make horses disappear and the automobile become commonplace inspired the entire Ford design team to work until late at night.[63] Ford's big, hairy, audacious dream revolutionised the automobile industry.

Vision doesn't always have to do with starting something new. Visionaries like Ford often use dreams and the power of vision to permanently transform an industry that already exists. At one point, Charles Sorenson, a member of Ford's team, remembered, "Mr. Ford and I [once] worked about forty-two hours without letup."[64] During this period of time, many of the other car manufacturers watched their market share erode as Ford rose to the number one position in the industry.

Ironically, however, once Ford achieved its goal of democratising the automobile, it didn't set a new BHAG; it became complacent and watched others pass it by.

I want to emphasise here that a BHAG only helps you until it is achieved. Once accomplished, another BHAG needs to be set to keep the momentum and sustain the power of vision.

Ford suffered from what is called the "we've arrived" syndrome—a complacent lethargy that can arise once you achieve one BHAG but don't replace it with another. Imagine it like celebrating the top-of-the-mountain experience when you are only just starting to climb. As a side note, if you currently have a BHAG, you might want to think about what's next before you complete it. Conversely, if you are feeling stuck in life, experiencing stagnancy and in a state of malaise, you might ask yourself if you once had a BHAG—either implicit or explicit—that you've attained and not replaced with a new one. In short, have you set a goal for yourself that is an estimation of the big picture you see for yourself? Are you stuck in your dreams? You may want to assess whether you are stuck because it's not coming from your core.

Let's look at another example of audaciousness in the young

company led by Masaru Ibuka. In the late 1950s, shortly after World War II, Tokyo Tsushin Kogyo (a relatively small company, largely unknown outside of its home country) took the costly step of discarding its original name in favor of a new one: Sony Corporation.

The company's bank objected to the idea: "It's taken you ten years since the company's founding to make the name Tokyo Tsushin Kogyo widely known in the trade. Why do you have to change now? After all this time, what do you mean by proposing such a nonsensical change?"

Sony's founders, Ibuka and his partner, Akio Morita, responded simply that it would enable the company to expand worldwide, whereas the prior name could not be easily pronounced in foreign lands.[65]

You're probably thinking that such a move does not represent something particularly audacious; after all, most small and midsize companies eventually look to overseas markets. And it's not that big of a deal to change a corporate name from Tokyo Tsushin Kogyo to Sony. But look closely at the reason they gave for this move, for therein lies an immense BHAG. Here's what Morita said in 1986, referring to changing their name to Sony:

> *Although our company was still small and we saw Japan as quite a large and potentially active market ... it became obvious to me that if we did not set our sights on marketing abroad, we would not grow into the kind of company Ibuka and I had envisioned. We wanted to change the image [around the world] of Japanese products as poor in quality.*[66]

In the 1950s, "Made in Japan" meant "cheap, junky, poor quality." In reading through materials on the company, I concluded that Sony not only wanted to be successful in its own right; it wanted to become known for changing the image of Japanese consumer products as being poor quality. Having less than a thousand employees and no overseas presence to speak of, this was a not a trivial ambition.

But it is important to note that this wasn't Ibuka's first BHAG in Sony's history.

In 1952, for example, its limited engineering staff created a "pocket" radio—a radio that could fit in a shirt pocket and be easy to carry.[67] In the 1990s, we take such miniaturisation for granted, but in the early 1950s, radios depended on vacuum tubes. To build such a miniature radio required long periods of painstaking trial and error, and significant innovation. No company in the world had yet successfully applied transistor technology to a consumer radio, but Ibuka led Sony's team to such accomplishment.

"Let's work on a transistor radio, whatever the difficulties we may face,' proclaimed Masaru Ibuka. *'I am sure we can produce transistors for radios."*68

When Ibuka told an outside adviser about the bold idea, the adviser responded, *"Transistor radio? Are you sure? Even in America transistors are used only for defense purposes, where money is no object. Even if you come out with a consumer product using transistors, who could afford to buy such a machine with such expensive devices?"*

"That's what people think," responded Ibuka. *"People are saying that transistors won't be commercially viable.... This will make the business all the more interesting."* 69

Ibuka dreamt of a pocket radio, and in August 1955, he fulfilled this dream with the launch of Sony's TR-55. Sony's pocket radio became a pervasive product worldwide. (As an outgrowth of this effort, one of Sony's scientists made breakthroughs in the development of transistors that eventually led to a Nobel Prize.)

With the same BHAG attitude in 1959, just four years after the transistor radio was launched, Ibuka spoke in a magazine interview about yet another dream: a transistor TV. While Ibuka talked about his dream in public, behind the scenes, things were already taking shape at Sony, and progress had already been made towards realising the transistor TV dream.

This point helps us to spot how a visionary's BHAG is different from just any ordinary BHAG. Since everyone demonstrate some level of BHAG, it is important to make the distinction. True BHAGs, unlike mere goals or wishy-washy ambitions, come out of a conviction based on personal estimation, not just bragging. Bravado set goals without understanding. Truly great people set goals with a quiet understanding of their passion (values), gifts (potential) and purpose (what us referred to as The Three Circles discussed in-depth in Chapter 14).

In April 1959, the first prototype of Sony's transistor TV was completed, and numerous improvements and design studies were carried out. On December 25, Ibuka's New Year's dream came true with the announcement of Sony's first TV: the world's first direct-view TV. When it went on sale in May 1960, the TV8-301 eight-inch portable transistor TV launched Sony's TV business.

As it happened, a group of market researchers representing foreign TV manufacturers was visiting Japan while the transistor TV was under development. Ibuka asked them whether they thought small TVs would sell or not. To a man, they said they would fail.

Looking back on this, Ibuka identified yet another important point, which is this: You don't have to build your life around what people want. By sheer power of vision, together with your depth of conviction, you can create a product and build a market for it. This is quite counterintuitive, as many business experts say to first do extensive market research to find what people need. But visionaries start with the end in mind by first creating the future and anticipating what could be. Ibuka's approach as a visionary shows us that while it was common practice to plan new products on the basis of market research, another way is to carry out market research by actually putting something on the market. Since then, he said, he believed new products always involved market creation. Ibuka said, "I'm now firmly convinced that brand new products must always create new markets."[70]

> ...visionaries start with the end in mind by first creating the future and anticipating what could be.

Henry Ford appear to share a similar sentiment with his famous quote, "If I had asked people what they wanted, they would have said faster horses."[71] And Steve Jobs too had this well-known quote: "It's really hard to design products by focus groups. A lot of times, people don't know what they want until you show it to them." What these extraordinary individuals teach us is that there will always be problems that people try to explain in detail, but only very few people know exactly how to solve it. To solve problems means we have to think better thoughts than the ones that caused the problem in the first place. It takes the power of solitude and the creative visualisation of vision to find sustainable solutions.

Even though the first iteration of our solution may not be the perfect remedy, making a real contribution and being proactive helps to identify what works and what doesn't. By aligning with principles of personal purpose, you can take responsibility for your life's outcomes, understand what works, collect the impact data into a feedback system, keep iterating the loop, and build momentum until you break through.

Two years after the transistor radio was launched in 1960, Sony launched the TV5-303, which was even smaller than the TV8-301; it became a huge hit in the United States.

The transistor TV appeared to prove that Sony had something to offer, and in 1968, when Sony launched the Trinitron TV, its role as a global leader was solidified, and Japan shot to the top on the international market, just exactly as Ibuka had envisioned.

> To solve problems means we have to think better thoughts than the ones that caused the problem in the first place.

The Trinitron was an instant hit. The improvements it offered in picture quality justified charging a premium. In 1973, it became the first consumer electronics device to win an Emmy. Sony eventually sold 280 million Trinitrons, as both TVs and, later, computer monitors.

If the Trinitron was nothing more than a huge leap in TV technology and a monster commercial success, that would be enough to assure it a place in the hall of fame. But it was so much more than that. It vaulted Sony into the first rank of technology providers. Trinitron sales helped finance Sony's run of success that few consumer electronics manufacturers have matched for innovation, across such a wide variety of products over so many decades. Furthermore, Ibuka's success at Sony was Japan's too. Prior to the Trinitron, most electronic products from the country were inexpensive and of suspect quality. The Trinitron was one of the foundational products establishing Japan as a world-class source of advanced electronics.

> One BHAG after another after another and another. That is how visionaries power on to greatness.

Fast forward to today. In what many analysts termed the greatest surprise of the January 2020 Consumer Electronic Show (CES) held in Las Vegas, Sony unveiled Vision-S, its first fully electric concept car. Needless to say, Ibuka's vision continues to speak today.[72] In what has been regarded record crushing, Sony Playstation 5 released surpassed all historical records set for a game console.[73] Not to talk of the Bravia TV Sony will be releasing in 2021.[74]

One BHAG after another after another and another. That is how visionaries power on to greatness.

Dreaming Big Also Requires Big Commitments and Big Risks

It's not just the presence of a goal that stimulates progress; it is also the level of commitment and focus (VAD) to the goal. Indeed, a goal cannot be classified as a BHAG without a high level of commitment and focus.

Being single-handedly tapped to lead the MIA would have been a nice accomplishment for Martin Luther King Jr. So also would have been his decision to lead the Montgomery Bus Boycott. But his commitment to "walk for 368 days to work without taking the public transport system" turned into a full-fledged BHAG. And in fact, King confirmed that their feet were tired after such a long walk. Many also speculated on the impact of their long period of action; would public transportation ever be desegregated? They were confronted by the risk of failure, yet they did it anyways. King led the campaign with all of his heart. Could they have failed? Yes. Would they have done it all the same? Absolutely yes.

The Montgomery Bus Boycott was the accomplishment that put Martin Luther King Jr. in the spotlight, not only nationally but internationally. It was so significant that it has been referred to as having a seismic impact on civil rights in America. Yet the decision to take such an approach looks much different from the perspective of 1955. As with Martin Luther King Jr., the risk does not come without pain. Staying in your comfort zone will not stimulate progress or allow the power of vision to take effect.

Walt Disney achieved great results through the same forward thrust, informed by a BHAG. He followed a pattern of making bold—and often risky—commitments to audacious projects.

In 1934, Walt Disney aimed to do something never done before in the movie industry: create a successful full-length animated feature film. In creating Snow White, Disney invested most of his company's resources and defied those in the industry who called it "Disney's Folly." After all, who would want to see a full-length cartoon? Two decades later, after a string of full-length animated films, including Pinocchio, Fantasia, and Bambi, Disney made yet another risky commitment to one of Disney's "bizarre ideas": to build a radically new kind of amusement park, later to become known to all of us as Disneyland. In the 1960s, Disney repeated the process again, with a commitment to fulfil Disney's dying dream: EPCOT Center in Florida. Although he passed away before EPCOT was completed, Walt's brother, Roy, continued running the company.

After Disney passed away, several challenges including rivals, competition, and a potential buyout rocked the boat. Disney's company, being infused with his spirit of "Imagineering," continued to move forward, after it defeated a corporate takeover and pursued bold new adventures, including Japan Disney and EuroDisney. Yet, in what appears to be another difficult move that comes from Disney's core DNA, during the COVID-19 global pandemic, Disney Shanghai was among the first companies to reopen for business on May 11, 2020. The reopening carried immense symbolic importance. It sent a message to Disney's furloughed park employees—forty-three thousand in Florida alone—about the future: There will be one.

"It has been an emotional morning," Joe Schott, president and general manager of the Shanghai Disney Resort, said in a phone interview on the morning of the reopening. *"There is light at the end of the tunnel. Life can get you down. Our brand is about hope."*[75]

By pursuing new adventures or risking an all-or-nothing investment on a new idea, visionaries stimulate progress and are propelled forward by their vision.

As discussed in the chapter on disciplined thoughts, a visionary's behaviour doesn't come from external value forces or motivations. The number one objective is always about the visionary's inner intuition or core value or belief: who they truly are at the core. That was what Steve Jobs did when he launched the iPad on January 27, 2010.

When customers tried out the iPad, they saw how wrong the pundits and critics had been. Once again, the world saw how right Steve Jobs turned out to be, launching back-to-back hit products. Despite many others who went ahead of Jobs but flopped with a tablet idea, he placed his bets with yet another BHAG with the launch of the iPad. Despite the critics, despite being late to the whole idea of tablets, Apple made the iPad, and we bought it in our millions. It's had some ups and downs since that 2010 launch, but it's also got progressively more spectacular as new versions were released.

> **The number one objective is always about the visionary's inner intuition or core value or belief: who they truly are at the core.**

Jobs said that Apple had found a third category of device, one that fit between a phone and a laptop computer. It did, and in the nine years since it shipped that first iPad to customers, Apple has released twenty different models of this slate device.

As 2011 approached, analysts asked Jobs about the supposed avalanche of tablets poised to enter the market. Again, in a visionary style, he answered that there were really "only a handful of credible entrants," but noted that they use seven-inch screens, which he said "isn't sufficient to create great tablet apps." Jobs stated categorically (and almost prophetically), "We think the seven-inch tablets will be dead on arrival, and manufacturers will realise they're too small and abandon them next year. They'll then increase the size, abandoning the customers and developers who bought into the smaller format."

It ended up taking more than a year for many manufacturers to give up on seven-inch tablets—other tech manufacturers kept trying to sell them until the end of 2014—but Jobs's anticipation of what would be successful in tablets ended up being presciently correct.

Jobs powered Apple with a clear vision and was confident to take on BHAGs that allowed his company to make long-term plans, which included customising silicon specifically to deliver that vision. The chasm between Apple's BHAGs, the risks and commitment and strategic focus when compared to the scattershot, somewhat mediocre, and seemingly random efforts by others continues to grow, as we will see when we move into the future.

Overbearing Pride, Confidence, or Arrogance? (The Hubris Factor)

Looking from afar, one may be tempted to conclude that a visionary's self-confidence is bordering on hubris: an excess of pride or overconfidence or arrogance.

To dream big dreams and set big, hairy, audacious goals requires a certain level of unreasonable confidence. It was not reasonable for a pastor to lead the Civil Rights movement. Walking to work for 368 days in order to protest a public bus system was not prudent, nor was it humble for Masaru Ibuka to think his company would dominate the international market and change the worldwide image of Japanese products as being of poor quality.

It was not cautious for Walt Disney to create his first feature film, spending all his resources, facing the possibility of a failure, and doing it while facing harsh criticism. It wasn't modest to declare, "We will democratise the automobile," as Henry Ford did. It was foolhardy and almost absurd for Steve Jobs to announce a tablet product when many other industry leaders tried and failed at it.

Therein lies of the maddening, counterintuitive paradox about the power of vision:

It may look crazy to outsiders, but BHAGs don't seem so to visionaries, who see it as something they set out to do.

Let's take a cue from mountain climbing, which comes in handy when discussing the power of vision. Imagine watching a rock climber scale a cliff without a rope; if she falls, she dies. To the uninformed spectator, the climber looks bold and seems to be seeking risks, if not foolhardy. But suppose that climber is on a route that appears extremely doable, well within her range of ability. From the climber's perspective, she has no doubts that, with proper training and concentration, she can make the climb. To her, the climb is not too risky. It does stimulate her to know that if she falls, she dies, but she has confidence in her ability. The highly visionary individuals who set bold BHAGs are much like that climber.

> **It may look crazy to outsiders, but BHAGs don't seem so to visionaries, who see it as something they set out to do.**

The BHAGs of visionaries are not formed out of pride, arrogance, or hubris; they are an estimation of their true selves and what they can do, based on their potential.

It's the Power of Vision, Not the Individual

At this point, I wish to provide some insight on a counterintuitive aspect of vision. Rather than cause you to brag, vision makes you humble. Also, it doesn't matter whether you are charismatic or not. It is easy to assume that visionaries set BHAGs because they're trying to be braggarts. They don't want to add points to their personal profile or show off. I cannot deny that Walt Disney had a charismatic sentiment, nor can we deny that he deserves much of the credit for popularising the word "imagineering" and setting bold goals of Space Mountain.

Disney died in 1966; he was no longer present to inspire or lead the Space Mountain project. After he passed away, did the Space Mountain mission seem any less inspiring? Did it grind to a halt? Of course not. The beauty of big dreams and visions in an individual's life, if it follows the power of vision framework, it continues to stimulate progress, irrespective of who carries on the legacy. The vision itself should be the motivating mechanism. A friend of mine reflected on his father's vision and concluded, "Vision is the greatest gift a father can pass down to his son."[76]

Vision is not about the individual; it usually transcends the individual. A well-articulated vision can create a powerful force that transcends generations. True vision takes on a life of its own, even after the initial dreamer passes away.

> **True vision takes on a life of its own, even after the initial dreamer passes away.**

Ibuka made use of BHAGs to institutionalise his own habits and way of life. Reflecting on the founder's life, Dr. Makato Kikuchi, Sony's director of research in the mid-1970s, said, "Ibuka taught us that, once the commitment to go ahead is made, never give up. This pervades all the research and development work at Sony."

Although we can certainly trace the conception of dreams, visions, and BHAGs to individuals, the vision of truly great people takes on a life of its own and propels generations forward, long into the future.

***

This chapter covered a lot about dreaming big and BHAGs, yet you may still wonder what I mean by "dream big". Here are a few takeaways:

1. Your vision should be clear, be compelling, and require no explanation. Always keep in mind that a BHAG is a goal—like climbing a mountain or going to the moon—not just a statement. BHAGs are the building blocks, the mental images and thoughts of what you can potentially accomplish. If it doesn't get you excited and make the juices flow in everyone who buys into the vision, then it's just not a true vision or BHAG.

2. Your big dreams and BHAGs should fall well outside your comfort zone. They should trigger the expansionary power of vision. As components of your vision, your BHAGs should be small enough to live out daily yet big enough to take a lifetime to accomplish.

3. Your vision should be so big, bold, and exciting in its own right that it would continue to propel your progress, motivate your growth, and stimulate your purposeful works, even after you are gone (in which case it functionally becomes a dream).

4. The inherent danger in BHAGs is that, once achieved, people drift away (as seen in some part of Henry Ford's life in the 1920s); they can stall and create the "I've arrived" syndrome. Be prepared to do what I call re-vision: a process of getting new knowledge and deeper insight into your life vision and purpose. Through re-vision, the vision usually remains the same, but the objectives and strategy can go higher. And more importantly, by following other principles and practices shared in this book, subsequent BHAGs can follow once the initial BHAG is completed.

5. Finally, and most important of all, your visions and dreams should be consistent with your core values and beliefs, who you truly are at the core.

BHAGs are not just goals. They keep you focused, disciplined, and consistent; it is important to preserve the core while stimulating progress. As we established in the definition of vision, it is a mental picture of the future. The mind, the core of your being, should always be the driving force. Again, the mountain analogy: BHAGs set the maps atop of the mountain, but it is the mind that provides the engine power.

Chapter 14
VISION, GIFTS, TALENTS, AND POTENTIAL

The fulfilment of your vision works in practical terms based on the application of your gifts and talents. Inside everyone resides some special ability or genius. What I found in my study of extraordinary individuals is that they were not just disciplined in their thinking; they also had a special ability to do certain things better. They exhibited a certain level of grace in doing things that others found difficult. For some, it is one key area of life; for others, it is in multiple areas. For those who show exceptional abilities in multiple areas, I found that there was a blend, a flow, or a mix in their giftedness that helped them accomplish their vision and purpose in life. It is however important to note that many great people didn't launch out because of their gifts, they just start working and doing the little they had to do. But through continuous effort and practice they eventually discover and develop their core gifts and unique abilities.

To be extraordinary in life requires more than just competence. It goes beyond just being skilled at something. Just because you've done something for a long time doesn't mean you are the best in the world at it. If you cannot be the best in the world at your core, who you are truly born to be, then you cannot become extraordinary in life. There is no other way to be extraordinary at something unless you are the best in the world at it. Being the best at something doesn't call for excessive competition. It calls for the discovery and the excellence of your gift.

> **Inside everyone resides some special ability or genius.**

Extraordinary individuals frequently produce spectacular outcomes in unspectacular areas of life simply because they operate in the areas of their talents and potential.

Through the process of vision, as you begin to see with your mind's eye, what follows the realisation of your true self is a clear estimation of what you possess to fulfil your vision. Vision in its true sense is not just about being futuristic; vision comes with strategies and plans, and most importantly, you clearly identify what you uniquely possess to make that vision come to pass. To put it in a better way, what follows vision is a discovery of what you have been genetically encoded with, that which you need to stir up or develop rapidly so you get to the higher, extraordinary state you picture in your mind's eye.

It almost appears like a new discovery that comes with a light-bulb moment: that sudden awareness that "I can actually do this; this is what I was born for." Imagine it's like when Aladdin rubs the lamp, and a genie comes out. It is like rubbing your own internal lamp to bring out the genie in you. Every single individual is born to be a genius of a kind. It only takes a disciplined, focused mind to activate it. It takes the power of vision.

As you become fully aware of what you are genetically encoded for, you naturally gravitate towards that which you are inherently wired to do. You begin to acknowledge you're different from people around you, who lack the gift you have. As a result, you become more aware of what you are genetically good at doing.

What you are good at can be termed a skill. Many people can be skilled at one thing, but very few people are gifted at that thing. Your gift and your potential make you a rare commodity. A lot of people only stay at what they're good at and never attain what they're the best at doing. Only until you discover your vision will you be able to follow a pathway in life that informs the use of your special ability.

> **Extraordinary individuals frequently produce spectacular outcomes in unspectacular areas of life simply because they operate in the areas of their talents and potential.**

Gifts are not necessarily the same as skills. In narrowing down what differentiates gifts from skills, Dr. Samuel Ekundayo and I identified nine ways gifts are different from skills. See the summary table below:

Gift vs. Skill

	Gift	Skill
1	You were born with it, and it gets refined through training and practice.	You learned it and get better at it through training and practice.

2	It takes less effort to fine-tune when the environment is right.	Even in the right environment, difficulty level and effort usually vary and can range from minimum to maximum.
3	It may not be given to everybody. In essence, what is given to each person can vary, and when they do look alike, their talent mix is usually different, hence it is unique and distinct.	It can be acquired by almost anyone.
4	Usually relevant for life work, which you can't necessarily retire from.	Relevant for jobs which you can retire from.
5	Duplication and replace-ability is low.	Duplication and replace-ability can range from medium to high.
6	Compensation for the application of one's gift and talent is usually out of proportion, either too high or too low, since it is usually unmeasurable or unquantifiable.	Compensation is usually proportionate to the skills applied, possibly because of its measurability (based on time; e.g., working 9-5 or two hours a day).
7	It is a precursor for being significant and for the establishment of long-lasting legacies.	It helps to attain success (not necessarily significance or legacy) and somewhat helps to qualify gifts/talents.
8	It is the source of one's uniqueness and influence.	It brings about position and promotion, but not necessarily influence.
9	Examples include musical and design gifts.	Examples include driving skills.

Note that what you are gifted at could start as a skill you pick up somewhere, but with time, you realise that when you connect back to the passion and the impact you're able to make (more on this in the three circles discussed below), you see that you are more passionate about it than others. With time, you realise that you simply are the best in the world at it. You move from being skilled at that thing to being gifted at it. The application of a gift is also what determines if what you are doing is your life's work or just a job. Note again that for some, what you call a job is actually your life's work; it's just a matter of clarity and understanding. Do you feel your job is something you don't want to retire from? Do you love it and enjoy doing it? Does it define the legacy you want to leave behind? Do you feel your job can be described as something you want to call your contribution to humanity? If you answer yes to those questions, your current job can potentially be your life's purposeful work. In effect, the ability of vision to inspire unique gifts and fulfil your potential helps you distinguish between your work and your job. Work is passion that is generated by a unique purpose. Work reveals your potential. Jobs tend towards skills. Although you can be highly interested in your job, you will soon find that if you lack core ideological belief in what you do, it wouldn't take long before it starts to bore you, and your interest will diminish. Vision is the juice of life. Gifts, talents, and potential are what makes vision even juicier.

It is the power of vision that helps you to identify and focus more on your gift than skills. Keep in mind that while you could be multitalented, one gift is usually dominant among the many gifts you have.

Gifts are often referred to as potential, and based on my understanding of physics gravitational force and potential,[77] I came up with this explanation: What is inside of you is called potential because it can be seen as a centre of gravity, whose force, based on a potential difference or height, attracts certain things to you. Your potential, like a gravitational force within you, pulls certain thing towards you and makes you handle and transform them with a special type of energy.

The power of vision is parallel to the force of your potential. Your ability to do things without any formal training or education is by virtue of the potential in you. Vision allows you to apply your gifts and potential in such a way that the clearer the intuition and mental picture, the stronger the potential to get things done and accomplished. In essence, the clarity of what you see possible in your mind's eye allows you to do what only you have the inherent ability to do, thereby making you use your special ability called a gift or potential. And because it consistently demands of you, when it is well articulated and applied to the order of excellence, you don't get squashed in the natural talent mindset trap.[78] The natural talent mindset trap is what makes people feel like they are anointed geniuses which inadvertently causes their potential not to develop. Natural talent mindset trap causes people become arrogant, defensive, non-learners who ultimately fall into a doom loop.

Your gift and potential are as unique as your DNA. Only you possess it to fulfil your life's purpose.

Your gift can liberate you from the shackles of mediocrity and complacency. Many are complacent because they are involved in a redundant routine that does not challenge them; it's just another day job that is mentally depressing and not stimulating or reinvigorating. If you find something that consistently draws on your imagination and creative ability, you will rarely get tired or bored. That's why kids never get tired because they're in a state of perpetual exploration, developing their senses and relishing the outcome of their adventures.

> **The power of vision is parallel to the force of your potential.**

This is exactly what vision does to you. You will know that you are actively making progress and accomplishing your life's purpose, even if others may not see it, especially at the beginning. But you will find that you hardly get tired. Opening and closing time becomes blurred out because there is always fresh passion and excitement that comes with what you do. It's no longer a job that you want to retire from; it becomes purposeful work (something that although it's done daily, it takes a lifetime to accomplish), which you don't want to end.

Resign? No way. People resign from jobs but not from their purpose and vision, which are cumulative experiences and adventures, made beautiful and magical because you are applying what has been genetically added into you: your gift.

Your Gift Makes You Worth More

After studying the practical essence of giftedness in the lives of extraordinary people, I had to revise my knowledge of economics, specifically monopoly, moat and price theory. Vision and gifts help you develop what is called an economic moat – an advantage that is difficult to copy or emulate. Vision and gifts also made me realise that you tend to become a monopoly of some sort and the theory of perfect competition pricing does not apply to visionaries. But let me explain before marketers, economists, and business gurus blitz me out.

If you spend five minutes doing what another person spent five hours doing, and you get the same five hours' pay, you are definitely going to be labelled as a cheat. (And this is what vision and your gift make you become on the outside: a cheat). Imagine that you attain that level of productivity not because you went to school for it or were trained in any special way but because you have natural talent at it (again, it can overlap as your skill). There is no economic theory that justifies paying you an amount for five minutes of effort and paying someone else who spent five hours doing the same thing the same amount. But what if your work output is the same (or even better) despite the time difference? Think about it. Giftedness. In essence, your gift is what makes you efficient per amount of labour input. Vision and the application of gift or potential is highly needed if we desire to see workers in an economy produce more widgets—from lumber to ideas—per amount of labour. The better we are at transforming the raw materials we have to the things we actually want and need, in an efficient and scalable way, the higher our standard of living.

By appropriating the power of vision and living in the reality of your potential, your value will increase over time.

The power of vision and its creative visualisation capabilities help you see the end first and activate a special ability in you (which gets refined through training and practice), thereby making your output and productivity extraordinary, primarily because you applied your inherent gifts. You didn't labour for it. The private labours, constrictionary, lonely efforts of vision (which in some cases last for many years) prepared you for one particular action that appears spectacular to others.

This finding is what we notice with athletes. They use creative visualisation and focus on their core strengths and abilities. They're known for one thing and one thing alone. They practice the same thing daily (only if we are privy to the rigorous training athletes go through). They focus on one dominant gift and through discipline, practice, and patience, they fine-tune it into excellence. Only for them to participate in an event that lasts for less than an hour and then earn an amount that is equivalent to someone else's entire life's worth.

> Your gift, brought to limelight by just making the decision to follow your vision, is what will make room for you.

Your gift, brought to limelight by just making the decision to follow your vision, is what will make room for you. Your gift will enable you to fulfil you vision. The application of your gift makes you able to do what appears impossible to others. Exercising this gift (no matter how small or latent it appears in the beginning) gives you real fulfilment, purpose, and contentment in your work (not just a job).

Vision Makes You Depend on Something That Is Not Taught or Learnt in School

Another counterintuitive dimension or paradigmatic shift about vision is this: Your degree, educational qualifications, or academic background becomes less relevant in the arena of greatness. In fact, when you come to the arena of living in the reality of your vision, degrees and certification fade away; they're obsolete. And this finding is in line with other researchers who conclude that Ivy League schools are possibly overrated.[79] Don't get me wrong, though; there is a place for formal schooling, which I will highlight shortly. But I want you to keep in mind that whether you have a degree or not, you are still qualified to fulfil your vision.

Education is a word that has often been misunderstood and taken to mean "formal schooling." Education is a word derived from the Latin word "educo," which means to educe, draw out, or develop from within. Someone who demonstrates highly developed faculties of the mind, helping them to accomplish great things within the frames of moral justification and without violating the rights of others, can be regarded as being educated.

Formal schooling might be the place to get the experience you need to make the shift towards your vision, but it is not a prerequisite for accomplishing your vision. University, as the name suggests, is universal knowledge (or general knowledge); visionaries are specific in their application of information and knowledge (what is referred to as specialised knowledge). And this has been proven in the life of truly great people. School is great (as you will find that I myself am a career academic), but identifying your true life's purpose transcends any prior training you might have had. The nature of vision is such that it creates pathways never created before, and only by relying on something within you that doesn't yet exist can you truly fulfil your life's unique purpose. Schools don't have curriculum titled "how to fulfil your life's vision and purpose and be great." You'll have to figure that out yourself.

> In fact, when you come to the arena of living in the reality of your vision, degrees and certification fade away; they're obsolete.

> Schools don't have curriculum titled "how to fulfil your life's vision and purpose and be great." You'll have to figure that out yourself.

What is common in our world today is the excessive focus on school degrees and qualifications as the only medium to break through in life. This has resulted in many missed destinies and wasted potential. The COVID-19 pandemic has brought about such a remarkable change in how we view careers. Young people have become particularly at risk. The New York Times reported on May 20, 2020, that young people are saddled with college debt and are not getting opportunity in "a job market devastated by the pandemic."

In a rather interesting move, on June 25, news broke that the US government, the nation's largest employer, with 2.1 million civilian workers (excluding postal service employees), will be modernising its hiring practices to focus on skills over degrees. The objective is to "find candidates with the relevant competencies and knowledge, rather than simply recruiting based on degree requirements."[80]

This news follows what is now becoming an increasing trend. On October 2018, CNBC reported that leading organisations such as Apple, Google, and IBM were no longer requiring a college degree and changed their job description to exclude college degrees as requirements.[81] In 2019, IBM reported that 15 percent of its new US hires had nontraditional backgrounds and were evaluated based on skills instead of degrees.[82] Think about that for a minute. And if you have been following the gift versus skills discussion above, you will know that what government officials and experts are referring to as skills can be interpreted to mean gifts.

These are companies many people try for years to land a job with. What could be the reason for this? What are the implications for you, schools and the educational system, and the job market in general? The reason, I assume, is that organisations are looking for the right people, the right "whos" that can drive new innovation and progress. They are aware of acute shortages of extraordinary individuals who understand corporate destiny and are able to not only fit roles but can take the organisations to new frontiers.

These recent developments underscore the fact that a lot of learning is happening outside of formal classrooms, and governments all around the world are beginning to recognise it. Those who make the effort to discover, develop, and distinguish their gifts (and not only skills) will in the end position themselves for greater opportunities. People who pursue their vision and refine their gifts are most likely to win and lead others into the new era.

> **People who pursue their vision and refine their gifts are most likely to win and lead others into the new era.**

On June 2, 2020, the CEO of Tesla, Elon Musk, also reiterated that you don't need a college degree (he has maintained this stand for many years). Musk added that he looked for "evidence of exceptional ability" in a potential employee, rather than a degree from a prestigious university.[83]

The US officials pushing for skill-based hiring are also recommending increased opportunities for apprenticeships and promoting training and vocational education as alternatives to traditional college programs. It's not surprising that experts and researchers are quick to jump on the bandwagon and are already tossing around alternatives to help prepare young employees. Many of them recommend apprenticeship programs, which mix school and on-the-job training, as a better way to prepare the workforce of the future. Before you know it, the apprenticeship world gets flooded with ordinary individuals who are willing to join the rat race. Not that it's bad to become an apprentice; the issue lies in joining it without a plan, strategy, or vision.

As you have found in this book, you don't have to follow the recommendations of so called experts. What you need to do is review and consolidate what is within you in the face of current realities. It is not usually an action that is required but a change in perspective that puts you on track for greatness. The earlier you understand the principles and power of vision, the quicker you realise that you don't need to run from pillar to post, trying a thousand and one things that get you frustrated and more confused. You only have to continue to align with your intrinsic values and gifts, seeing basic connections that allow your potential to find full expression. People who are powered by vision can meet all of these criteria.

By aligning with your vision and abiding by the principles and practices that bring your dreams to life, you're not only going to live a life full of opportunities; you'll be able to have fun doing what you love and at the same time be able to make a meaningful contribution to your world. It is not about predicting or estimating what the next wave of opportunity will be; vision demands that you are ready and are the best, all the time, in your area of personal purpose. Vision is not just about predicting the future; vision empowers you to create the future. Vision is what brings about the discipline, focus, and excellence that comes with greatness.

> **Vision is not just about predicting the future; vision empowers you to create the future.**

Depending only on what you are taught, without the discovery of what distinguishes you from the multitude, can leave you in perpetual mediocrity. In a fascinating, significant paradigm shift, you may find that your formal education doesn't make your dream come to pass, but putting your gift to work does.

Culturescapes and influences during our upbringing and what the community models to us created the impression that school is everything. This leads many to hand their destinies over to instructors or lecturers, who themselves are teaching from curriculums that have long been outdated. Somehow, we have been made to believe that going to school and getting a degree is the only way to success.

If you are intelligent but not exercising your gift, you're probably going to be poor. If you're educated but have not developed your talent, you're likely to be depressed, frustrated, and tired. Education, degrees, and certificates, in themselves, don't guarantee anything; it is your God-given gifts that provide keys to your greatness. Being exceptional, as Elon Musk wants of his potential employees, requires operating with an outside-the-box mindset that only true visionaries possess. Vision provides you with the mental firepower and discipline to engage and become more, simply by following the dreams and core persuasions in your heart.

This should be a cause for relief, for many people think their failure in school means failure in life. Vision makes your life simple and levels the playing ground for everyone to become an active agent and force for greatness. You can become great because the pathway of greatness is not labelled by degrees or certifications but by the application of what is already inherent in you. You not only need to be liberated from what I already explained as external negative value forces (that make you think you need something when you really don't), but you also need to understand that not following your dreams is why you hate Monday mornings and can't wait for Fridays. For true visionaries, every day is an opportunity to build something truly great and legendary because in the scope of their unique vision, their picture of the future is already clear.

Depending only on what you are taught, without the discovery of what distinguishes you from the multitude, can leave you in perpetual mediocrity.

And with the power of BHAGs, visionaries become excited, as their creative juices flow from one accomplishment to another.

Think about it. There are so many educated people out there who are bright and intelligent but very miserable and perplexed because they don't have vision and don't understand their purpose. Some have degrees in banking and finance, wealth management and treasuries, yet don't have money in their accounts.

If you're intelligent but are not exercising your gift, you're probably going to be poor. If you're educated but have not developed your talent, you're likely going to be depressed, frustrated, and tired.

To be extraordinary, you must break loose from your initial wiring and shift the paradigms that make you hold on to a mediocre, average lifestyle. You must not become perplexed by the complexity of modern times. Visionaries become even more relevant as chaos and complexity increase because of the sheer power of their simplicity and the accuracy of their thoughts, which have been refined through discipline. As explained in early chapters, you must make the effort to rewire your mind with the power of thought and focus (VAD), so that you can hold a new and better paradigm. Discover your gift, and put it to work. Through continuous service, take any opportunity that comes before you to use your gift (no matter how small); fine-tune your gift from latency to potency.

> **You can become great because the pathway of greatness is not labelled by degrees or certifications but by the application of what is already inherent in you.**

I found that some people are limited by money when they attempt to explore their gift. Money locks you into the rat race; some people who have only begun to apply their gifts can easily get carried away by money and as a result fail to reach the fullness of their purpose and potential. In the economics of visionaries, when the time of manifestation comes, you will be able to charge whatever amount comes to your mind. Not only are you able to charge, you are also able to give more and serve more freely. Always remember that your gift is inherently yours.

The potential inside you is a strong force. The gift inside of you is loaded. Dr. Myles Munroe put it better when he wrote the following:[84]

> *The world won't move over for you because you're smart. Whenever you exercise your gift, however, the world will make room for you. Anyone—yourself included—who discovers his or her gift and develops it will become a commodity. If you're a young person in high school or college who is planning your career, don't do what people say will make you wealthy. Do what you were born to do, because that is where you will make your money and find your life's fulfilment. No matter how big the world is, there's a place for you in it when you discover and manifest your gift.*

You are special. Dream big. The world needs your unique contribution through the exercise and application of your gift. But if you lack vision, it will remain in latent form until you discover it. A gift in its raw form is latent. Gifts that has been discovered and refined become talent and potential. Your gift, talent, or potential is the special ability or energy that comes from your core; it is part of what defines you as a special individual, full of life, passion, and zeal. Your potential is a strong force, a staying power that makes you do exploits and wonders. It is a beautiful thing to be powered by your vision and propelled by your gift.

> **It is a beautiful thing to be powered by your vision and propelled by your gift.**

All the extraordinary individuals I researched accomplished great results not just because of what they studied in school. They applied their gifts. They proved over and over again that more than other human and material resources, potential is what's required to fulfil your purpose in life. They became dominant in one area of life, not because they were skilled or because of any special training or education. They revolutionised a sector of life with this special ability. Their vision, brought to light through the application of their gift, makes them remembered many years after they are gone. They created new roads where one never existed before, not because there wasn't a challenge or obstacle but in spite of it.

Apart from all the opposition, be aware that your vision and gift will be criticised and tested. People who don't have a clue about your vision may call it a waste of time. Meanwhile, you are training and preparing yourself by taking on tasks that may not fetch financial returns (at least in the beginning). All great people appear to go through a level of criticism in trying to bring their vision to life.

When Henry Ford was just a farm boy, he started out fixing wristwatches. Most people probably thought he was crazy, as he continued to experiment with combustion engines in his garage. He was applying his gift and refining it. No one remembers all the people who thought he was crazy; we remember only the man who had vision enough to create the Model T and through which a whole new industrial era emerged.

Martin Luther King Jr. had the oratory gift, together with other complementary gifts, which helped him accomplish most of his life's purpose. It took years of training and practice.

Each of these extraordinary individuals had a unique gift, which they applied in fulfilling their life vision.

And this brings to what is called the *Hedgehog Concept*.

The Hedgehog Concept

The Hedgehog Concept is an idea popularised by Jim Collins in his book *Good to Great*.[85] Jim developed this concept from Isaiah Berlin's famous essay "The Hedgehog and the Fox."

Berlin divided the world into hedgehogs and foxes, based upon an ancient Greek parable:

The fox knows many things, but the hedgehog knows one big thing. The fox is a cunning creature, able to devise myriad complex strategies for sneak attacks upon the hedgehog. Day in and day out, the fox circles around the hedgehog's den, waiting for the perfect moment to pounce. Fast, sleek, beautiful, fleet of foot, and crafty, the fox looks like the sure winner. The hedgehog, on the other hand, is a dowdier creature, looking like a genetic mix-up between a porcupine and a small armadillo. He waddles along, going about his simple day, searching for lunch and taking care of his home.

The fox waits in cunning silence at the juncture in the trail. The hedgehog, minding his own business, wanders right into the fox's path.

Aha!, I've got you now, thinks the fox. He leaps out, bounding across the ground, lightning fast. The little hedgehog, sensing danger, looks up and thinks, Here we go again. Will he ever learn?

Rolling up into a perfect little ball, the hedgehog becomes a sphere of sharp spikes, pointing outward in all directions. The fox, bounding towards his prey, sees the hedgehog's defense and calls off the assault. Retreating back to the forest, the fox begins to calculate a new line of attack. Each day, some version of this battle between the hedgehog and the fox takes place, and despite the greater cunning of the fox, the hedgehog always wins.

Berlin extrapolated from this little parable to divide people into two basic groups: foxes and hedgehogs. Foxes pursue many ends, at the same time, and see life as complex. They are "scattered or diffused, moving on many levels," says Berlin, never integrating their thinking into one overall concept or unifying vision. Hedgehogs, on the other hand, simplify a complex world into a single organising idea, a basic concept that unifies and guides everything. It doesn't matter how complex the world is; a hedgehog reduces all challenges and dilemmas to simple—indeed almost simplistic—hedgehog ideas. For a hedgehog, anything that does not somehow relate to the hedgehog idea holds no relevance.

It is important to clarify that hedgehogs are not stupid. Quite the contrary. They understand that the essence of profound insight is simplicity. I found this simplicity in the extraordinary individuals I researched for this book. This was how I felt when I held an iPhone for the first time in 2010 (when I didn't even know who Steve Jobs was): "Could another phone be simpler to use yet so sophisticated and powerful?" What could be simpler than Mother Teresa's decision to love the poor, sick, dying, and children loitering the streets without hope? How about Joseph's "my bundle stood straight up, and your bundles circled around it and bowed down to mine"? In most Disney shows, I'm sure you watch and ask, "What could be simpler than making kids and families happy?"

> **...understand that the essence of profound insight is simplicity**

No, the hedgehogs aren't simpletons; they have a piercing insight that allows them to see through complexity and discern underlying patterns. Hedgehogs see what is essential and ignore the rest.

What does all this talk of hedgehogs and foxes have to do with vision and being extraordinary? Virtually everything. Almost everything we have discussed since the beginning of this book fits neatly together in the Hedgehog Concept.

Extraordinary people are hedgehogs. The clarity and power of their vision made them become hedgehogs, which they used to drive forward what is called the Hedgehog Concept. Ordinary people who remain in obscurity are like foxes; they never use the clarifying power of vision to develop their Hedgehog Concept, and as result, they're scattered, diffused, and inconsistent.

Let's go back to my research and consider the cases of Hellen Keller and Mother Teresa.

One might think that Helen Keller, who became deaf and blind at nineteen months of age, would not amount to anything. It is possible she had a hard start, as accounts recorded how she was restless and unruly. But with time, she began to focus her energy on core areas of strengths: feeling things with her hands and communicating back through Braille. In classic hedgehog style, Keller took this simple concept and implemented it with fanatical consistency. She embarked on a reading and writing program never seen before in human history. Not only was she ahead of her peers, she became the first person with a major disability to graduate from college.

While in school, she combined the arduous tasks of attending class and writing her first book: *The Story of My Life*, which was published in 1903. The book was later recognised by the New York Public Library as one of the hundred most important books of the twentieth century. On June 28, 1904, she became the first person with a serious disability to earn an undergraduate degree. Having developed skills never approached by any similarly disabled person, Keller began to write about her blindness, a subject then taboo in women's magazines because of the relationship of many cases to venereal disease. Edward W. Bok accepted her articles for Ladies' Home Journal, and other major magazines—The Century, McClure's, and The Atlantic Monthly—followed suit. Applying the same Hedgehog Concept, she became a lecturer. At the time of her passing in 1964, Keller had written books, gave multiple lectures, traveled to over thirty countries, and visited many institutions as guest lecturer. She personally lobbied and became an activist for better treatment of people with disabilities. She instituted the organisation for the deaf and blind and through her work many policies for the handicapped were repealed and revamped.

> **Ordinary people who remain in obscurity are like foxes; they never use the clarifying power of vision to develop their Hedgehog Concept**

Here is one of her famous quotes:
"The most miserable person in the world is the one with sight but no vision."

Helen Keller focused on her core abilities. With focus, she developed her skills as her mind's eye was able to see and dream. And in the simplistic and focused style of the Hedgehog Concept, she made valuable contributions to the life of many.

Let's take a look at Mother Teresa.

She was committed to her profession of vows to serve for the rest of her life (which conferred on her the title "Mother") and in 1944 served as a principal of Saint Mary's School. But in a typical hedgehog fashion, she sought to be more effective and focus on what was essential to her life's purpose. On September 10, 1946, Mother Teresa experienced a call inside of another call (or what I like to call a re-vision), which brought about more specificity in what she was called to do. She was riding in a train from Calcutta to the Himalayan foothills for a retreat when she said she got the inspiration to abandon her teaching and work in the slums of Calcutta, aiding the city's poorest and sickest people.

> **Hedgehogs know exactly what to do; not wasting time in complexities, she focused her strength.**

After nearly a year and a half of lobbying, in January 1948, she finally received approval to pursue this new calling. That August, donning the blue-and-white sari that she would wear in public for the rest of her life, she left the Loreto Convent and wandered out into the city. After six months of basic medical training, she voyaged for the first time into Calcutta's slums with no more specific a goal than to aid those in need and the less privileged.

Mother Teresa quickly translated her calling into concrete actions to help the city's poor. She began an open-air school and established a hospice for the destitute in a dilapidated building she convinced the city government to donate to her cause. In October 1950, she won canonical recognition for a new congregation, the Missionaries of Charity, which she founded with only a handful of members—most of them former teachers or pupils from St. Mary's School.

As the ranks of her congregation swelled and donations poured in from around India and across the globe, the scope of Mother Teresa's charitable activities expanded exponentially. Over the course of the 1950s and 1960s, she established a leper colony, an orphanage, a nursing home, a family clinic, and a string of mobile health clinics.

In 1971, Mother Teresa traveled to New York City to open her first American-based house of charity, and in the summer of 1982, she secretly went to Beirut, Lebanon, where she crossed between Christian East Beirut and Muslim West Beirut to aid children of both faiths. In 1985, Mother Teresa returned to New York and spoke at the fortieth anniversary of the United Nations General Assembly. While there, she also opened Gift of Love, a home to care for those infected with HIV/AIDS.

In February 1965, Pope Paul VI bestowed the Decree of Praise upon the Missionaries of Charity, which prompted Mother Teresa to begin expanding internationally. By the time of her death in 1997, the Missionaries of Charity numbered more than four thousand—in addition to thousands more lay volunteers—with 610 foundations in 123 countries around the world.

Mother Teresa was a model hedgehog; she simply acknowledged, based on deep insight and conviction, that this was the essential thing she was the best at doing in the world.

It could be one gift or a mix of gifts; extraordinary people come to discover that which they're genetically encoded to do, that which comes to them naturally, and then focus their time, energy, and resources doing that same thing over and over again, until they're world famous, and they don't stop, even then. Remember that it's your life's work, not a job.

> ...wouldn't it be refreshing to see individuals succeed so brilliantly by taking one simple concept and just doing it with excellence and imagination?

The question I ask myself as I come face to face with the simplicity and power of vision, as it pertains to the Hedgehog Concept, is that in a world overrun by success hacks, personality hacks, personal management faddists, social media ranters, futurists, fearmongers, motivational gurus, and all the rest, wouldn't it be refreshing to see individuals succeed so brilliantly by taking one simple concept and just doing it with excellence and imagination? Becoming the best in the world at reading and writing in Braille and publishing books and giving lectures. Heading to the slums, cleaning them up, and providing basic amenities to poor people. What could be more obvious and straightforward?

Chapter 15
THE THREE CIRCLES OF EXTRAORDINARY INDIVIDUALS

Reviewing Jim Collins's 2001 Hedgehog Concept and the three circles which he applied to companies, I found his 2011 keynote lecture at the Peter Drucker Centennial,[86] where he provided a model I have now developed and call the Three Circles of Extraordinary Individuals. In a way, it captures the entire message of this book.

What distinguishes extraordinary individuals are two fundamental things. First, they spent their time figuring out and understanding three key dimensions, what I call the three circles. Second, they translated that understanding into a simple, crystalline concept that guided all their efforts; hence, the term Hedgehog Concept.

More precisely, a Hedgehog Concept is a simple, crystalline concept that flows from a deep understanding about the intersection of the following three circles:

1. What gift do you possess that you can be the best in the world at (and, equally important, what you cannot be the best in the world at)? This discerning standard goes far beyond core competence. Just possessing a core competence doesn't necessarily mean you are the best in the world at it. Conversely, what you can be the best at might not even be something you currently do. So this requires self-awareness and deep reflection, which takes time.

2. What significant value or contribution can you make in the lives of others? All extraordinary individuals attained piercing insight into how to make a meaningful impact in the lives of others. They had a consistent measurement and feedback system from their target audience and focused on delivering consistent value within their niche. They had an important value orientation that cannot be measured in

social or economic terms. This is how they felt useful, and the feedback added to the entire flywheel process.

3. What you are deeply passionate about? Extraordinary individuals focused on those activities that ignited their passion. The idea here is not to simulate passion but to discover what makes you passionate. They essentially aligned with things that fell into their core beliefs and made them feel they are who they truly are when involved in such activities.

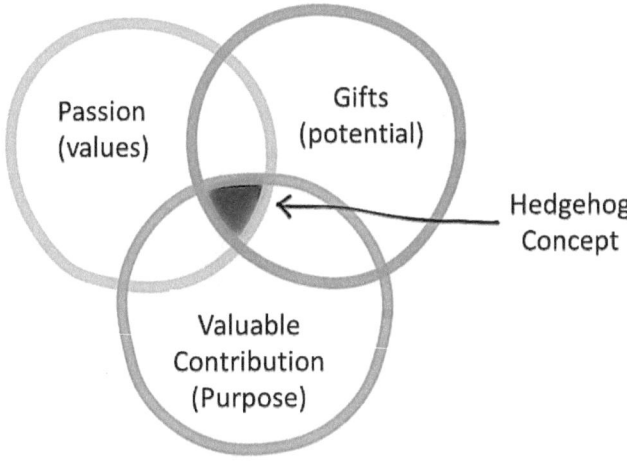

FIGURE 14: Three Circles of Extraordinary Individuals and The Hedgehog Concept

To quickly grasp the three circles, consider the following analogy: Suppose you were able to construct a work life that achieved these three goal: First, you are doing work for which you have a genetic or God-given talent, and you might become one of the best in the world in applying that talent. ("I feel that I was just born to be doing this.") Second, every time you do such work, it feels like a dream because you can make a tangible contribution to people in significant ways. And especially when you get paid for impacting lives, you think it's so amazing to do what you love and actually get paid. ("I get paid to do this? Am I dreaming?") Third, you are doing work you are passionate about and absolutely love to do, enjoying the actual process for its own sake. ("I look forward to getting up and throwing myself into my daily work, and I really believe in what I'm doing.") If you could drive towards the intersection of these three circles and translate that intersection into a simple, crystalline concept that guided your life choices, then you'd have a Hedgehog Concept for yourself.

Your passion.
Your gift.
Your unique valuable contribution.

What Are You Wired For? Understanding What You Can (and Cannot) Be the Best At

Stick with what you know you have the innate capability to execute effortlessly. The way to figure this out is to ask important questions, like: What can I potentially do better than any other person? What do I accomplish gracefully that requires the use of my gift? And another equally important question is: What can't I be the best at than another individual? This is not a question of competition. This introspection occurs in your solitude moments. These questions evaluate your self-awareness.

Through an iterative process of continuous practice, you can begin to zero in on what you know in your heart you truly are the best at. That was how Helen Keller did it. That was the same approach Mother Teresa used. Let me add one more example from my research, that of Steve Jobs.

Although many called Steve Jobs a marketer, I will argue based on research that his gift was more in the aspects of design, process, and strategy. He initially chose a college that was so expensive that it cost all his working-class parents' savings to pay his tuition. After six months at college, he didn't see the value in it and decided to drop out. Although he admitted it was pretty scary at the time, looking back, he recalled it was one of the best decisions he made. Not an easy road. He later spoke about this experience in his speech at Stanford University's 2005 Commencement:[87]

> **What can't I be the best at than another individual?**

It wasn't all romantic. I didn't have a dorm room, so I slept on the floor in friends' rooms, I returned Coke bottles for the 5¢ deposits to buy food with, and I would walk the 7 miles across town every Sunday night to get one good meal a week at the Hare Krishna temple. I loved it. And much of what I stumbled into by following my curiosity and intuition turned out to be priceless later on.

While many others would have spent their entire parents' savings and more on a college that they wouldn't feel committed to, in a typical hedgehog style, Jobs found Reed College, which offered the best course in calligraphy. Jobs went ahead to say:[88]

> Because I had dropped out and didn't have to take the normal classes, I decided to take a calligraphy class to learn how to do this. I learned about serif and sans serif typefaces, about varying the amount of space between different letter combinations, about what makes great typography great. It was beautiful, historical, artistically subtle in a way that science can't capture, and I found it fascinating. None of this had even a hope of any practical application in my life. But 10 years later, when we were designing the first Macintosh computer, it all came back to me. And we designed it all into the Mac. It was the first computer with beautiful typography.

The Macintosh computer was a machine that came with something unprecedented: a wide choice of fonts. As well as including familiar choices such as Times New Roman and Helvetica, Jobs introduced several new designs and evidently took some care in their appearance and naming. Some were named after cities he loved, such as Chicago and Toronto. He wanted each of them to be as distinct and beautiful as the calligraphy he had encountered a decade earlier, and at least two of the fonts—Venice and Los Angeles—had a handwritten look to them.

It was the beginning of something, a seismic shift in our everyday relationship with letters and with type. An innovation that, within another decade or so, would place the word font—previously a piece of technical language limited to the design and printing trade—in the vocabulary of every computer user.

In a special report, Simon Garfield concluded, "The ability to change fonts at all seemed like technology from another planet. Before the Macintosh of 1984, primitive computers offered up one dull typeface, and good luck trying to italicise it. But now there was a choice of alphabets that did their best to re-create something we were used to from the real world."[89]

By following a rather evolutionary approach, using the power of focus, intuition, and aligning with what he truly believed in his heart,

Jobs went ahead to revolutionise multiple industries throughout his lifetime. This gradual but consistent evolution of his gift resulted in more revolution. Even critics acknowledge Jobs's enduring penchant for specifics in design and production. He knew what his core gift was and, in a typical hedgehog style, developed and matured it. By the time of his death on October 5, 2011, Steve Jobs revolutionised six industries with his counterintuitive approach. The industries include: animated movies, digital publishing, music, personal computers, phones, and tablet computing.

This principle of finding out what they were the best at in the world was not only limited to Mother Teresa, Helen Keller, or Steve Jobs. Indeed, all extraordinary individuals possess these unique, hedgehog-style attributes that make them flourish. Mandela had the combination of literacy, law, comradery, and a passion for freedom for his people. Martin Luther King Jr. was a gifted orator, a passionate preacher, and an advocate for freedom-for-all. Joseph had the gift of interpretation of dreams. Masaru Ibuka was special in the area of electronics. Henry Ford was gifted in the area of mechanics. This special ability came together with their vision, and its application propelled them to greatness.

At this point, it is important to draw out this vital note:

The Hedgehog Concept is not a plan, strategy, or intention to be the best. It is an understanding of what you can be the best at.

As you can imagine, everyone would like to be the best at something, but only very few people actually understand—with piercing insight and egoless clarity—what they actually have the potential to be the best at and, just as important, what they cannot be the best at. And it comes through deep insight and reflections. Note that in most cases, this giftedness was hidden and had to be discovered, understood, and brought to light.

Understanding Your Unique Contribution

Your unique contribution is also the value you creation. It is the product of your purposeful work.

During the hardest times, that is the very moment you see

extraordinary individuals thrive. In fact, that was why I chose the word extraordinary. Because when you expect them to act the same way or for business as usual to continue, great people act counterintuitively, finding joy and fulfilment in going the extra mile in order to create new value and to make meaningful contributions. Just when you expect her to enjoy her new role as a principal, Mother Teresa decided to go attend to those in the slums. In her day, no one born blind and deaf had ever written a book; that was when Keller's publication began to flourish. Just when it looked like no one could ever speak against the status quo or the laws of the land, King and Mandela chose imprisonment rather than follow the status quo.

This brings me to another important point: People who became extraordinary didn't do so because circumstances were favourable, but because they understood what area of life demanded their unique contribution and then focused in that area. They were able to do this because of their vision and clarity of insight into what actions they needed to take that will make them fulfilled. They figured out what could make the greatest impact or bring the greatest returns per unit effort. And they didn't measure value only in terms of money.

> During the hardest times, that is the very moment you see extraordinary individuals thrive.

Imagine it as what you could do quite efficiently and make the greatest return per your labour cost (usually the application or exercise of your gift). Imagine it as what you know will bring remarkable value and real benefits to people around you.

The implication of this is that you don't need to wait for the perfect opportunity to make what is called a "valuable contribution" in the general sense. You just need keep taking every opportunity you get to serve as it pertains to the other two circles. It is important to remain consistent in these three circles. For the flywheel to keep building momentum and bringing energy back into the system, you have to keep at it; otherwise, there is a risk of falling back. The only way to remain great is to keep applying the fundamental principles that makes you great.

Vision and gifts help you make a meaningful contribution to others; this is one of the most important aspects of vision. After all is said and done, vision's sole purpose is to help you gravitate towards your true self. But it doesn't just end there. Living in the reality of your true self, within your Hedgehog Concept, makes you impact your world in authentic ways. Your contribution becomes significant and remarkable. In essence, the cumulation of your action serves others. You become a Level 7 leader because your motivation for why you do what you do is deeper, as it comes from the heart. Heart-to-heart impact is more profound than other types of impact. I discussed this more in Chapter 28.

In the words of Jack Canfield, "When you truly are on purpose, the people, resources, and opportunities you need naturally gravitate towards you. The world benefits, too, because when you act in alignment with your true life purpose, all of your actions automatically serve others."[90]

Understanding Your Passion

As we already discussed, your passion is what lies at the very epicenter of your being. In short, it is who you truly are at the core. You know you are wired for it, and it directly checks the mark with your beliefs and values. It's not saying, "I want to get passionate about what I am doing"; it is the other way round: "I should only do what I can get passionate about." Mother Teresa didn't make the total commitment to helping people in the slums because it was fun, nice, and easy. In fact, it wasn't because it showed her charisma (some people probably saw it that way). It was simply because of her passion.

> **Passion is integral to the entire process of becoming extraordinary.**

Passion is integral to the entire process of becoming extraordinary. It is a critical component of the Hedgehog Concept. Passion cannot be manufactured, nor can you motivate people to feel passionate. Passion can only be discovered at the core. You can only discover things that ignite your passion, as well as the passion of those around you. It doesn't really matter what this is; it could be anything. The point is that you feel deeply and genuinely passionate about what you are doing.

The Triumph of Understanding over Bravado

While the Hedgehog Concept and the three circles look very simple in theory, in practice, it can be difficult. But if you take the patience to arrive at it, you will find your vision beginning to manifest in phases[91] and move towards becoming extraordinary. In reality, there are "prehedgehog" and "posthedgehog" states. In the prehedgehog state, it's like groping through the fog. You're making progress on a long march, but you can't see all that well. At each juncture in the trail, you can only see a little bit ahead and must move at a deliberate, slow crawl. Then, with the hedge, you break into a clearing, the fog lifts, and you can see for miles. From then on, each juncture requires less deliberation, and you can shift from crawl to walk, and from walk to run. In the posthedgehog state, miles of trail move swiftly beneath your feet, forks in the road fly past as you quickly make decisions that you would not have seen in the fog.

Ordinary individuals never come out of the fog. They do so many things, trying to claim it as clarity; and instead of seeking understanding, they adopt more strategies and quick fixes. Some go all out to borrow external forces, driven by the impression that something is terribly wrong with them when they only need to be patient and discipline their thoughts. Many veer off the trail, banging into trees and tumbling down ravines, all trying to become great in life.

> **Average people don't ask themselves the right questions, questions prompted by the three circles.**

Extraordinary individuals are in the same complex world as ordinary individuals, but they seek simplicity and clarity, while the ordinary individuals remain in perpetual complexity.

The bottom line: Average people don't ask themselves the right questions, questions prompted by the three circles. Extraordinary individuals start with these questions. Ordinary people tend to display false bravado and make high-sounding statements without really understanding.

In today's world where growth industry hacks try to preach success at all cost to you; it is such a relief to realise that becoming obsessed with growth alone will not make you extraordinary. You must focus on sustained growth, with the benefit of your Hedgehog Concept. If you have the right Hedgehog Concept and make decisions consistent with it, you will create such momentum that your main problem will not be how to grow, but how not to grow too fast.

It is important to point out that transitioning into your own personal Hedgehog Concept will take time, but keep working at it; this is how your flywheel is going to turn from ordinary to extraordinary. And as important as Hedgehog Concepts are, it will be a terrible mistake to jump right into it, thoughtlessly. Insights don't just happen; they take time. They essentially build on what we have discussed so far in this book.

Like scientific insight, a Hedgehog Concept simplifies a complex world and makes decisions much easier. Once you have it, it has crystalline clarity and elegant simplicity, but getting the concept can be devilishly difficult. It takes time. Recognise that getting a Hedgehog Concept is an inherently iterative process, not an event. If you wonder how to stay the course and not get burned out, what you need to do is to essentially iterate the Vision Flywheel to greatness. Revise your thoughts, become a disciplined person, and take action. One step at a time, step-by-step. To support the Vision Flywheel process, I developed a value-adding toolkit (VAT) that ensures your flywheel turns and does not stall. I found that truly great people developed their Hedgehog Concept by periodically doing a personal evaluation. And this is why although they do experience personal shortcomings that could have negative impacts on their flywheel to greatness, they learnt to reflect and review how they can better serve (what areas actually produces their best impact).

Imagine VAT like a vigorous mental debate where you are asking questions relating to your three circles (as discussed above), starting with self-awareness and evaluation. With self-evaluation, you are asking yourself questions, such as in the last action you took, what was the learning experience or benefit? What didn't go well and needs to be improved? The end result of the self-evaluation will help determine precisely what area you need to add value to yourself. If you felt certain actions were not in line with your core values, you do fewer things that will cause such actions to be taken in the future. If you felt that certain actions produced the right results, do more things that will cause such action to be taken in the future.

In essence, VAT helps you to identify and drop what didn't work and add more value to yourself. Keep in mind that adding value to yourself is not primarily about what you are adding, per se; it's about what you are subtracting, since such activity didn't align with your vision and values. Then you take action and serve with your gift in the areas that truly matter.

Iteratively doing this will bring illumination at every stage or cycle in the VAT. To get even better, apply the VAT in solitude. Be guided by the three circles, iteratively and over time, carry out analysis and autopsies of events in your life, and figure out vital issues and decisions facing you as an individual. Greatness may not come overnight, as we have seen in the stories of extraordinary models, but it will eventually happen if you follow these practices.[92]

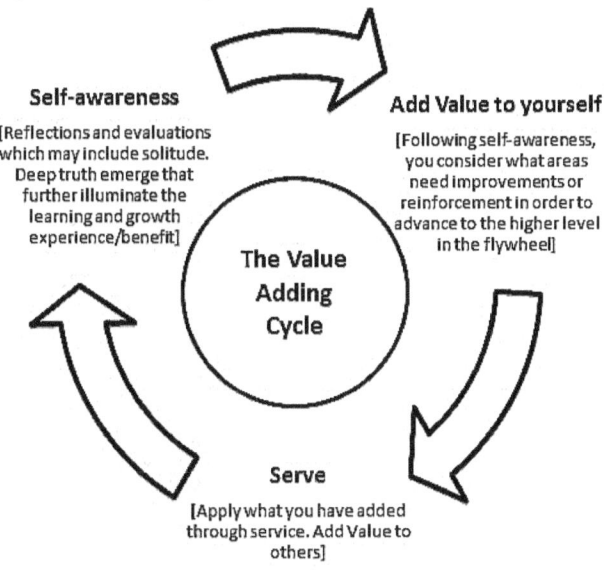

FIGURE 15: The Value-Adding Toolkit (VAT)

***

Gifts and natural talents are central. But they didn't come because these great people searched for or excessively focused on them. While gifts are inherent, it is passion and hard work that gives them full expression. The place of constant and continuous work (not just job) is essential to having extraordinary outcomes. The ability to continuous build momentum through the application of one's gift and to combine that with diligent work takes a culture of discipline. The rest of the book—principles of personal management, discipline, and disciplined actions (a culture of discipline) —only makes sense when you understand the place of your gift, the Hedgehog Concept, and how everything fits into the overall Vision Flywheel.

While gifts are inherent, it is passion and hard work that gives them full expression.

PART 3
PUBLIC MANIFESTATIONS

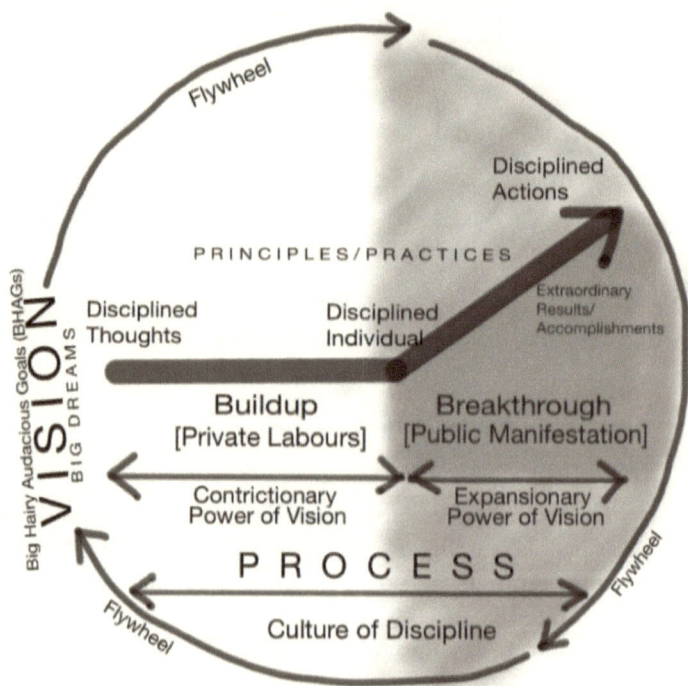

Chapter 16
PRINCIPLES OF PERSONAL MANAGEMENT AND SUSTAINABLE GROWTH

A number of scientific research have point to the fact that a person's trait will tend to improve over time, indicating an implicit belief that, regardless of its current surface features, the true self's positive nature will eventually shine through.[93] While this statement holds true, a costly assumption will be to think that growth will happen by itself. The positive nature of who you truly are, as you become powered by your vision, will shine through but there is need for personal management for growth to be sustained. To truly grow sustainably, we have to take responsibility for how we grow, making sure that it's unceasing and in the right direction. More importantly, we must note that in the school of effective growth, improvement and change go hand in hand. To enter the new is to break from comfort.

Measuring growth, fine-tuning growth directions, and making growth sustainable are processes that can sound ambiguous and quite overwhelming. However, we wouldn't want to experience taking one step forward and later two steps backward. If that is the case, we may end up being worse off, and rather than grow, we retrogress. That is why we must take responsibility for our personal growth, ensuring that it is measurable and specific.

We need to be vigilant as we make progress. We need to constantly check that what we call growth is not actually a short-term fix that doesn't last. Principles of personal management and growth are predicated upon our ability to set a sustainable course of

> **Sustainable growth occurs only when you identify your personal growth trajectory based the vision of your destiny.**

growth, in the reality of our purpose and potential. It is defined by not leaving growth to chance but taking responsibility to manage our resources as well as engage in activities that have long-term benefits for our lives. Sustainable growth occurs only when you identify your personal growth trajectory based the vision of your destiny.

For example, how do you classify a real estate agent who religiously accompanies his family to church, but only because being perceived as a God-fearing, family-oriented man is "good for business." The agent has completely designed his life around getting ahead in business and somehow managed to entangle his family, the church, and community into that bracket. This should not be so. Many start out their businesses and careers with the mentality of getting ahead, believing that they can fake righteous living (going to church) in order to get a couple business referrals. The question we need to ask ourselves is this: looking at things holistically, is it sustainable to only get ahead in business by manipulating our family and community? This illustration shows a lack of personal integrity, where what you have in mind (your values at the core) is not congruent with your actions. Such growth cannot be sustained.

The right perspective is to first understand what our values are (based on the principles of personal purpose and disciplined thoughts) and then become personally effective and efficient in utilising the gifts and resources we have towards accomplishing our purpose. Because each life is made unique—a divine original—we have to identify the very best we can be in life.

Vision provides us the inner compass to navigate our lives by using our time and resources in the most effective way. If we live by the principles of personal management and growth, we realise that growth is not just an annual thing, but a daily and weekly process within a continuum. Abiding by this principle helps us to understand that growth for the vision is a function of fulfilling our purpose in phases. Purpose is not static; purpose is dynamic, and with a Vision Flywheel, we can set multiple BHAGs or growth objectives that take us from one level to another.

Vision provides us the inner compass to navigate our lives by using our time and resources in the most effective way.

Having the right perspective and being ethical applies to life in general. Our motive for careers and jobs, companies to work for, mentors to learn from, and so on shouldn't be based on just the desire to make money or get ahead. We must take responsibility for our growth, which sometimes means sacrificing comfort and financial certainty for the opportunity to learn and grow.

Personal development and growth shouldn't just be goals; they should be part of your lifestyle. It should be a habit that everything you do in life filters through. Taking charge of your own growth is so rewarding. When you learn how to take responsibility for your growth, you strengthen your confidence and overall outcome in life. In short, when you commit to growth, everybody wins. This is because as you grow, your ability to create value and to be a blessing to others increases. The positive externality we generate further creates inspiration for others around us to grow themselves. The ripple effect of committing to growth inadvertently creates an environment where growth is modelled and expected. So start right now. Make sure whatever you want to experience growth in is measurable, is in the right direction, and is sustainable.

> ...when you commit to growth, everybody wins.

Avoid Placing Goals before Growth

I have heard many refer to the current generation as the "microwave generation." I believe it's based on our desire for instant gratification. Not that some of us don't like principles and processes; it's just that sometimes, we jump from pillar to post out of peer pressure. When we take the time to first understand the proper way things should be done, the principles that hold things together, we find that we can then develop the speed and momentum we need as time goes by. We eventually meet all our life desires in a more sustainable way, without borrowed forces, when we first go for growth instead of just setting goals.

Some people totally ignore the process and run after the rewards. They inappropriately place goals before growth, when it should be the other way around. It is our commitment to growth that will consistently enlarge our capability and enable us to achieve not only current goals but also future goals. Growth requires change. Change requires leaving our comfort zone. Growth takes effort and requires careful planning. Goals have a binary outcome; you either achieve them or you fail.

Growth considers very small incremental improvements, even if the outcome does not lead to accomplishing the goal. Note also that growth in this context is not a function of age. It is a matter of the grind, the ability to accept responsibilities.

Growth gradually becomes an outward manifestation of time of private labours. With time, spending weeks and months of personal study and asking questions ultimately strengthens you for the challenges to come.

> **Growth gradually becomes an outward manifestation of time of private labours.**

Setting goals is great, but more than that, it is important to grow up. When boys grow up, they develop the spiritual and physical stamina to avoid short-lived relationships and marriages. They will be there (full-time) for their kids through the journey of life (not part-time). When girls grow up, they become the foundation and pillars of not only a thriving home but also a community that is well nurtured and successful. Growing up with patience, perseverance, and compassion produces good, strong character.

So will you commit to growth and not just goals? Start today by drawing a growth plan, not just a goal plan.

Visionaries Embrace Change as a Component of Sustainable Growth

It's one thing to embrace change; it's another thing to see change as an opportunity for growth. One can change without growing, but growth cannot occur without change. To truly experience effective growth, one must be committed to change, again and again.

Our comfort zone is where we are safe. Comfort zones limit our dreams and potential; they encourage mediocrity. Things are easy and predictable, and we spend most of our time in the comfort zone (see Figure 17: comfort zone versus learning zone versus breaking point). Our comfort zone is a state of rest, inertia, where there is no change in momentum. Staying in the comfort zone is like going to the gym every day and doing the same exercises for months. There would be no significant change or improvement. Coming out of our comfort zone is to enter the new: the learning zone. This is where you push the boundaries of your existing skills and experience. This is where real learning and growth takes place.

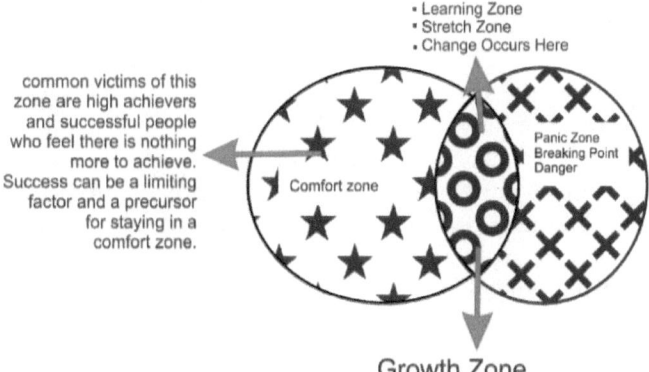

FIGURE 17: Change: comfort zone versus learning zone versus breaking point

Daniel H. Pink put it well in his book *Drive: The Surprising Truth about What Motivates Us*, with the following:

"We need a place of productive discomfort, if you're too comfortable, you're not productive. And if you're too uncomfortable, you're not productive. Like Goldilocks [and the bears], we can't be too hot or too cold."[94]

If you've ever pushed yourself to get to the next level in sports, fitness, or learning, you know what it's like to step outside your comfort zone. You know what it's like in the learning zone. To transition away into being a novice can be tough. Breaking from your comfort zone and entering the new can be a truly daunting process. Yet it is the most rewarding. Growth can be exhilarating yet painful, gainful yet uncomfortable. However, once you take the leap, the development often adds to the richness of your experience. Discomforting yourself can truly open a world of opportunities.

> Growth can be exhilarating yet painful, gainful yet uncomfortable.

Transitioning from Comfort Zone to Growth Zone

I would like to share the following process which I extrapolated from this research, tried them myself and now recommend for you.

First, recognise that remaining in your comfort zone will create negative impacts on your ability to live purposefully and to reach your full potential. Do a cost-benefit analysis by asking the question, will the benefit of changing outweigh the cost? Do a personal audit and identify areas that you can make small, marginal adjustments that will expose you to new experiences; experiences that will challenge you to grow. Small adjustments may include, for example, adding more distance to your jogging route or coming home from work early to cook dinner.

Second, understand the principle and power of proximity. The law of proximity is such that we become the average of people we spend time with the most. You will need to assess your environment, relationships, and social networks; be willing and ready to make necessary changes. It is ideal to break from relationships that don't help you grow and focus on the ones that strengthen your resolve to get better. Be aware of close family and friends who encourage you to stay in your comfort zone and praise you when you didn't do anything more than the average. Look for environments that will challenge you to go from Level 1 to Level 2 and up and on. Look for social circles that consist of people who embrace change and consistently demand better of themselves and the people around them. You will know in your heart when you get into an environment that, although you feel less accomplished and somewhat lower in rank, is more of a product of personal assessment rather than what the environment imposed. You will know when you are in a place that you are challenged to do better. Growth environments consist of visionaries who are moving forward. This type of environment is usually the best to learn and grow in.

Third, set small, achievable growth objectives, little changes, incremental steps, and measurable milestones that can be sustained over time. This is what author James Clear refers to as Atomic Habits – tiny changes, marginal gains or one percent improvements. He puts it in context that: "it is easy to overestimate the importance of one defining moment and underestimate the value of making small improvements on a daily basis. Too often, we convince ourselves that massive success requires massive action."[95] This calls for the importance of maintaining focus and a disciplined mindset because a disciplined mindset is a growth mindset. So aim to become a better, more responsible, and empowered individual. In the end, you will reap all the benefits of effective growth through a positive change process.

Chapter 17
A CULTURE OF DISCIPLINE

Earlier, we established vision as a conception inspired in the mind through disciplined thoughts. Following the discovery of your true self, your big-picture destination, as well as your inherent potential, vision ultimately sets you on a journey towards greatness. But it takes the utilisation of BHAGs, Hedgehogs Concepts, and other tools to propel you forward along the flywheel.

It is one thing to start out on the flywheel; it is a totally different thing staying the course until you become truly great. It was a culture of discipline that helped extraordinary individuals to accomplish great outcomes.

Disciplined Individual

Gifts are inherent. You are born with them. You are genetically coded for them. They are the special edge that extraordinary people discovered, developed and distinguished (3D) themselves with. Like every one of us, their gift was there and buried within at the beginning, but then they discovered it and brought it to light. A self-disciplined lifestyle showed their willingness to go to extreme lengths to fulfil their responsibilities. Disciplined individuals demonstrate the strength of character that eventually leads to greatness. Disciplined individuals base their lives on their values, beliefs, and ideology, which all agree with their Wise Advocate. Attempting to be a disciplined individual without first having a disciplined thought life is impossible. Similarly, without disciplined thoughts that make you become a disciplined person, there cannot be disciplined actions.

> **Disciplined individuals demonstrate the strength of character that eventually leads to greatness.**

Ultimately, to break through and become legendary means having the discipline to make a series of good decisions consistent with your Hedgehog Concept. Disciplined actions follow from disciplined individuals who exercise disciplined thoughts. That is the entire essence of the breakthrough process.

> Attempting to be a disciplined individual without first having a disciplined thought life is impossible.

Some of the legends here might appear like extremes. Their lives seemed to contradict popular culture. For example, Mother Teresa wore a sari for most of her life. Whether in public or private, she had a simple appearance that you could almost identify with her personal brand. Steve Jobs had a similar lifestyle. Most people recall Jobs's long-sleeve black turtlenecks. You will identify Martin Luther King with his suit. When new fashions are introduced, extraordinary people don't bother. When they eventually do appear with whatever they wear, culture follows them. This is a very interesting find. It points into the direction of holding to your core values yet becoming a force of change. It shows how vision constricts you and how this very constriction defines the order of the day through its expansionary power.

Joseph, the Old Testament character, had a dream that showed he was going to be a leader. Initially appearing like a child who was spoilt by his parents, Joseph shared his vision openly with his brothers and told them they would all bow down to him. It requires a great deal of training, discipline, and practice for vision to move an individual from an ordinary state to greatness. So the events in Joseph's life made him become more disciplined; his ultimate action not only saved his immediate household but also the entire nation of Israel. By holding on to his vision, he was able to withstand the struggles of each day, knowing fully well that there was more to his life. While holding on to BHAGs, Joseph didn't ignore current events, including his role as the one in charge of Potiphar's house. Joseph modelled the paradox of the "and" that is common with visionaries. They have the commitment to make the most of the day "and" the commitment to make the most in the future. It is not either/or. Being vision oriented means you are effective today, in your current role or the task in front of you and also effective in actively creating a better future. And this can only be achieved with a disciplined personal lifestyle. By doing so, Joseph attended to both current needs and future needs, building each passing day towards his destiny. Joseph, "Daddy's favourite," learnt the humility and discipline that made his life become extraordinary.

Proximity and environment have important roles to play in maintaining a disciplined lifestyle. Again, we come to the external value force discussed earlier. But this time, we are talking about positive external value forces (EVFs). There are certain people around you who provide the environment that allows you to recognise the uniqueness of your vision and who are equally invested in ensuring that it comes to reality. These people may recognise your gifts and potential and provide the necessary environment for them to flourish. They help your character and integrity, and together, you re-enforce a culture of excellence. I speak more about these individuals a little more in the chapter on Corporate Destiny.

However, the responsibility of activating your gift is primarily reserved for you and only you. Nobody else will discover it for you. Your growth environment will allow it to germinate; you are the one who has to discover and apply it. This brings about the second step along the Vision Flywheel to greatness: the disciplined individual vision makes you become.

> **Proximity and environment have important roles to play in maintaining a disciplined lifestyle.**

Disciplined Individual Lifestyle

Disciplined individuals apply their Hedgehog Concepts and utilise their power of choice, decision, and gift to engage in activities and events that align with their core values and beliefs. Disciplined people have integrity and ethics; you will find them doing only what they know is part of their vision and BHAGs.

> **Critical thinking is a component of disciplined thought.**

Disciplined people stir up their gift by developing it, refining it, enriching it, and using it. That's where education comes in. Formal education may not give you gifts, but it can help you develop them. To an extent, schools provide the space to think constructively. Critical thinking is a component of disciplined thought. The learning and teaching environment can create constrictionary forces in the private labour room of vision. In short, school cannot give you your gift because it is inside of you, but it can help you polish and refine it.

Now here's the beauty of vision and your gift when it comes to personal discipline: It removes envy and jealousy from your life, which are the cause of strife and discord in many homes, families, and relationships. Earlier, I pointed out that you are not to copy someone else's core values. The same apply for gifts. You already have it; you just have to stir it up and develop it.

Unfortunately, many people spend their lives mimicking the gifts of other people. Some engage in jealousy and envy. Jealousy and envy of someone else's gift makes you covet what is not yours. It drains your energy and wastes your time. Envy eventually drains life and passion out of you. Other people's gifts can inspire you, but they cannot belong to you. What is yours is uniquely yours. As found in the case of Joseph and his brothers, envy drains energy out of you and is an indication that you lack the understanding of how you will uniquely impact the world. When you have vision and foresight, you don't need to be envious. You only need to fan the embers of what you have into a flame of excellence.

Take time to find your true vision. The principles and practices shared in this book will help you break out of mediocrity and apply your gift to greatness.

Work for the vision within you. Let it push you to greatness.

The power of vision will make your life elegant, simple, and effective; it will cause you to engage in activities that align with your values and passion. You'll spend less time quarreling, being jealous, and engaging in petty fights because you'll be fully aware of your potential and capabilities.

Your gift will inevitably make you famous, but the quality of your character will keep you grounded.

Your energy is reserved for works that align with the vision inspired within you and not by inferior, exterior reasons, such as money or fame. Your gift will inevitably make you famous, but the quality of your character will keep you grounded.

In the realm of visionaries, there is no room for envy or strife; everyone becomes partners and contributes towards a set destiny.

There's no rivalry, only disciplined individuals taking disciplined actions and results.

It's all about the disciplined person vision makes you become.

With time, if you keep at it, your vision will stir up your gift. Your vision will make room for you. As you iteratively go over the Vision Flywheel, you'll experience an upward spiral that makes you stand among people who demand the application of your gift. Your vision will propel you to this level of greatness.

I'm not talking about discipline in the sense of always waking up at the same time or arriving at work as scheduled or never missing an appointment. All of these are great signs of discipline though. But I'm talking about being the master of your destiny, being proactive in pursuing your vision and staying the course. It is the type of discipline that rather than being obsessed with course corrections, you are committed to getting better through focused application of your energy and resources, even if that means going from failure to failure without losing esteem.

It is the type of discipline that helps you escape the rat race.

So while it's important to dream big, it's equally important to be a disciplined individual. Don't let people say you shouldn't have high expectations. Always expect more than what you have. No matter who you are or where you're from, your dreams are valid. You only need the discipline to keep you on the flywheel to greatness.

Although we are all born as originals, people become imitations due to copying. I used to think about becoming like everyone else and joining the rat race. I experienced the phenomenon Vishen Lakhiani (Founder of MindValley) called "living in the culturescape"[96] by allowing the crippling, limiting and unnecessary expectations of saturate and influence my life. But I soon realised that if all the rats are in the race, and you win, you simply become the Big Rat. I recommend that you get out of the rat race and stop competing with the community you are supposed to serve or lead. Stop being in a contest with society; stop trying to follow all the fads and trends in the world. Stop trying to please everybody. Be disciplined.

Decide that you're not going to be a rat. Say to yourself, "I'm going to find my own niche, my own hedgehog space." Even though the journey will be lonely in the beginning, be committed to stay within your three circles. Decide that you're going to live based on principles and values. Make room for yourself in the world by using your gift, being inspired by your vision.

If you're reading this and think that you're too old, it may be because you've been told you're past your prime. You've concluded that you don't have the energy to pursue your vision or time to stir up your gift.

Don't believe the lies you've been told. No matter your age, you can still make a unique contribution to humanity. You can still leave an enduring legacy for the next generation.

You may have worked hard all your life but have little to show for it. Let me encourage you that as long as you can maintain a disciplined lifestyle in the fulfilment of your vision and dreams, you can become extraordinary. As long as you can read this book and apply its principles and practices, you're not too old to fulfil your dreams.

> Say to yourself, "I'm going to find my own niche, my own hedgehog space."

Many of the extraordinary individuals I researched had a build-up process from a young age, but later in their lives, they started living in the reality of their vision and accomplished great things. Becoming great is a mental process that does not first and foremost require an action but a change in perception or paradigm. Simply seeing a different mental picture allows you to commit to a course and pathway in life that sets you apart for greatness. You will find the opportunity to use your gift in ways that make your results and outcomes more profound.

> Becoming great is a mental process that does not first and foremost require an action but a change in perception or paradigm.

Be inspired and encouraged. You might have a horrible past, but take a look ahead of you and see that there is so much in store for you. By starting today, you can activate the power of vision to make your future and your later years better.

Irrespective of the state of the economy, the demands of your current career, or the job market situation, you will not be hindered by an initial lack of resources or by what people say about you. The power of vision can push you past these issues.

Decide today to become a disciplined person; part ways with the norm, the rat race, envy, mediocrity, and all activities that shortchange your destiny. The private discipline and sacrifices will soon pay off.

Vision will expand you. It will help you maximise your potential. No matter what stage of life you are in, the power of vision can work for you.

Be challenged to achieve the greatness you were born for. The practices of vision will help you transcend current trends and conventional wisdom.

Because you have become a disciplined person, you have the confidence to enter into unfamiliar terrain.

Discipline is what allows you to follow an evolutionary process rather than a revolutionary process. What people term revolutionary is just another cycle in the visionary's evolution. That's what makes visionaries extraordinary.

Greatness doesn't mean you're not exposed to the same short-term pressure from the outside world, but it means you have the patience and discipline to follow the build-up and breakthrough Vision Flywheel model, despite these pressures. That's how you attain extraordinary results.

Disciplined Actions and Results

When ordinary people are able to discipline their thoughts through the power of focus and begin to think big and dream big, they become disciplined through the discovery, development, and distinguishing attributes of their gifts and the Hedgehog Concept; their actions will become disciplined and produce extraordinary results. In short, ordinary individuals become what we have called in this book legends.

Powered by simple acts of vision, ordinary people can transform into something greater than their own ability. They become a special commodity and are able to meet specific needs and demands only they can meet.

Disciplined action is the third big chunk in the Vision Flywheel framework; it only makes sense in the context of disciplined thought and discipline individual. More importantly, disciplined actions are a product of the Hedgehog Concept, which itself is a principle of a disciplined individual.

You cannot produce a remarkable result if you operate outside of your three circles. It would be a terrible mistake to thoughtlessly attempt to jump right to a Hedgehog Concept without being a disciplined individual yourself. It's a process you must stick to if you want to be extraordinary. And it's the lack of discipline to follow through this process that makes a lot of people today seek alternative quick fixes. It is common for people to attend seminars upon seminars, read books upon books, trying to build their personality, when the focus should be on developing intrinsic qualities and habits that truly sustain greatness.

Extraordinary outcomes don't just happen; they follow disciplined actions. It took Steve Jobs several attempts to finally get the hang of what the final product he wanted to create would be. In some cases, the product was launched only as a vision while research continued for the next-generation model.

> **Extraordinary outcomes don't just happen; they follow disciplined actions.**

Remember that Masaru Ibuka applied this counterintuitive approach of disciplined thoughts, disciplined individual, and disciplined actions to create products that people didn't know they wanted; they found themselves eventually loving them.

Disciplined action was what depicted the life of Joseph, which ultimately landed him before the king. He was a hard-working young man, but the envy of his older brothers caused them to kidnap him and sell him into slavery. He worked in Potiphar's house and became trustworthy, until Potiphar's wife blackmailed him when he wouldn't have an affair with her. Joseph was found guilty and sent to prison. In prison, the culture of discipline that characterised his life was still obvious. In typical hedgehog style, he knew exactly what his values were, together with his gift and the unique contributions he could make. Who would have thought that the dream of "the sun and moon and eleven stars bowing down"[97] would be fulfilled through a prison sentence? This set of actions allowed him to continue to build up until his eventual breakthrough.

Joseph's vision eventually came to pass. After his gift brought him before the king, and he successfully interpreted the king's dream, he was appointed second in command. Not long after, his brothers came to him to seek help. Joseph eventually saved his entire household from a terrible famine. In the account of this story, we saw the emergence of what I call Level 7 leadership, the type of transcendent leadership where you are humble yet proactive in the fulfilment of your unique purpose or a larger cause with the sole aim of bringing glory to an unseen deity called God. He was not only bowed down to[98]; he delivered them – the people that hated him. Joseph, the ordinary boy who was showing off his dream, had become a disciplined individual showing a level of humility and persuasion common among truly great people.

Disciplined outcomes may look simple to accomplish, but remember, it takes months and years of simplifying a complex world through difficult choices and decisions. And while it has a crystalline clarity and elegant simplicity once you get a handle on it, operating from the core, the Hedgehog Concept and living a disciplined life can radically help you accomplish great results. But I must remind you that getting the hang of it takes repetition; it's an iterative sequence, not an event. It's an evolutionary process, not a revolutionary one.[99] It takes continuously going over the loop till you accomplish great results. When you look back on previous disciplined actions, you find that they built a trail of revolutionary impacts (i.e. evolution within helps you create revolution without). Disciplined action paints the picture of a life's purpose, as described earlier.

> **Disciplined outcomes may look simple to accomplish, but remember, it takes months and years of simplifying a complex world through difficult choices and decisions.**

The essence of process and each iterative loop is to help you realign with your core values and ask important questions about the three circles. This brings us back to self-awareness. With every step in the loop, disciplined individuals continue to create larger, more significant impacts.

Does Being Disciplined and Focused on Your Vision Make You Tyrannical?

Does pursuing your vision make you become tyrannical, cold blooded, or ruthless? This is a question that lingers in the hearts of many people I've spoken about vision to. Someone outrightly said to me, "Some people [leaders] are just tyrants and drive everyone crazy because of their vision." I'd like to approach this with what I found while researching this book.

Henry Ford, for example, has been generally misunderstood to be ruthless and cold-blooded.[100] His habit was to follow through his vision with a high level of persistence and detail. And this usually happens even when a lot of people disagree with his vision. In most cases the outcome of the vision speak for itself. It would be inaccurate to call Henry Ford a tyrant for pursuing his vision and applying the principles and practices that brought that vision to life.

Walter Isaacson's biography of Steve Jobs presents sections that described both his dark and bright sides. One of Jobs's dark side was described in his biography as "reality distortion field."

Bud Tribble, a software engineer under Jobs, recalled that he adopted the phrase "reality distortion field" from "Managerie," an episode of Star Trek, "in which the aliens create their own new world through sheer mental force." Tribble explained, "Steve has a reality distortion field." He further adds, "In his presence, reality is malleable. He can convince anyone of practically anything. It wears off when he's not around, but it makes it hard to have a realistic schedule."[101]

What's intriguing is how Jobs broke the so-called leadership rulebook by not inspiring or coaching employees to achieve something, and instead flatly insisting that it could and would be done. Negotiation was out. Failure was not an option. Naysayers were turfed.

Steve Wozniak, who co-founded Apple with Steve Jobs, explained it this way: "[Jobs's] reality distortion is when he has an illogical vision of the future, such as telling me that I could design the Breakout game in just a few days. You realize that it can't be true, but he somehow makes it true."[102]

Like Wozniak, Debi Coleman (an early Mac team manager who took over Apple manufacturing) believed that the reality distortion field was empowering: It enabled Jobs to inspire his team to change the course of computer history with a fraction of the resources of Xerox or IBM. "It was a self-fulfilling distortion," she claimed. "You did the impossible, because you didn't realize it was impossible."[103]

Jobs's use of foul language was also well known. This is clearly not the most desirable way to provide feedback. However, Apple employees (at least some) learned that what Jobs was really trying to say was, "Tell me why this is the best way to do it." What Jobs was attempting was to challenge employees to be creative and to find the optimal way to achieve something, to make something perfect.

Jobs had a weird if not bizarre approach to inspiring his employees. You could easily conclude it's tyrannical to paint a picture in your mind and require every other thing around you to conform to that mental image. Yet as biographer Isaacson stated, "It infused Apple employees with an abiding passion to create groundbreaking products and a belief that they could accomplish what seemed impossible. They had T-shirts made that read '90 hours a week and loving it.'"[104]

It's easy for us to question Jobs's motivational tactics, which were jaw-dropping at times. We can quickly jump to conclusions that Henry

Ford was cold-blooded and ruthless. But then look at how Jobs resuscitated Apple, which was on the brink of death in the nineties, and then led it to become the most valuable company in the world. Look at the monumental accomplishments of Henry Ford, not only in the automobile world but also how he profoundly shaped the twentieth century and continues to affect our lives today, a man with less than a sixth grade education.

Rather than smirk at Jobs's reality distortion field or scorn Ford for being high-handed, perhaps there's something to learn from them about vision, life, legacy, and their approach to leadership. The business world is strewn with the entrails of visionless leaders who beat up team members and employees, decimated their organisations, and only lived for the next quarter's results. They never worked towards any long-term objective. And in a matter of time, they leave with a golden parachute, a phenomenon described in this book as doom loop.

Perhaps we can learn about the basis of persistence and the power of will, which when mixed together in a human mind become an irresistible force. I have come to realise that people who pursue their daily work with determination to bring their vision to full manifestation are often misunderstood. To truly fulfil one's life vision, some level of what people generally call tyranny might be required. At a time when majority of people are ready to throw their aims and purposes overboard, and give up at the first sign of opposition or misfortune, visionaries carry on despite all opposition, until they attain their goal and fulfil destiny.

Like every one of us, Steve Jobs and Henry Ford were far from perfect. Towards the end of Jobs's life, he shared some of his misgivings with Isaacson, acknowledging his mistakes. But he remains one of the greatest enigmas as a corporate leader. His vision powered him to greatness. What he lacked in people skills and empathy, he **...visionaries carry on despite all opposition.** made up for with a compelling vision for the future and the pursuit of excellence. Ford was once associated with anti-Semitism but later retracted his comments and showed evidence of change.[105]

With a culture of discipline that revolves around their Hedgehog Concept, great people start from practically nothing and change the world. Truly great people go from an ordinary state to extraordinary by following a build-up and breakthrough process. But what does build-up to breakthrough really look like?

Chapter 18

FROM GROWTH TO BUILD-UP TO BREAKTHROUGH TO EXTRAORDINARY LIFE

There is an illusory and deceptive tactic out there today that tricks people into believing that getting high-quality results involves personality hacks, without going through principles, practices, and the natural process of work and growth that make it possible.

The journey to being great or extraordinary requires sequential stages of growth and development. This truth of life is demonstrated by every living thing; I even observed it in my nine-month-old child. I watched as he began to turn himself over when laid on his back when he was a few weeks old. Months later, he started sitting up as he gained more muscle strength. Then from crawling, he began to hold onto objects and then could leave whatever he held onto and take one or two wobbly steps before falling to the ground. As a father, no matter what I did, I could not break that process. Each step is important and cannot be skipped; it takes time.

> **The journey to being great or extraordinary requires sequential stages of growth and development.**

We acknowledge and accept the principles of process in the growth of a child, but it gets harder in the areas of character formation, emotions, and human relations. Even if we acknowledge processes in these areas, accepting and living with them seems difficult and daunting. As a result, we seek shortcuts or hacks or time-saving techniques that skip vital steps, yet we expect extraordinary, quality outcomes. Vision takes process. From conception and light-bulb experiences, to the many changes, discomforts, and sacrifices we have to endure, it's easy to abandon processes in the very areas of life where they matter the most.

The challenge of following through with process increases when we have to face a world so used to shortcuts. The power of vision can sustain you if you get the right mindset and follow the principles that guide vision.

> **Vision takes process.**

Becoming Extraordinary Does Not Require Exasperation

Process involves one turn and another. And with practice, principles become embedded into our daily lives. Principles are deep, fundamental truths that have universal application. They apply to individuals of every kind. Principles are guidelines of human conduct that are proven to have enduring, permanent value. When truths that form principles are internalised, they become habits and character traits, empowering people to create a wide variety of practices. Light-bulb moment bring about processes that if we follow through consistently can lead to principles and fundamental truths. Principles are like geographic locations; values are like maps of those locations. It is vision that help us to not only see maps but to also connect them to their actual geographic locations. Vision is the mental big picture of our true, extraordinary state, guided by core values, principles, practices, and processes, which in turn make the mental picture become a reality. Living by principles that guide our vision helps us to successfully navigate through processes.

> **When truths that form principles are internalised, they become habits and character traits, empowering people to create a wide variety of practices.**

The power of vision does not require borrowed strength. It requires understanding principles and following through with specific actions. The sad reality I came across in our modern time is where people attempt to do great things by thinking of their status or position of power (or their proximity to it) as the way to fast-track their growth. A lot of people want to achieve more and become more without following fundamental truths of vision, but character development follows a step-by-step process. For example, you can't get to a destination if you don't first know where you are going. You wouldn't know when you arrived. What's worse is that everywhere along the way would look like the destination just because you don't know where it is.

I have watched as people of all ages try to shortcut the build-up process in the name of mentorship. Mentorship is good, if properly practiced, to the extent that it helps both the mentee and the mentor discover their own unique calling and walk in the reality of their life purpose. Many so-called mentees don't enter such relationships to understand or accept processes; they just want to borrow strength.

Borrowing strength (which is manifested in our credentials, positions, authority, past achievements, etc.), or using force, shows an inherent weakness. It builds weakness in the person being forced to acquiesce and undercuts organic natural process of reasoning and internal discipline. In short, borrowed strength shows dependency on external factors (external value forces) to produce results and accomplishments. This is not sustainable in the long term. You will not be able to produce at your natural frequency.

> **Borrowing strength... It builds weakness in the person being forced to acquiesce and undercuts organic natural process of reasoning and internal discipline.**

Process helps us rely on our own intrinsic strengths, to take the steps required to sustain and nurture growth. Because external influences, borrowed strength, or external forces won't last for long. Process requires patience, perseverance, and some painful sacrifices, but in the end, it produces staying power. The results of following through with process is that it produces sustained greatness, which is uncommon today.

The Build-Up and Breakthrough of Vision

Revisiting the Vision Flywheel of Greatness framework that became the backbone of the research I did for this book, we identified how an ordinary individual's perception can change by virtue of a light-bulb experience. Then comes the build-up through personal, private labour, and ultimately a breakthrough. Instead of following fads and trends, truly great people maintain a consistent course, continually building themselves and focusing on their core competency until breakthrough.

For example, you will find that as you operate with the power of vision, your dependency on technology will also drop. Not that technology is not important. It is, but visionaries only see it as an accelerator or multiplier and not their driving force. It was startling to find that while most of the visionaries discussed in this book championed a new course, including the technology domain, they didn't know about computing and didn't rely on technology. They pioneered new technological innovation primarily by designing or defining its purpose rather than depending on it for their breakthrough.

Instead of following fads and trends, truly great people maintain a consistent course, continually building themselves and focusing on their core competency until breakthrough.

I am not saying that you don't use technology or computers. Indeed, your initial ideas have to be put together using technology, but you will find that at the time of full manifestation, you no longer depend on technology as you innovatively create and focus on critical aspects of your purpose and destiny. For some, indeed, your manifestation is in the areas of technology and computing; stick with it. Follow the process, and you'll be well on your way.

The force of vision on its own has the intrinsic potential energy and power to propel visionaries forward and equally attract human, natural, and material resources to make their vision come to pass. From Joseph in the Bible to Helen Keller and Mother Teresa, many of the extraordinary individuals in this book used no technology for their breakthrough.

The problem is that a due to lack of understanding of the principles of vision, many today adopt technology at a great cost, but it doesn't produce extraordinary results.

Let's take another case from Masaru Ibuka, founder of Sony. When he began his company, he started out not knowing exactly what to start with. He didn't have a clear idea of which product to sell. Since 1945, Ibuka followed the process after experiencing light-bulb moments that brought a new perspective on how to restore the ruins of Japan after the world war. While he had the vision, which is intricately tied to the light-bulb experience, it took more iterations and refining of his thought. His thoughts were disciplined and focused, and that allowed him to try as many products as possible, not minding which one failed or succeeded. He was consistently driving towards the breakthrough, quietly, silently.

Through patience, perseverance, and many pains of growth, coupled with consistent actions, Sony kept advancing. Ibuka applied his inherent gifts and also attracted similar minded, talented individuals as they together pushed towards a great corporate destiny. That was how they became extraordinary. Extraordinary outcomes are produced by focused people whose thoughts are disciplined and whose principled lifestyle leads them to become disciplined individuals and whose actions are disciplined, targeted, precise, and remarkable over time. Without vision, there would be no scope or dimension to guide your range. There would be no discipline or focus.

In contrast to Ibuka, founders of Kenwood Corp. appeared to have a specific category of products in mind. They christened the company with the name "Kasuga Wireless Electric Works" in 1946 and "since its foundation," according to the Japan Electronics Almanac, "Kenwood has always been a specialist pioneer in audio technology." In 2007, JVC Kenwood discontinued its line of consumer audio receivers, home theater systems, and other home electronics.[106]

> …chasing efficiency may not be the answer to getting more things done; nor does it equate to growth.

I cannot overemphasise the importance of process. I have seen so many people resort to tools, attend seminars, or employ strategies to circumvent process. Some call it being efficient. But chasing efficiency may not be the answer to getting more things done; nor does it equate to growth.

The Visionary Flywheel and the Wishers Doom Loop

I'll just use the word wishers to capture those who don't want to follow process, people who lack character or determination and are always seeking a shortcut. As described in prior chapters, wishers are constantly circumventing process through get-rich-quick schemes. They never experience light-bulb moments and as a result stick with old thoughts while expecting new results.

But the same old thinking produces the same old results.

Although it starts with unfamiliar experiences, being able to change one's mindset through deliberate and consistent process, as extraordinary individuals did, can make one's life follow this simple truth: power exists in the fact of continued improvement and the delivery of results.

In the beginning, your accomplishments may appear inconsequential, insignificant, almost intangible. But as you follow the process of vision as described in this book, iterating through the flywheel, you find that your vision enables you to have hindsight that produces insight that creates foresight. Over time, intangibles and inconsequential events of life fit into the context of an overall concept that creates extraordinary outcomes.

When you operate with vision, with time, people begin to see and feel your momentum build up. The power and energy radiating from the epicentre of a visionary is contagious. An increasing body of scientific evidence shows that we can communicate on an unseen energetic level. This cognitive coherence has been found to create a circle of influence. With time, people will line up with enthusiasm, and the product of their enthusiasm is to keep adding more momentum to the power of vision that is already at work.

Then, the first breakthrough appears. And because it is based on values and principles that won't get carried away with fads and trends, other breakthroughs will follow, and the momentum will continue to build. Small, little, inconsequential steps have snowballed into extraordinary outcomes. This process of building momentum around your vision, inspiring enthusiasm in others, and allowing the feedback loop to inspire you to keep following through the pathway to your destiny keeps you constantly growing. This gradual, sustainable growth, stimulating the evolutionary process, is captured in Figure 18 and the upward spiral diagram is presented in Appendix 3. The continuous loop of progress is called the flywheel effect.[107]

> **The continuous loop of progress is called the flywheel effect.**

Let me demonstrate the flywheel effect in the lives of extraordinary people in my research.

Let's take Masaru Ibuka again as an example. After the first breakthrough with the transistor radio, Ibuka and team built a process that entrenched Sony's core principles and values, and they continued with the practice and work ethics. Not long after the transistor radio, the Walkman followed. Same process, and Sony moved from one hit product to another. The flywheel effect that started with Ibuka continues to churn out innovative products that loyal customers are willing to buy. I remember how I felt when I held a Sony Discman for the first time in the 1990s. I became a fan. And together with many others like myself, we added to Sony's momentum and its Vision Flywheel.

Another example: Mother Teresa, demonstrating a similar flywheel effect, started with just herself and a core conviction. Little by little, students from the school she left started to volunteer with her in the slums. In no time, their number grew, and they began to attract more resources; they garnered worldwide support, and their momentum continued to feed back into the overall power of vision, from one result and accomplishment to the other.

The life of each extraordinary individual in my research showed this consistent flywheel pattern. They didn't have to do anything more than what they were doing; they only maintained the consistent strategy they built. Their core belief was very important. It was who they became (the tree), and the outcome they recorded was just a fruit of their tree; they continued to yield fruit.

On the other hand, I have observed many people fall into the doom loop; as a result, they never accomplish anything great in life. Instead of a quiet, deliberate process of figuring out what their life vision is and determining their core gift or competency, many employ mechanical tactics and external, borrowed strength or force to create impressive scenes. Instead of doing the work they need to do within, so their outside accomplishment can be sustained, people assume that doing something radically new will create great fanfare and hoopla aimed at motivating the troops, who will not be motivated or inspired after the fanfare is over.

> **...although the power of vision is resident within, it requires an arduous build-up stage.**

It is not strange today to see people finding the answer to their problems by tirelessly seeking a single defining action, or endlessly searching for the grand program or one killer idea or what is termed a miracle moment that they expect to put them in the spotlight.

Vision takes process. And although the power of vision is resident within, it requires an arduous build-up stage. No steps can be skipped. Many fail in the build-up stage by cutting corners. Cutting corners eventually pushes them to premature stardom, only for them to jump out of the flywheel. Once they are out of the flywheel, they lose direction, then they stop, change course, and are thrown in a new direction, and then they stop, change course, and are thrown in a new direction, and so the spiral goes, as shown in Figure 19. After years of lurching back and forth, people who remain ordinary are those who fail to build sustained momentum, and as a result fall instead into what is called the doom loop. These are the wishers, the undecided, multitalented people who try but fail to balance everything.

Consider this example that is common to many people today: Someone attends university, and while in school, she learns how to play an instrument while studying for a degree. Upon graduation, she picks a career in banking, and on weekends, she plays in a band. Apart from that, she does catering during her spare time and wants to become a professional soccer star.

Another example is this subtle but common situation with people who are multitalented: they focus on their gifts more than the process that will fine-tune it to excellence and greatness.

I have come across various strands of these personal errors many times. And when I try to preach simplicity and focus, including all the details in the power of vision, people think I am killing their gifts and talents. Little do they know that there is always one dominant gift per person, per time, and all other gifts and talents are supportive. It takes the power of vision to help you align and synchronise your innate capabilities as an effective, creative, and sustainable force.

The good part is that this book can help you figure things out, if you are trapped in the doom loop. Not only will you understand your vision; you will develop convictions and core values that bring your vision to life. By getting your own vision, you can begin to discipline your thoughts and focus on the things that truly matter. Essentially, the power of vision is the effective force to get you started on your extraordinary pathway; it is what you need to stay on the flywheel to greatness.

> ...the power of vision is the effective force to get you started on your extraordinary pathway

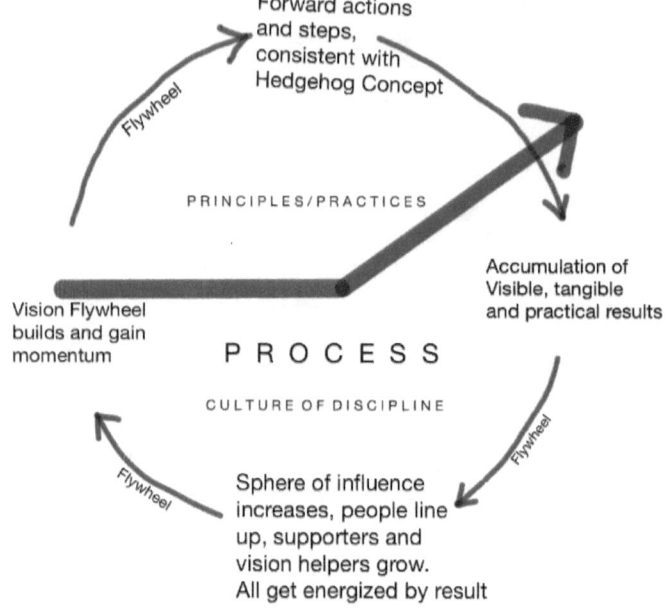

FIGURE 18: The Vision Flywheel Effect

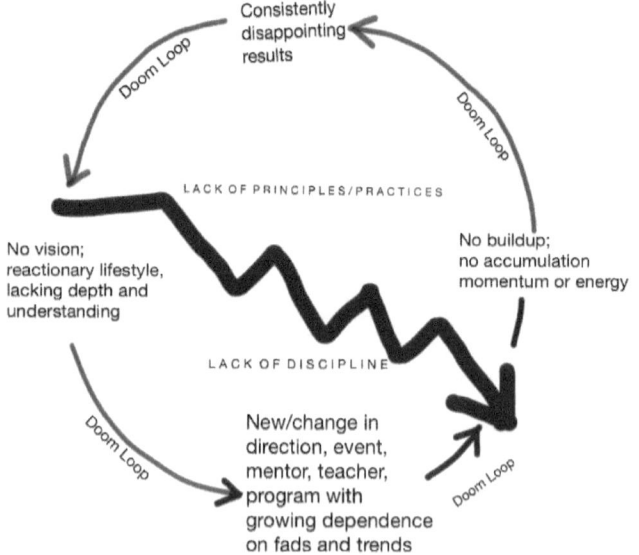

FIGURE 19: The Doom Loop

Chapter 19
RE-VISION

Vision is alive. It evolves. As a result, one of the most important aspects of vision is what I call re-vision. Look at it from this angle: The picture, what you see, can be the same, but with re-vision, you change the picture frame. Every single one of us has to constantly review and realign our vision as we gain more clarity, wisdom, and understanding. Certain things in life will happen that cause your scope to grow; your horizon will enlarge. This often leads to new perspectives and paradigms. Take such opportunities to review, restrategize, and reprioritise. Expand your vision. Don't settle for techniques and approaches that are obsolete. Re-vision gives you the opportunity to review all the concepts and frameworks discussed in this book, but in a rather sequential fashion to refine and sharpen your vision.

Re-vision help you to reactivate the entire iterative loop of the Vision Flywheel. Disciplined thoughts: ensuring my values and core beliefs are intact and congruent with my purposeful work. Disciplined individual: using the power of VAD and staying where the magic is, the intersection of gifts, passion, and valuable contributions. Disciplined actions: accomplishing BHAGs, using resources at my disposal to produce tangible results efficiently, effectively, and sustainably. Each iterative process becomes what I call a re-vision.

> **Re-vision help you to reactivate the entire iterative loop of the Vision Flywheel**

In a nutshell, re-vision is when a new perspective emerges that changes your paradigm and further clarifies and qualifies your vision. While your life vision remain fixed, re-vision allows you to apply vital new information while conceptualising your original vision, ultimately producing a stronger, clearer, and more effective life vision and purpose.

Re-vision starts with the concept of solitude, discussed earlier. The power of solitude starts by you asking purpose-related questions from the three circles: Do I really understand that I can be the best in the world, more than being merely successful? Do I appreciate what my values and passions are? Am I truly making a significant contribution that elevates the hopes and lives of others?

> In a nutshell, re-vision is when a new perspective emerges that changes your paradigm and further clarifies and qualifies your vision

What I found consistent among extraordinary individuals was how their culture of discipline allowed them to carry out ongoing re-visions. As new knowledge emerged, their conviction became stronger, and they were able to pivot along the flywheel to extraordinary accomplishments.

As we discussed, Mother Teresa was already a nun and had gone through some processes along the Vision Flywheel. She was already in the right place, India, and was already fulfilling her purpose, serving others. But with re-vision, what has been referred as a call inside of another call for Mother Teresa, she went further to become more specific in which area she wanted to serve.

Having a paradigm shift, arriving at a new BHAG after accomplishing an old one, or just completing a VAT exercise on your three circles and the Hedgehog Concept, there will always be moments where you realise there's more to life and you determine what direction things should go. Re-vision is that ongoing step that helps to fit all the pieces together in the long term.

Re-vision, like everything discussed in the book, is built on principles and practices, and it takes a culture of discipline as well as an understanding of time.

PART 4

PRACTICES OF VISION THAT MAKE ORDINARY INDIVIDUALS BECOME EXTRAORDINARY

[P R A X I S]

1. Plan and take action
2. Understanding the concept of time in the realm of visionaries
3. Persistence and passion
4. Genius of the AND versus tyranny of the OR
5. Character over charisma
6. Triumphing despite naysayers and negative external forces
7. Anticipate and enjoy the provision of vision: Pro-Vision
8. Be, do, have

Chapter 20
PLAN AND TAKE ACTION

A critical component of greatness is the ability to break big or complex ideas into small actionable items. This is called planning. Planning is basically estimating the costs, strategies, available resources, and actions that will make the vision come to reality. For visionaries, the planning is not usually according to limited resources but applying the expansionary power of vision. And this comes after a strong core built on clear perspective and intuition. Plan and then start with what you have and where you are. Planning helps in taking consistent core, value-based actions that fall within one's Hedgehog Concept.

Most of the time, vision, the mental big picture conceived in your mind, already includes everything you need, including the strategy and ideas, but you require proper planning to cultivate and develop them. The expansionary power of vision has a way of positioning people with vision who live nearby and can make the vision come to pass, either by stirring up gifts or by bringing you in contact with vision helpers. Most of the time, you only need to be keenly aware of people, places, and processes that will enhance your vision. And this also means you need to continuously apply the 3D of vision so you know how far along you have come and where you are heading.

Take Mother Teresa; she was already in India, where her vision was supposed to come to pass. And when she caught the vision, she already had people, past students and volunteers, who were willing to support it. With proper planning and action, the processes began to come together.

Planning also helps bring to your vivid consciousness things that fall outside of your Hedgehog Concept. Don't be afraid to say no to what doesn't align with your vision and purpose, but be keenly aware of opportunities as they emerge.

Act, no matter how small the dot is on the Hedgehog Concept. As long as the three circles intersect, be confident in your choice and action. Always give every opportunity your best shot.

Planning becomes essential as you iterate the flywheel with many seemingly avoidable hedgehog-like opportunities. Not every opportunity is right for you to accept, but you have to plan and prepare. Without proper planning, you may miss the right chances and opportunities when they appear.

> **When you lack a plan, you miss opportunities.**

Develop a plan, a blueprint of what activities you want to engage in. When you lack a plan, you miss opportunities. Estimate what stage you want to be on the flywheel and VAT. Write your plans, ideas, and strategy on paper. Your plan can be kept private, but don't hesitate to share your vision and dreams. The reason is because your plans can change, but your vision remains consistent.

Ideas are seeds of destiny and greatness that drop in your mind. And remember, with a disciplined thought life, your ideas cease to be ordinary as well; they become value-based. Ideas are products of imagination, and if properly developed and planned, they become your vision made manifest in phases. When you have a disciplined mind, your ideas, wishes, expectations, and thoughts become components of your vision. Planning is important because without it, you won't be able to put your thoughts on paper and test your dreams. The cultivation of your vision requires planning; otherwise, it will not develop properly and will fade away like a cloud.

> **Ideas are seeds of destiny and greatness that drop in your mind.**

And when it fades away, you miss the chance to build on them, and you inadvertently miss future opportunities.

Vision Manifests in Phases[108]

It is important to understand that breakthroughs don't occur all at once, even though it's possible in some cases. Everyone desires an instant breakthrough. But that's not always the case. This is only applicable in theory. In real life, and in the many individual examples given in this book, the breakthrough of vision comes in phases. And without proper planning and development, you will not be able to capture this moment. You will potentially lose momentum along the flywheel for the next phase of your breakthrough if you fail to plan. An extraordinary state is accomplished through the accumulation of multiple smaller breakthroughs. Vision manifests in phases, which is why you need to properly plan.

After BHAGs are set in scope, it takes proper planning to make them become reality. Otherwise, they become another wish that only floats around without any concrete backing.

> Everyone desires an instant breakthrough. But that's not always the case.

Let's take another cue from the mountain climbing illustration. Just because you have a compass (vision) and a body that serves as hardware to bring the vision to pass, doesn't mean that you don't need to plan. The practice of planning helps you not only put the resources needed together (the water, climbing ropes, etc.), it also helps to coordinate the compass and do the climb in sync and in the right direction.

Your Dreams Are Worth Writing Down

Create a dream map for yourself. In moments of solitude or personal evaluation, write your plan of action and outline the steps you want to take to bring your vision to pass. Review it as often as required, until it resonates with your core values and potential. Beware that even after you write it and make it known, people who are going nowhere (negative external value forces) may encourage you to throw it away and remain average. Only average people who are going nowhere do such things; they're the ones who aren't doing anything and want other people to stay idle too. The worst thing to do is present your big vision for review and approval by people with small minds. Not everyone is qualified to share your vision with, especially in the early state of formation. You can share it with people called destiny partners. Destiny partners are discussed in the subsequent chapter on corporate destiny.

> The worst thing to do is present your big vision for review and approval by people with small minds.

Not everybody will understand your visions and dreams, but make the effort and put it down in writing anyway. Your dream is worth writing down. You can develop a personal document that you call your dream book; write your plan in its pages. You can call it "My Business [Company or Title] in the next five years" or "By the year ----, this is where I want to be." Don't be afraid to share your vision; it will remain consistent because according to the process of its conceptualisation, it comes out of your convictions and your Hedgehog Concept. But be weary of sharing your plans, as they will often change from time to time, and your followers may get confused.

Don't Be Afraid to Dare and Plan for Something Others Term Impossible

Fear has been depicted as False Evidence Appearing Real. What I found on my personal journey is that everything we've ever longed for or wished would happen, including creativity, breakthroughs, and innovations, all lies at the other side of fear. Eleanor Roosevelt put it this way:

> *"You gain strength, courage, and confidence by every experience in which you look fear in the face. You must do the thing which you think you cannot do"*[109]

Yes, it may sound crazy even to yourself, and you may feel that you won't accomplish your big vision. But if you work towards it, you will realise that you ultimately grow into new levels. It may require some changing, stretching, and adjusting, and you must exit your comfort zone into a learning zone. But keep in mind that just the opportunity to dream and envision new possibilities is empowering on its own. We can raise the limits and set a new personal best for ourselves. Daring the impossible also allows us tap new energy, gain new inspiration, and clarify our vision as we raise the bar higher. The motivation is in daring and doing. Don't let fear paralyse you or crush your creativity and imagination. You were created for more. As shown in Figure 20, after you conceive your vision, you go ahead to plan and then take action. Don't just set goals; do what has been inspired in your heart. Plan, and then take action.

FIGURE 20: Bring your vision to life with planning and action

Because of the power of vision at work in you, you will be inspired to take a stand, to take action, and to do things a little differently. It is these points of decisions and the accompanying small but consistent actions that turn ordinary people into living legends. The accumulation of those daily actions builds experience and motivates you to do what most people say is impossible, the things that only appear in their dreams.

So go ahead and dare the impossible. How do you start to dare the impossible, you ask? Take action towards your plans, visions, and goals today. If you don't have vision and BHAGs yet, setting growth goals is a good way to start. Make decisions. Be proactive in bringing your vision to life. Nobody else has been given this unique vision to impact the world. It has been given to you. Take any event facing you today, and work towards it with the intention of going over and beyond the norm. Tell yourself, "I can do it." Speak to yourself from the core of your heart. When you want something to show up in your outward life, deposit the seed of word in your inner self. The time is now. Dare the impossible. Go for it.

> **Take action towards your plans, visions, and goals today.**

Chapter 21
UNDERSTANDING THE CONCEPT OF TIME

One thing that should have become obvious in the entire Vision Flywheel process is that it takes time. Understanding the concept of time is highly important when it comes to the realm of visionaries. Visionaries don't see time the way others do. In fact, visionaries don't work with the time of others. Extraordinary people seem to use a time frame that is opposite to the rest of us. When others are busy running around like foxes, great people like hedgehogs are basically conserving their energy, doing things that fall within their three circles, things that build up into something great. From build-up to breakthrough takes time, especially when private labours don't yield immediate results. This calls for the exercise of patience, a virtue aspiring visionaries require more than anything.

It's like the time of private labour takes so long. Then as the flywheel turns, the breakthrough comes, and the time of public manifestation covers all the years of private labours and pain.

Patience is required because for visionaries, even though what they see with their mind's eye is achievable and real, it will take some time before other parties and stakeholders come to the same viewpoint (if they ever level up).

But patience does pay off. Understand that it will only take a matter of time before your vision comes into reality. Because if you follow the process, principles, and practices, it will surely come to pass. This helps the visionary to remain patience and steadfast.

When some people make plans to carry out their vision, they appear to create a timetable that imposes force on others around them in order to bring the vision to pass, especially in a corporate setting.

> **Visionaries don't see time the way others do. In fact, visionaries don't work with the time of others.**

However, vision cannot be rushed. It takes time. Just arriving at a light-bulb experience powerful enough to change your perspective and the resulting change in paradigm that follows a new perspective all take time. Are you willing to commit to time, work, and wait patiently?

Applying the practice of time and being patient doesn't mean you are not doing anything. You must be willing to progress at the pace of your unique vision. Remember that in its first inception, vision can appear like a cloud; it will take continuous re-vision and refining of one's gift for us to arrive at its full manifestation.

> **While the practice of planning and estimation helps us to put deadlines on our goals, patience and time help us to be willing to rearrange deadlines.**

While the practice of planning and estimation helps us to put deadlines on our goals, patience and time help us to be willing to rearrange deadlines. A balance of both keeps you steadfast and consistent, not wavering back and forth to every whim and caprice of life. Good character and personal habits distinguish truly great people, who are formed through these practices.

Understanding time and being patient is what will help you; for example, if you are going through a lot of difficulties and hardship at your job, you should remain focused and at peace, knowing that you are going somewhere bigger and better. Like the hedgehog who simply minds his business, even in the face of uncertainty, you can be aware of underlying life principles that will help you succeed.

Nelson Mandela was in prison for twenty-seven years, yet he was patient and waited for the right time for his vision to come to pass. Not an easy deal. He declined the opportunity to be released earlier, simply because he felt it was not yet the right time. P. W. Botha, the president of South Africa at the time, offered to release him from prison in 1985 to defuse racial tensions in the country. Seeing that it was more of a show, Mandela chose to remain in prison. And when the time was right, on February 11, 1990, Mandela walked out

> **...even though you can be laid off from a job, no one can lay you off from your vision.**

a free man. He went ahead to became the first black president of South African. When you are patient in the fulfilment of your vision, you can be calm in the midst of uncertainty. For example, you can be at peace when everyone else is worrying about being laid off at your current job. Remember, even though you can be laid off from a job, no one can lay you off from your vision.

Chapter 22
PERSISTENCE AND PASSION

It is private labours that prepare us for extraordinary public manifestations. Sticking with the process and enduring the private labour pains is how the laboratory of an extraordinary life works.

It is pretty simple: If you are not doing anything, you will hardly face any challenges. If you are not moving in a direction, you will experience no resistance. If you don't want to face any problems or challenges, just stay an average person. Mediocrity in life means not aiming for anything, for the sole purpose of avoiding challenges, troubles, and difficult situations. That is why many people remain a nobody for so long. When you decide to follow through with your vision, there will be naysayers, stress, disappointments, and pressures.

> **Sticking with the process and enduring the private labour pains is how the laboratory of an extraordinary life works.**

Be willing to pay the price of your vision. To do that effectively requires planning and taking action, as mentioned earlier. But more than that, you need to understand that time and patience are required to bring your vision to reality. In addition to them, you need to develop persistence in your passion. Persistence will keep you moving forward, yet you need passion to feed your persistence.

> **If you are not moving in a direction, you will experience no resistance.**

Passion will help pay the price of time and help you persevere. Passion keeps you focused.

As we discussed in previous chapters, your vision is uniquely yours and is derived from your core (including values and beliefs). As a result, you require a sustainable source of power that helps you to keep the momentum. Passion is the stamina that helps you remain committed to the purpose of your heart. Many people today have gotten one opportunity or the other, but due to a lack of passion, they remain in mediocrity. Being passionate is having genuine commitment to the vision inspired upon your heart. You must put your whole heart and life into your vision.

> **Persistence will keep you moving forward, yet you need passion to feed your persistence.**

Visionaries demonstrate a high level of dislike for their current state because it is indicative of a lesser existence. Some visionaries demonstrate their passion through anger. But true visionaries turn this anger into fuel that drives their vision forward and takes them to a new level along the flywheel.

Passion is unquantifiable. Yet being fueled by passion makes you want to not settle but keep moving forward. Steve Jobs was regarded as lacking the human touch or normal emotions with the people he worked with. Yet we see a man who was passionate about his vision. It wasn't a surprise to find that each product launch had a lot of iterations and mock-ups, many of which never saw the light of day. New products went through many iterations before they eventually got launched. Jobs was committed to his vision and followed through with pristine precision and passion.

Most of the people on earth have no passion for life because there is no vision inspired in their hearts. They have not discovered anything important in life to commit themselves to and as a result are just going through the motions. Instead of responding, they merely react. A reaction is typically quick, without much thought; it's tense and aggressive. A response is thoughtful, calm, and non-threatening. Responding differs by involving mindfulness and a level of VAD.

> **Passion is unquantifiable.**

Visions are tested over time, but having genuine and true passion helps you stay faithful and excited about your vision. And faithfulness to your vision is one of the marks of its legitimacy. In essence, the mark of a great vision is the ability to go from failure to failure without losing focus or passion.

> **...the mark of a great vision is the ability to go from failure to failure without losing focus or passion.**

If members of a group or corporate partners are passionate about the corporate vision, they may be so positively occupied that they don't have time for backbiting, envy, gossip, or anger.

Chapter 23
THE GENIUS OF THE "AND" VERSUS THE TYRANNY OF THE "OR"

The story of Henry Ford and his automobile factory helps to properly explain the genius of the "and" vision praxis.

On the frigid Monday of January 5, 1914 in Detroit, thousands lined up in the bitter cold outside to take Henry Ford up on an extraordinary offer: five dollars a day for eight hours of work in a busy factory. That was more than double the average factory wage at that time, and for US workers, it was a defining moment of the twentieth century. Prior to that, Ford had already transformed the American way of life for 15 million families with the affordable Model T (the "people's car"), primarily by reducing prices by 58 percent from 1908 to 1916. At a time where there were more orders that it could fill, it would have made sense for Ford to raise prices. Ford kept lowering prices, even in the face of a shareholder suit against the practice. All of these events shocked and outraged the industrial world. Various publications at that time accused Ford of "economic blunder if not crimes"[110] and said that he had injected "spiritual principles into a field where they do not belong."[111]

Not to claim that Ford made no errors, and he had a spotty historical record, but his handling of employee wages was what many call a major tipping point in the automobile industry. Bob Kreipke, corporate historian for the Ford Motor Co., put it this way: "It was an absolute, total success.... In fact, it was better than anybody had even thought."[112]

University of California, Berkeley, labour economist Harley Shaiken described the Ford wage increases this way: "What that gave us was an industrial middle class, and an economy that was driven by consumer demand."

What does this story have to with the genius of the "and"? A lot. Ford demonstrated that vision is not only about being the best in the future. It is in fact about being the best today AND being the best in the future. Vision is about working towards a better state AND maintaining a strong presence today. This idea of using the genius of the AND was what I found to be unique among truly great people.

As we established earlier, visionaries start out with core values and an unwavering truth that anchors their lives. Despite having these defining beliefs, visionaries create a resounding impact and change their world. Despite having intrinsic, unchanging beliefs, they are able to stimulate progress in their world. The reason is because visionaries practice the genius of the AND. They don't say: "I will only focus on the future." Instead, visionaries are effective today and effective in the future. They are the best today and the best in the future. They preserve the core and stimulate progress. They hold on to a central belief system that never bends and are pragmatic enough to take real action. Visionaries eventually do impossible things, not because it is easy or the conditions are favourable, but because they have core ideologies that drive their actions.

> **Vision is about working towards a better state AND maintaining a strong presence today.**

We also spoke earlier about jobs versus work and indicated that your work should be the focus. But what if you have a job now? What do you do? Abandon it because you've gotten a vision? No. Visionaries are effective in their job and also effective in their work.

Ordinary people operate with the tyranny of the OR. They will say, "You either go to school or get a job." You either choose your expected future or create your current reality. And as a result live a one-sided life that hardly builds up to anything. Focusing only on the future is fantasy. Dwelling on only current realities, even if they are good, will make you admire your current accomplishments, which will soon become events of the pasts. Visionaries are pragmatic and optimistic at the same time.

The ability to effectively apply the genius of the AND is the beauty of a disciplined individual. We're not talking about mere balance here. "Balance" implies going to the midpoint, 50-50, halfway. Visionaries don't seek balance between short-term and long-term. They seek to do very well in the short-term and very well in the long-term. Visionaries don't simply balance between idealism and profitability; they seek to be highly idealistic and highly profitable. Visionaries don't simply balance between preserving a tightly held core ideology and stimulating vigorous change; they do both, to an extreme.

Irrational? Possibly. Uncommon? Yes. Hard to do? Absolutely.

As F. Scott Fitzgerald pointed out:

"The test of a first-rate intelligence is the ability to hold two opposed ideas in the mind at the same time, and still retain the ability to function."

The practice of applying the genius of the AND is what made ordinary people become extraordinary. The ability to hold two opposing ideas in your mind, opening up for change, and keeping your core values intact can help you advance in your Vision Flywheel.

Visionaries end up influencing culture not because they chose culture over their core beliefs (in which case, they too would have been carried away by fads and fashion), but because they did the opposite. Visionaries started with their core beliefs and also opened it up to the culture they operated in.

Visionaries operate in counterintuitive, countercyclical, and countercultural ways because despite being part of a system, cycle, or culture, they can at the same time initiate action that appears opposite to that system. The genius of the AND gives them the ability to do so.

The Stockdale Paradox

The application of the genius of the AND is what brought about the Stockdale paradox. The Stockdale paradox is one the many concepts that, at first glance, take some linguistic mental jumping jacks to fully grasp. This paradox was first put forward in Jim Collins's book *Good to Great*, a seminal self-help and corporate leadership book.[113] The Stockdale Paradox was named after Admiral James Stockdale, who was the highest-ranking military officer in the Hanoi Hilton. During the Vietnam War, Stockdale was held captive as a prisoner of war (POW) for over seven years.

During this horrific period, Stockdale was repeatedly tortured and had no reason to believe he'd make it out alive. Held in the clutches of the grim reality of this hellish world, he found a way to stay alive by balancing the harshness of his situation with healthy optimism.

Stockdale explained this idea as the following: "You must never confuse faith that you will prevail in the end—which you can never afford to lose—with the discipline to confront the most brutal facts of your current reality, whatever they might be."

In the simplest explanation of this paradox, it's the idea of hoping for the best, but acknowledging and preparing for the worst.

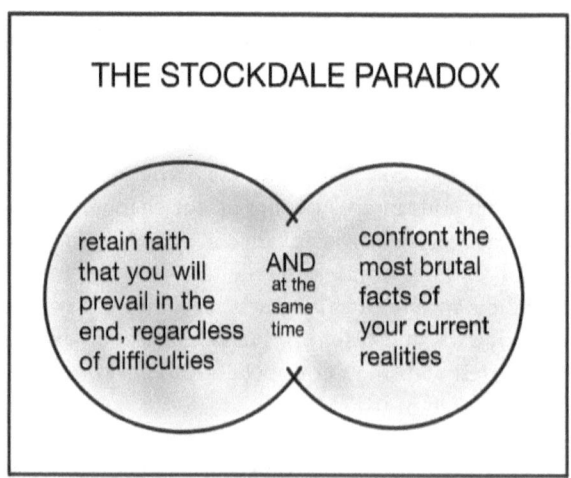

FIGURE 21: The Stockale Paradox Genius of "And"

The ability to acknowledge your situation and balance optimism with realism comes from an understanding of the Stockdale paradox. This contradictory way of thinking was the strength that led the admiral through those trying years. Such paradoxical thinking, whether you consciously know it or not, has been one of the defining philosophies for great leaders making it through hardship and reaching their goals.

Whether it's weathering torture and imprisonment in a POW camp or going through your own trials and tribulations, the Stockdale paradox has merit as a way of thinking and acting for any trying times in your life.

The contradictory dichotomy inherent in the paradox holds a great lesson for how to overcome difficult obstacles and achieve success. It also flies right in the face of unbridled optimists and those positivity peddlers whose advice pervades nearly every self-help book or guru spiel out there.

In a discussion with Collins for his book, Stockdale spoke about how the optimists fared in camp. The dialogue went like this:

"Who didn't make it out?"

"Oh, that's easy," he said. "The optimists."

"The optimists? I don't understand," I said....

"The optimists. Oh, they were the ones who said, 'We're going to be out by Christmas.' And Christmas would come, and Christmas would go. Then they'd say, 'We're going to be out by Easter.' And Easter would come, and Easter would go. And then Thanksgiving, and then it would be Christmas again. And they died of a broken heart."

As I explained, one of the purposes for writing this book is to provide hope in crisis; no other time appears to be more appropriate for the Stockdale paradox to be applicable. The Coronavirus pandemic has brought a high level of uncertainty to our lives.

Pessimists will be unable to cope because they lost hope too early. Optimists who initially claimed the COVID-19 would disappear soon realised that their unwillingness to acknowledge the deep downturn and extended timeframe of the crisis impaired their ability to adapt to new conditions.

These are scary times, with an overwhelming amount of brutal facts, including the fastest economic decline since the Great Depression.

True vision lets you prevail through the uncertainties of crises; you learn to appreciate the brutal facts and at the same time stay optimistic that you will prevail in the long-term. Vision in its true form helps you accept the reality, commit to being resilient, and develop a plan that reflects your commitment to stay in the fight, irrespective of the downturn.

> **Vision in its true form helps you accept the reality, commit to being resilient, and develop a plan that reflects your commitment to stay in the fight, irrespective of the downturn.**

Chapter 24
CHARACTER OVER CHARISMA

Our character, basically, is a composite of our habits. "Sow a thought, reap an action; sow an action, reap a habit; sow a habit, reap a character; sow a character, reap a destiny," the maxim goes.

Habits are powerful factors in our lives. Because they are consistent, often unconscious patterns, they express our character and influence our effectiveness (and ineffectiveness) every day.

Private labours and the activities of the mind that clarify and qualify your vision also provide the appropriate environment and nutrients for essential character growth. The limbic portion of the brain also houses our habit centre. The habit centre of the brain is like the reservoir of our prior actions, out of which the neocortex takes messages and interprets them as received. What this means is that our actions (what our neocortex does) is a function of our habits, which eventually forms our character.

Research indicates that the authenticity of the messages stored in our mind (including our vision), the entire operations at the core, and the extent to which we consistently align with our internal ideology counts more than anything else in life.[114] Essentially, this validates the diversity of our visions, gifts, and abilities; it also helps you appreciate that whether you got a call to Calcutta like Mother Teresa or a light bulb moment to create Mickey Mouse like Walt Disney, you are still on track to a life of impact and purpose. The important thing is, you continue to align your internal energetics so that what you hold at the core informs your action.

Habits are powerful factors in our lives.

But instead of building character, what we have today is the chase after charisma, the need to be liked or to appear good before everyone. Greatness is not at all about being charismatic, funny, jovial, or loved by everybody. True greatness is not all about exercising charm, seeking attention, and courting the admiration of others in order to inspire their devotion. Simply, greatness is all about understanding your vision and purpose, your true self, and what you are born to accomplish, and then following through to the benefit of humanity, being a source of blessing to as many as you can touch. In this sense, true greatness becomes a reflection of the integrity of your character rather than charisma.

Again, we go entirely by what the research presented. What I immediately found was that these extraordinary people were not all charismatic.

Even those who appeared to be charismatic, like Mother Teresa, did not do so in order to attract attention or admiration; it was simply a reflection of their core values, who they truly are.

> ...extraordinary people were not all charismatic

You may say Steve Jobs and Henry Ford lacked charisma, but they made sure the workers in their companies were well-paid. They didn't do it to appear in the headlines; it was just the right thing to do based on their core beliefs and values. Walt Disney, who one would have expected to be charismatic because he was in the business of making people happy, had an appearance code known as the Disney Look, a non-charismatic policy that prohibited employees from having a mustache, among other issues (when Disney himself sported a mustache). And we can go on and on with the charisma versus character nexus, but the main thing to understand is that you don't have to be charismatic or loved by everyone to be truly great. The call, as surprising as it might sound, is not first to please people.[115]

Your vision is most important. You first become the right "who" before your service can become true and effective. And this is why character is important.

Many people today lack character primarily because they don't know who they are. And you can only know who you are through self-awareness and the rewiring process that aligns you with your true self (the first principle discussed earlier). Carrying out this rewiring process is also the foundation for developing a clear mental big picture of your future. Vision is an actual estimation of your true self, and as such, it is established in your purpose. Vision helps you to gain a critical balance (the intersection of the three circles) in doing what you're passionate about, what you are uniquely gifted to do, and that which makes a significant contribution to others (your Hedgehog Concept).

Character derives from this basic principle of effective living: People can only experience true success and enduring happiness—and live an extraordinary life—as they learn and integrate other principles that bring their true self to life. No matter how many strategies and tactics we use to get other people to do what we want, either for them to work harder or to be more motivated, if our character is fundamentally flawed, marked by duplicity and insincerity, then, in the long run, we cannot be successful.

For example, if I am living a life of duplicity, it will breed distrust, and everything I do—even using so-called good human relations techniques—will be perceived as manipulative. It simply makes no difference how good the rhetoric is or even how good the intentions are; if there is little or no trust, there is no foundation for permanent success. Only basic goodness gives life to technique. Extraordinary people don't have duplicity in life. They stand on core values and principles that are obvious for all to see. That is why character is key in vision praxis.

> **It is character that communicates most eloquently.**

It is character that communicates most eloquently. As Ralph Waldo Emerson put it, "What you are shouts so loudly in my ears that I cannot hear what you say."

You can lack communication skills and other techniques of human interaction, which undoubtedly affects the quality of your relationships and how people perceive you, but they are secondary when they acknowledge your integrity, which is a product of your strength of character.

Eventually, if there isn't deep integrity and fundamental character strength, the challenges of life will cause true motives to surface, and human relationship failure will replace short-term success.

The core values, assumptions, and beliefs you hold about yourself are inseparable from your character. Being is seeing in the human dimension. And what we see is highly interrelated to what we are.

Your character governs your effectiveness in life. These inner introspections of vision allow us to position ourselves to live a life congruent to who we truly are. That way, we can easily flow into other character qualities like patience, openness, and increasing desire to understand others and genuinely listen to them. Together, they develop our character to a higher level.

It's a principle-centered, character-based, inside-out approach to personal and interpersonal effectiveness. "Inside-out" means to start first with self; even more fundamentally, to start with the most inside part of self, with your paradigms, your character, and your motives.

True Character Gives Rise to Effective Interdependence

When you know who you are and know the abundant, infinite nature of your inherent gift, you don't find it difficult to share. It is your character that positions you for effective service through shared beliefs and values. Our world teaches us to be independent, but people who are strong in their character anticipate interdependence and collective greater good for all.

True, independence of character empowers us to act rather than be acted upon. It frees us from our dependence on circumstances and other people and is a worthy, liberating goal. But it is not the ultimate goal in bringing our vision to full manifestation through effective living.

Independent thinking alone is not suited to our interdependent reality. Independent people who do not have the maturity to think and act interdependently may be good individual producers, but they won't be good leaders, team players, or corporate leaders. The reason is because they're not coming from the interdependence necessary to succeed in marriage, family, institutional, or organisational reality.

If we take time to look deeper at life, we will discover that by nature, life is highly interdependent. Trying to achieve maximum effectiveness and expanded influence through independence is like trying to play tennis with a golf club; the tool is not suited to the reality.

> **Independent thinking alone is not suited to our interdependent reality.**

Interdependence is a far more mature, more advanced, vision propelling concept. If I am physically interdependent, I am self-reliant and capable, but I also realise that you and I working together can accomplish far more than I can ever accomplish alone, even at my best. If I am emotionally interdependent, I derive a great sense of worth within myself, but I also recognise the need for love, for giving, and for receiving love from others. If I am intellectually interdependent, I realise that I need the best thinking of other people to join with my own.

interdependence is the root of what Stephen R. Covey refers to as the "Win-Win" mindset[116] which flows out of an abundance mentality—the idea that there's plenty for everyone. Many view the world like a pie—if you win some, there is less for me. It's limited. The whole idea of interdependence, abundance mentality and thinking win-win is that you can grow the pie—we can all win abundantly. There's more creativity and possibility out there than we might have imagined. The beauty of the power of vision is everyone can fulfil their dreams, providing the opportunity for everyone to win. A person with a solid character, despite having deep core values will still be open to seeing the third dimension or what I often refer to as "seeing in thirds" – when it is not about my way or your way but a third alternative which is usually a better or higher way suitable for both. Remember, vision is all about embracing the core but stimulating progress with new knowledge.

Martin Luther King could have just used the privilege of the pulpit to preach about civil rights but he went ahead to lead the movement himself. Not just the Baptist Church or the civil right but a more advanced, third alternative that included, quiet counterintuitively at that time, non-violence. Nelson Mandela could have easily pushed for imprisonment for his jailers but he aligned with a third alternative which was strange to both his captors and his compatriots. He chose unity. Same applies for various extraordinary people researched in this book.

As an interdependent person, I have the opportunity to share myself deeply, meaningfully, with others, and I have access to the vast resources and potential of other human beings.

Interdependence is a choice only independent people can make. Dependent people cannot choose to become interdependent. They don't have the character to do it; they don't own enough of themselves.

Your Vision Flywheel will keep turning and gaining momentum until you accomplish an extraordinary life; this requires you to operate with effective interdependence.

Pursuing Your Vision Helps Build Your Character, and Character Strengthens Your Vision

Vision has to do with the mastery of yourself through private and consistent efforts. The constrictionary power of vision imposes discipline and a lifestyle that not only allows you to establish new values and beliefs congruent with your destiny, it also helps you eliminate non-essentials that are not required. Private labour grounds our character and allows us to be proactive and effective. Conversely, vision comes with expansionary powers that allow private effectiveness to become obvious and of benefit to many. Your private habits form the strength of your character and produce the excellence and distinctiveness that make you flourish in certain areas of life where your gifts, talents, and potential begin to manifest in greater forms.

The strength of your character keeps you in the constant loop of the flywheel, with the awareness that you can only do so much and that it is corporate interdependent level of operations that leads to greater good. In the fullness of your vision, the expansionary property of vision helps us come in contact with other people with shared values and beliefs.

The character you develop through vision keeps you in an upward spiral of the flywheel, where you correctly see the map of what is and what ought to be and maximise the opportunity to integrate the principles of vision, leading to sustainable growth in your life.[117]

As you come in contact with different people who hold various other paradigms in their lives, character holds you steady. And as you have come to learn, you don't live your life based on external value forces. Keep in mind that some may hold genuine interests in your progress and in the fulfilment of your vision (positive value forces); others are merely just living out their negative paradigm and way of life. Although you clearly know that they are only living out their wrong wiring, you have to operate with such people, nonetheless. It is the strength of your character that is the most important way of engaging with and avoiding these types of external forces.

The place to always focus on is your core, who you truly are. Strength of character allows you to exude your positive values. By doing so, you are ensuring that you deposit into the emotional bank accounts of others through genuine courtesy, respect, and appreciation for that person and for other points of view. Ensure a continuous communication process as you listen with greater depth. You express yourself with greater courage when you focus on truly helping people.

To make any significant social or economic contributions as visionaries do requires that you are not fundamentally reactive but that you go deeper inside yourself for strength of character and to be proactive. You keep hammering it out until the other person realises that you are genuinely interested in their progress.

And the stronger you are, the more genuine your character, the higher your level of proactivity, the more committed you really will be in seeing others succeed.

Visionaries exert their influence on others not with force but with the strength of their character. It is what helps them to move from just transacting to transforming. Strength of character crystallises in the power of influence that transforms other individuals involved and by extension other systems and institutions along the way.

People will hardly trust you if you don't have character. And your vision will become a doom loop rather than a flywheel.

Vision helps you discover your gift, but it is character that helps you sustain it.

Vision helps you discover your gift, but it is character that helps you sustain it.

Chapter 25
TRIUMPHING DESPITE NAYSAYERS AND NEGATIVE EXTERNAL FORCES

Vision wakes up opposition. For example, suppose you have been an office clerk for fifteen years, and everybody thinks you're content with your job. Then one day, you follow the flywheel process described in this book; your paradigm shifts, and you decide to dream big and do something out of the ordinary. Assume part of the goals towards your vision was to take a certification program. When your friends ask you why, you say something like, "I am going to get certified in management because I want to be the CEO one day." Suddenly, your friends become your rivals, or at best, they are confused and wonder if you are in your right mind. They begin to ask questions like, "Who do you think you are to believe you can become a CEO?" or they ask a common question we've all gotten used to in one way or the other: "Do you know how old you are? Do you realise your brain cannot handle that certification exam?" Your brother may say, "Why are you leaving that job? The pay is good and covers your bills." By the time they finish, you feel like returning to your clerk duties.

> **Vision wakes up opposition**

If these naysayers are distant friends, it wouldn't be an issue. It so happens that they are usually well-intentioned close friends and family members who assume they know you but have no idea of what you are becoming. Many family members, including parents, encourage their children not to do anything crazy and to stay where they are because the risk is too high some new. Some outrightly argue that we have lost our minds when we dare to do the impossible.

Everyone who ever dared to become great in life experienced

temporary defeat, failure, and criticism. Recognise that challenges and failure will arise, but by putting a proper plan in place, you can mitigate them. Criticism, however, is not within your control. But you can control how you respond to it. Don't quit on your visions and dreams before they come to manifestation because of people's criticism.

> **Everyone who ever dared to become great in life experienced temporary defeat, failure, and criticism.**

Let me encourage you to get used to the idea that people may gossip about you and treat you with malice because of your vision. It's all part of the process. See it as a proof that you're really engaged in something tangible in life. At the onset of your vision, when you step outside of other people's expectations, they begin to see you as a problem.

Negative external value forces will attempt to derail you from your purpose and destiny. You must resolve to stay focused on your vision. This is the constrictionary power of vision, the staying power of interiority, that despite the opposing forces and naysayers, you operate from within your heart, knowing fully well that your convictions are valid and true. As a side note, when you eventually become great, when your vision powers you to greatness, these people will appear to become the first set of beneficiaries. So for their sake, it is important we still take action that pertains to our big picture and not settle for mediocrity. The life of Joseph shows that people who try to kill our visions and dreams are usually the first in line to enjoy the benefits and rewards of our personal labour.

Even though you may appear crazy to many people, keep in mind that those who are crazy enough to follow their dreams are the ones who change the world. People who change the world declare independence from the opinions and expectations of others.

In the face of criticism, rumours, lies, accusations, oppositions, naysayers, and adversaries, keep your mind's eye focused, continue working, and keep building. And applying other practices discussed in this section: time, passion, patience, consistency; you will see that you silence them at the dawn of your manifestation.

If required, dissociate yourself from people or limit your association with environments that carry negative external forces or try to suppress your vision and purpose. Although you may need them to help you know that you are in the right place (i.e., opposition is proof that you are doing something right), you need to recognise that if staying within that environment is killing your dreams and passion, it's time to leave.

Although it may not be an easy step, especially when it involves loved ones or associates, you will need to ask yourself whether you want to trade your vision and destiny for the satisfaction of other people.

The beauty of the power of vision is that although it will first constrict out things (including resources, human and material) that are not relevant for your vision and destiny, then in the end, it will expand you. The expansionary power of vision brings in other people who will help bring your vision to manifestation. Seek or create an environment of destiny helpers and vision partners who will hold you accountable for your vision and demand nothing less than the fulfilment of your unique vision. Ask yourself, who are those I can share my vision with and who will commit to helping me bring it to pass, instead of discouraging me from achieving it? Who can I get close to who will provide a positive external influence upon my life?

Always guard your heart by watching the gates to your core. I introduced the sixth sense concept earlier in Chapter 11. Exercise the practice of your sixth sense, and let it strengthen the effectiveness of your other sense organs. Your ability to discern coded, invisible details will save you a lot of headache and missteps. Needless to say, the sixth sense itself becomes stronger through solitude moments.

Before we wrap this point, I will like to point out that while dealing with naysayers can be draining, it is always a good thing to have the ability to investigate what they say, which could still be useful. For example, if someone says your work output is poor, rather than take it as an end to your vision, take it as an opportunity to know that this area is not your area of unique contribution (i.e. use the VAT and The Three Circles to refine your VAD). In short, naysayers could potentially lead you in the right direction if you appreciate their negative feedback and use it to identify your true positive area. In that case, naysayers inevitably become support systems themselves without even knowing it.

Chapter 26

ANTICIPATE AND ENJOY THE PROVISION OF VISION: PRO-VISION

The provisions and resources at our disposal are never enough to fulfil our vision when we first receive them. To fulfil your vision, what you currently have may not be enough. You will most likely require more. Vision and provision therefore go together. Provision is usually hidden until you take action in line with your vision.

As the flywheel of vision continues to turn from private to public and you gain more momentum, the expansionary power of vision comes in force. Vision has a special way of attracting resources of all sorts to help bring the vision to pass or to reach a higher phase of manifestation. A higher phase of vision manifestation causes you vision to advance to others who share the same vision and are equally committed to a collective destination. The expansionary power of vision turns an individual vision to a corporate vision.

> **Vision has a special way of attracting resources of all sorts to help bring the vision to pass or to reach a higher phase of manifestation.**

Part of the provision that comes with vision and having BHAGs are people who share the corporate vision and find the fulfilment of their individual vision in a corporate setting. As a result, for an individual's vision to come to pass, it may advance from that individual and become a corporate vision. People who share in that vision are special providence.

A lot of people don't understand the practice of provision and stop dreaming. They cut their vision short and are confused about what they really want to do in life because they know they have few resources. Many are stuck because of the belief they have to pay for their visions with their present income, when they can barely make ends meet as it is. Similarly, when young people tell their parents what they dream of becoming, parents often become nervous because they feel their children's dreams are too big for them to finance.

Let us start by making this clear first: If what you currently have is enough to help fulfil your dream, then its not a true dream in the first place.

By its nature, visions hold our expansion packs. Your vision is designed to expand you. So it goes without saying that your vision will be bigger than you. Your part is not to do everything yourself; your part is to fundamentally understand the process, principles, and practices that guide vision. Essentially, writing a vision, making a plan of action, and taking the first few steps is what you are required to do.

A true vision has its own special way of setting you up for opportunities. With opportunities come momentum along the flywheel. True vision will attract pro-visions: resources (both human and material) required to bring your vision to pass. The word "pro" means "for." There are people for your vision. There are houses that are pro your vision. There are airlines that are pro your vision. Your part is to take the first step and believe. The impact of your purposeful work that originates from deep within has a resounding effect. This is where you need to focus your attention.

> **If what you currently have is enough to help fulfil your dream, then its not a true dream in the first place.**

From Joseph to Masaru Ibuka to Martin Luther King Jr. and the other extraordinary individuals reviewed in this book, they hardly depended on their own resources in accomplishing greater things. If your current assets are limited, you need access to more resources to help you get to your destiny. But access only comes by first using the little that is currently in your hand.

It is human nature to gather all you need before you start on a project or venture. But visions and dreams don't work that way. They work in the reverse order. You first see and complete what you want to accomplish in your mind before the resources come. The power of vision allows a creative visualisation process that causes things to first be created and completed in the mind before they become visible. The ability to develop a mental picture is not only empowering enough on its own; it also attracts materials and resources that allow the mental image to become a reality. Provision for your vision is usually hidden until you act on it. Whatever you were born to do attracts what you need to do it. You must develop the practice of vision that causes you to first establish what you want to do before resources come to catch up with it. This underscores the need for writing your vision and planning.

> **It is human nature to gather all you need before you start on a project or venture. But visions and dreams don't work that way.**

Provision versus Prosperity of Vision

Our world has a false impression about prosperity. What we term prosperity or wealth is actually in excess of what we really need. And this is the root cause of why many worry that the money they have in the bank is not enough to fund their vision. They expect it to be in excess. Our understanding of prosperity is like hoarding. You don't have to own extravagant things in order to do extraordinary things. But vision does see prosperity that way.

What the research showed was quite convincing; money is not a prerequisite for your vision or greatness in life. The individuals I researched didn't start out seeking money. Steve Jobs, Henry Ford, Masaru Ibuka, and Walt Disney did not start out wealthy. They were not children of wealthy parents. And while you would have expected them to base their vision on wealth, they started out with their core values. Ibuka focused on Japan becoming an economic powerhouse, Ford focused on democratising the automobile, Disney focused on making people happy, and Jobs was all about amplifying the human ability using technology.

> **...money is not a prerequisite for your vision or greatness in life.**

In the end, there were more of them in this power of vision research who won the Nobel Peace Price than appeared on Forbes' list of the wealthy. And many of those who appeared on the list of the very wealthy arrived there based on the manifestation of their vision, which allowed them to accumulate wealth. Not the other way around.

Prosperity in real terms doesn't mean that future needs are met today; it means that today's need is met today. So you are inherently prosperous. You have what you need to get started. The opposite mindset, that you lack what it takes to start, keeps people from taking action towards their vision.

Provision is for vision. Provision is what comes to you as you work on your vision. You were not born to have too much or too little. You were born to fulfil your purpose, and doing so will make you prosperous. However, when you capture your vision—the part you're supposed to contribute to your generation and succeeding generations, the role you're supposed to play in history—when you capture that and are doing it, you will see that all your provisions are automatically built into it.

As a result, you won't work for money like ordinary people do. We become prosperous based on the work we do with our gifts and talents. If you have anything in excess, it is a sign that you are not utilising it effectively or you're greedy. That is not prosperity. We are as rich as our purpose in life (which itself is a function of the vision we see). Yet, until our vision reaches its full manifestation, provision continues to come that no one can hold back because of the expansionary power of vision.

> **Provision is what comes to you as you work on your vision.**

Don't abandon your vision because you seem to lack money. Don't fall for the general assumption that you must have all that you need to get started. Prosperity is that, for example, your parents are able to pay for your tuition, but provision comes when you begin to learn, have vision, and grow. Don't let the mental impression of not having excess deter you. Use what you already have to bring your vision to life because it unlocks provision for you.

> **We are as rich as our purpose in life**

Your ability to follow through with your vision not only unlocks provision; it also affects the lives of those around you. Provision for vision includes people who decide to work with you to bring the vision to a higher state of impact. They are not your possession in the sense of how we see things of material prosperity. They are pro, for, the vision. Nurture them, and take care of them. Ensure that their visions and purposes are being fulfilled also.

Visionaries never join the people who say they don't have enough. Some people ask for the wrong things that don't pertain to their life's purpose or vision. Some covet what is not theirs. Some pursue other people's vision and as a result find that they are short of provision or resources. It is someone else's vision, and the provision is secured with them, not you. Capturing your own vision is the most important step to not only being prosperous but also to obtaining provision.

> **Don't abandon your vision because you seem to lack money.**

Chapter 27
BE, DO, HAVE

It is not what do I need to HAVE before I can start, or what work do I need to DO, but who do I need to BE? What kind of person would have access to the kind of outcomes I want? Then being that kind of person, what would I be doing? And then the having takes care of itself.

Every single goal we set in life has two faces to it: the what (of what we want to accomplish, achieve, or have) and the who (who will be accomplishing it).

The who (or the be) that does the doing is what drives you and subsequently results in having or achieving.

Let's take a look at some examples. Say you have a weight loss or fitness goal you have been struggling with. The problem is that most people focus on the HAVE: losing weight, instead of the BE, which is the main driver for achieving a goal.

To increase your chances of succeeding, you first need to become the person who is willing to find better ways of handling stress instead of comfort eating and procrastinating about exercise.

In other words, be someone who can develop strategies to say no to that second piece of cake and yes to activity. The result is you will have a fit body.

Most of us think we need to have a certain thing or set of things (more money, love, time, experience, etc.), so that we can finally do something important (pursue our passion, start a business, go on vacation, create a relationship, buy a home), which will then allow us to be what we truly want in life (peaceful, fulfilled, inspired, generous, in love). In actuality, it works the other way around.

First, we become what we want (peaceful, fulfilled, inspired, generous, loving, or whatever), then we start doing things from this state of being, and soon we discover that what we're doing winds up bringing us the things we've always wanted to have.

If this concept is new to you or seems counterintuitive or confusing (or both), it's actually quite powerful and life-altering when we really get it and practice it in our lives.

Many of us hold the assumption that our visions, BHAGs, big dreams, and everything in between are supposed to be hard, painful, and dramatic. Right? Well, maybe it doesn't have to be that way.

What if we were able to live in alignment more often with this powerful principle of Be, Do, Have? What if we remembered that we have the capacity to experience any state of being at any time, not just when things work out perfectly or we achieve exactly what we're after. There's nothing wrong with pursuing goals and dreams with passion. However, when we erroneously think that the fulfilment of any specific goal, dream, or accomplishment will give us what we truly want to have in life, we delude ourselves and set ourselves up for failure, disappointment, and pain.

Remember that who and how we're being is a direct product of how we think, feel, and act. And what we think, feel, and act are direct reflection of what we are seeing at the core. They are the key raw materials for how we ultimately create our reality. Being gives us access to what we're really after. We don't have to suffer and struggle as much as we do; we actually have the capacity to live our life with a true sense of elegance (the deeper meaning of this word is not about appearing a certain way but about being able to put forth a small amount of focused effort and manifest an abundant result). What his means essentially is that changing seeing, can change being.

> **Being gives us access to what we're really after.**

Put your vision before you again. Reflect on your BHAGs one more time. Begin to embody that state of being. Don't wait till the accomplishment of this goal. For example, you may start being joyful (as if you already accomplished your goal). Note that this is not about faking it; it's about authentically embodying the desired states of being your true self, who you want to be in life. It is seeing it first from within.

From this state of being, think about, talk about, and speculate about the specific actions you might want to take. Allow yourself to sit with this for a while; don't be in too much of a hurry. If you really allow yourself to come from this empowered state of being, the actions will start to show up with ease, and your ability to both take them and allow them to work will increase exponentially.

> ...changing seeing, can change being.

Being a visionary doesn't mean life is all serious but no fun. Have fun. Be, do, have. Get support from those around you, talk to people about your vision and goals, and know that you will probably trip and fall many times along the way, just as many great people who went ahead did. You may miss a goal, learn from it, derive something to learn, and grow again. The goals can change, but keep the vision in focus.

We've all heard this many times, but it's important to reiterate here: We are human beings, not human doings. When we remember this, our life can really take off in a profound and fulfilling way.

> **We are human beings, not human doings.**

Chapter 28
LEVEL 7 LEADERSHIP

The Power of Vision Produces Level 7 Leadership. One of the greatest forces on earth is the force of vision. Visionaries usually become leaders because vision imposes a certain discipline and focus that crystallises in the excellence we all admire. Show me a person of vision, and I will show you someone destined for greatness. Inherent in the power of vision is the discipline to stay true to your purpose and calling. With this also comes the focus and discipline that allows you to utilise your gifts and potential for the greater good of humanity. The application of the principles and practices that guide vision and the passion to live in the reality of your purpose ultimately makes you become a Level 7 leader.

> **Visionaries usually become leaders because vision imposes a certain discipline and focus that crystallises in the excellence we all admire. Show me a person of vision, and I will show you someone destined for greatness.**

Modesto Maidique, visiting professor at the Harvard Business School, asked leaders these questions: "Who do you serve, yourself? Your group? Society?" Maidique built a six-level purpose-driven model of leadership.[118] The scale ranged from Level 1 Leader: Sociopath to Level 6 Leader: Transcendent. Not dabbling too much into all those levels, one thing to note is that a perfect example of a Level 1 Sociopath is Adolf Hitler, who ended up destroying his country, his tribe, his family, and, in time, himself. Indeed, he served no one. I spoke about the vision of Adolph Hitler earlier; you may recall how his purpose was self-gratifying and dehumanising; it held no positive, extraordinary virtues.

Apart from Maidique's levels of leadership, Jim Collins in his book *Good to Great* identified five levels of leadership.[119] At the top of his leadership hierarchy is Level 5, which are individuals who blend extreme personal humility with intense professional will. His research found that these types of leaders are at the helm of good-to-great companies, companies that emerged from poor performance to a much better performance over a long period of time.

Levels 1 through 4 have been discussed extensively by other leadership authors; they are rather self-explanatory.[120] In this chapter, I will briefly look into the Level 4 to 6 leadership traits and introduce you to an ideological Level 7 leadership. I found Level 7 to be a rare type of leadership that anyone desiring to be extraordinary should aim for in life.

Jim Collins's Five Levels of Leadership

Leadership Level	Name	Description
Level 5	Executives	Builds enduring greatness through a paradoxical blend of personal humility and professional will
Level 4	Effective Leader	Catalyzes commitment to and vigorous pursuit of a clear and compelling vision, stimulating higher performance standards
Level 3	Competent Manager	Organises people and resources towards the effective and efficient pursuit of predetermined objectives
Level 2	Contributing Team Member	Contributes individual capabilities to the achievement of group objectives, and works effectively with others in a group setting
Level 1	Highly Capable Individual	Makes productive contributions through talent, knowledge, skills, and good work habits

Maidique's Six Levels of Leadership

Leadership Level	Name	Focus	Description
Level 6	Trans-cendent Leader	Society	Transcendents go beyond the institution they govern by ensuring that the institution grows while contributing to the entire community.
Level 5	Builder Leader	Institution	Builders make decision that serve and help to build the institution.
Level 4	Achiever Leader	Command from above	Achievers are effective in getting the job done. They serve the goal commanded from above (e.g., a boss, a board, or the law) without broader consideration.
Level 3	Chame-leon Leader	Prevailing Winds	Chameleons adapt to their surroundings and serve whichever group they belong to. Chameleons are often used by others.
Level 2	Oppor-tunist Leader	Themselves	Opportunists exhibit no consideration of their friends, family, society, or institution. They serve themselves and think only about their own benefit.
Level 1	Socio-pathic Leader	No One	Sociopath is the catchword for a destructive person. Sociopaths serve neither themselves nor their surroundings.

Level 4 Leaders

Both Collins's and Maidique's research frames were largely unidentical, but I was able to find some similarities. Maidique's Level 4 leader, the Achiever, appears to be where most people reading this book might fall into. The critical thing about achievers is that in their drive towards a goal, they often substitute the needs of the whole with their personal striving to succeed.

The Level 4 Achiever fills the senior executive ranks. It's rare for these leaders to fail to achieve their goals, and they often exceed sales quotas, create generous profits, and are frequent stars at merit-award dinners. The Achiever, to use Peter Drucker's felicitous phrase, is often a "monomaniac with a mission" and is focused, energetic, results-oriented, and highly prized by top management. Achievers pursue goals established by their bosses or by themselves, in a single-minded manner. Therein lies their Achilles heel: They drive towards a goal without giving much consideration to the broader mission. According to Maidique, former Hewlett-Packard CEO Mark Hurd is an excellent example of a Level 4 leader. Under Hurd's watch, HP's stock price more than doubled, but he decimated the company's infrastructure and R&D (its intellectual seed corn) to do so. By simply cutting R&D to about 2.5 percent of revenue, down from 6 percent during the 1990s, the Carly Fiorina/Mark Hurd team "saved" HP about $4 billion—about the equivalent of half the profits earned during Hurd's last year. HP's once formidable technological and product strength was slowly sapped away.

> The critical thing about achievers is that in their drive towards a goal, they often substitute the needs of the whole with their personal striving to succeed.

When Dave Packard was asked in the early 1980s what accounted for HP's extraordinary run, he modestly replied, "I guess we found a way to make a better product." Where are those better products today? Referring to one of HP's most visible new product initiatives, the TouchPad, a late entry into the iPad-dominated tablet space, a senior HP executive reportedly told the Wall Street Journal, "We know we're the fifth man in a four-man race."

In Collins's term, Level 4 leaders are effective and have the peculiar ability to catalyse commitment to and vigorous pursuit of a clear and compelling vision, with the pure purpose of stimulating higher performance standards. Collins gave numerous examples of Level 4 leaders. Scott Paper, for example, had a CEO named Al Dunlap, who beat on his own chest and told anyone who would listen (and many who would prefer not to) about what he had accomplished. Quoted in BusinessWeek about his nineteen months atop Scott Paper, he boasted, "The Scott story will go down in the annals of American business history as one of the most successful, quickest turnarounds ever, [making] other turnarounds pale by comparison." According to BusinessWeek, Dunlap personally accrued $100 million for 603 days of work at Scott Paper (that's $165,000 per day), largely by slashing the workforce, cutting the R&D budget in half, and putting the company on growth steroids in preparation for sale.[121] After selling off the company and pocketing his quick millions, Dunlap wrote a book about himself, in which he trumpeted his nickname, Rambo in Pinstripes. "I love the Rambo movies," he wrote. "Here's a guy who has zero chance of success and always wins. Rambo goes into situations against all odds, expecting to get his brains blown out. But he doesn't. At the end of the day he succeeds, he gets rid of the bad guys. He creates peace out of war. That's what I do, too."[122]

> **Extraordinary people powered by a distinct vision lead with grace; it almost appears that they've been born to do it all their lives.**

The great irony is that the animosity and personal ambition that often drive people to positions of power stand at odds with the humility required for a higher level of leadership. Level 4 leaders stop short of personal humility, which is a critical cornerstone of visionary leaders. Level 4 leaders also lack the long-term, transgenerational perspective that is characteristic of visionaries. Extraordinary people powered by a distinct vision lead with grace; it almost appears that they've been born to do it all their lives.

Level 5 and 6 Leaders

While these leaders operate with some characteristics similar to the people mentioned in this book, Level 5 leaders are no match for those types of extraordinary individuals. It is important to note that this type of leadership can be rather common, and while their accomplishments move them and their institution forward, they don't always create an enduring legacy, characteristic of visionaries.

To an extent, Collins's Level 5 and Maidique's Level 6 leadership frames almost coincide in meaning. Collins talked about a combination of personal humility and professional will as the archetype for Level 5 leadership, saying such leaders set the standards of building an enduring company, based on channeling their ambition into the company and not for themselves. Quite similar to Collins's idea of Level 5 leadership, Maidique described Level 5 leaders as builders. He addressed them as legendary leaders such as IBM's Tom Watson Jr., GM's Alfred P. Sloan, and Oprah Winfrey. These people serve their institutions by managing for the long term and not allowing themselves to be seduced by the twin mirages of short-term profit and stock valuations. They have a grand vision for the future of their organisations, and they infect others with their energy, enthusiasm, and integrity. These are the leaders we write books about, study, try to understand, and lionise. Indeed, their compelling modesty and an unwavering resolve to do what must be done separates them from others. In Collins's model, Level 5 leaders embody all the attributes included in levels 1 through 4. The Level 5 leader, the Builder, strives not to reach a goal but to build an institution.

Maidique discussed Level 6 leadership and said it transcended Level 5 builders; in essence, Level 6 leaders are transcendent. Level 6 leaders transcend political partisanship, ethnic group, race, and even the institutions that so formed their life and ideology. They focus on how to benefit all of society, all of humanity. These are referred to as global citizens, but that title doesn't even cut it.

Rare Level 7 Leaders

I found another type of leadership prominent among the extraordinary individuals I researched. I would almost describe the type of leadership I found as Level 5 or 6 leadership, in which case I wouldn't need to stress it in this chapter, but I found it undeniably obvious in what the data provided. Let me add quickly that while I knew there were leadership lessons to be learnt from these extraordinary individuals, I wasn't sure what they would be until I began to analyze the data and reviewed the results. These extraordinary individuals served their world with the humility and excellence of their gift and talents (Level 5); they showed professional will and drive (qualities of Level 5 and 6 leaders); and they went further to demonstrate an additional trait, which I call super transcendency, the commitment to impact multiple generations for the sole purpose of bringing glory to something supreme, which a number of them called God. It might sound unacceptable to someone who doesn't believe in the existence of God or a deity, but the fact that you put your belief in something (no matter what you call it) indicates that you have a belief system.

Seven Levels of Leadership

Leader-ship Level	Name	Focus	Description
Level 7	Level 7 Leader	Universe/ Global	Combines the attributes of Level 5 and 6 but goes beyond institutions and societies to have universal, transgenerational influence, with the ultimate intent of bringing glory to some unseen force, greater influence, or deity.
Level 6	Transcendent Leader	Society	Transcendents go beyond the institution they govern by ensuring that the institution grows while contributing to the entire community.
Level 5	Builder Leader/Level 5 Executive	Institution	Builds enduring institutions through personality attributes and decisions that serve and help in such building process.
Level 4	Effective Leader	Command from Above	Commitment to and vigorous pursuit of a clear and compelling goal or vision. They rigorously follow commands from their superiors. They achieve

Level 3	Competent Manager	Prevailing Circum-stances	and stimulate higher performance but often lack consideration for the broader community. They quickly adapt to their surroundings, serve whichever group they belong to, and competently organise people and resources towards the effective and efficient pursuit of predetermined objectives. Like chameleons, they are often used by others.
Level 2	Contributing Opportunist	Themselves	That they belong to a team can be confusing because their focus is usually what they can accomplish for themselves by working in a group setting. Although their contributions are recognisable, their personal benefits are usually the driving force.
Level 1	Highly Capable Sociopath	No One	They are highly intelligent, smart, and skilled, and make productive contributions through good work habits, but in the end, they self-destruct, serving neither themselves nor their surroundings.

Dr. Martin Luther King Jr. was a prime example. Not only was he pursuing the abolition of segregation, his purpose stood for freedom for all humanity; he consistently reaffirmed that his commitment was to God. He fought for equal rights for all people. His purpose transcended just black people, so much so that a significant portion of the 1963 march to Washington where he gave his famous "I Have a Dream" speech included white people in its leadership and planning.[123] His ability to bring people from different walks of life to represent a shared value and to build on freedom, a core American philosophy, resonated with everyone. His ability to adopt a non-violent approach, even in the face of internal and external criticism, showed clearly that he was not only committed to achieving his goal, but achieving it the way God would approve of. Not only because he was a Baptist preacher, from a young age, he had challenged his beliefs and found that the best way to resolve bigger issues was to respond with love. Extraordinary individuals exhibited a special leadership quality that showed their lives had a higher influence beyond what science and theories could explain; it was a supernatural experience. This ultimately strengthened their resolve and made them committed to a higher calling.

There is no better example of what it takes to be supertranscendent than Nelson Mandela. He was able to soar above hatred for his white jailers, the political tug of the African National Congress, the pull of his racial and tribal group, and the rejection by the Afrikaners to build a South Africa for all South Africans. Like Martin Luther King Jr., Mandela wanted people to be judged by their character instead of their skin colour. Although Mandela never claimed any specific religious affiliation, many referred to his ability to reconcile and love those who held him captive for twenty-seven years as saintlike attributes.[124] Research showed that he had roots of religious faith.[125] It was obvious that something more, something spiritual, appealed to him.

> ...people don't arrive at Level 7 leadership positions only by educational qualifications or merits...

Mother Teresa made it clear that God appeared to her and demanded that she be the hand of love. She demonstrated a transcendent leadership, not just focused on the charity she poured her heart into, but to bring glory to God.

Joseph in the Bible was a good Level 7 model. He served to the highest level of his gift, with no reward or payment in view. From Potiphar to the prison stewards and ultimately to the palace. Yet when the time came, the very same people who tried to kill his vision were the chief beneficiaries of his sacrifices. One would have thought he would respond as he so desired. His impact transcended partisanship, ethnic loyalty, or racial group. What he saw, the true implication of the dream of his brothers bowing to him, transcended his family; it became the singular event that saved Israel from starvation due to the drought.

In a similar fashion to Level 5 and 6, people don't arrive at Level 7 leadership positions only by educational qualifications or merits seen by the general public; they turn out to perform the role better than the wildest imagination of observers and critics.

Level 7s never see themselves as though they deserve the title or are fit for the roles placed on them, but they do everything within their capacity to produce results over and beyond expectations. They execute with humility, knowing fully well that the vision they carry is way bigger and as such solicit support from their community.

> **Level 7s never see themselves as though they deserve the title or are fit for the roles placed on them...**

The prime objective of Level 7 leaders is to see a great number of people within their community, the larger society, and indeed everyone in the universe become more successful in the next generation; they're comfortable with the idea that most people won't even know that the roots of that success trace back to their efforts. They're not I-centric, and you will rarely find them talking about themselves.

Level 7 leadership captures the enduring significance of the power of vision. As I emphasized earlier, this book is not just about the businesses and institutions these individuals were part of. It's not even about these individuals, per se. It's primarily about their inner workings and intuitions. Without any clear intention to lead people; no initial plans to build or be a part of any institution, these individuals followed the light in their heart, their vision, and became leaders that not only impacted people around them but remained a source of transgenerational influence to many of us reading this today.

> **Level 7 leadership captures the enduring significance of the power of vision.**

Becoming a Level 7 Leader

A review of all seven levels of leadership shows that there are two possible categories of people when it comes to leadership development: those who don't have the seeds of Level 7, and those who do. The first category consists of people who could never in a million years bring themselves to subjugate their egoistic needs to the greater ambition of building something larger than themselves. For these people, jobs will always be first and foremost about what they get, because that is how they get their fame, fortune, adulation, power, whatever, not what they build, create, and contribute. Remember, one attribute of operating from the core is conviction, which is not necessarily quantifiable.

The second category of people, which I suspect includes most of the people reading this, consists of those who have the potential to evolve to Level 7. The capability to become a Level 7 resides within them, perhaps buried or ignored, but there nonetheless. And under the right circumstances (self-reflection, P-EVF, conscious personal development, a mentor, a great teacher, loving parents, a significant life experience, a Level 7 boss, or any number of other factors), they begin to develop. The fact that you are reading this book now falls into this category; the power of vision at work in you may provide the impetus and drive to become a Level 7.

Although I cannot prove that Level 7 leaders are prevalent in our society, keep in mind though, that they exist all around us. If only we knew what to look for. And what is that? Look for situations where extraordinary results exist but where no individual steps forth to claim credit. You will likely find a potential Level 7 leader at work. They will barely be known, and Level 7 leaders like it that way. They carry no airs of self-importance and find companionship among average people. They rarely cultivate hero status or executive celebrity status. Look at people who are diligently serving and blessing others with the excellence of their gifts, without any reward or recompense. Find people who are daily living in the reality of their dreams and inspiring others to do the same. You would be terribly mistaken to think of them as soft. Although they could be awkwardly shy and lack pretense, they may have a fierce, stoic

> ...one attribute of operating from the core is conviction, which is not necessarily quantifiable.

resolve towards life.

Level 7 leadership is a very satisfying idea, a powerful idea, and perhaps an essential idea. A "Seven Steps to Level 7" would trivialise the concept. My best advice, based on the research I did on extraordinary individuals, is to begin exercising your power of vision as well as the principles and practices surrounding it.

On the one hand, Level 7 traits enable you to implement the components of the Vision Flywheel and other findings discussed in this book; on the other hand, practicing those components may help you to become Level 7. Think of it this way: This chapter is about what Level 7 is; the rest of the book describes what they do to become it. Leading with process, principles, and practices of vision as well as maintaining a culture of discipline can help you move in the right direction. There is no guarantee that doing so will turn you into a full-fledged Level 7, but it gives you a tangible place to begin.

I cannot say for sure what percentage of people have the seed within, or how many of those can nurture it. I myself discovered Level 7 while doing this research, but I do not know whether I will succeed in fully evolving to Level 7. And yet, it has been deeply inspirational to unravel what Level 7 leadership is all about. Martin Luther King Jr., Nelson Mandela, Mother Teresa, Joseph, Masaru Ibuka, and all the other Level 7s I learned about have become models for me, something worthy to aspire toward. Whether or not I make it all the way to Level 7, the attempt will be worth the effort. Like all basic truths about what is best in human beings, when we catch a glimpse of that truth, we know that our own lives and all that we touch will be the better for the effort.

Chapter 29
CORPORATE VISION AND CORPORATE DESTINY

Visionaries become specialised and distinct. The constrictionary power of vision makes visionaries specially disciplined and focused in the aspect of their Hedgehog Concept. Discipline ultimately breeds excellence and specialisation, which brings visionaries before a large audience, who have been influenced or impacted by the gift of the visionary. As visionaries function at their best, the momentum of the expansionary power of vision also allows them to attract all types of essential resources that keep the Vision Flywheel going, ensuring their purpose is being fulfilled and legacies established. Top on the list of those resources is human resources. In essence, vision attracts people to you who will help in the fulfilment of your vision.

> ...vision attracts people to you who will help in the fulfilment of your vision.

I found this corporate sense in the lives of the people I researched for this book; I was able to further connect this to many foundational assumptions of what makes an institution great. Essentially, it became obvious that the vision of extraordinary individuals transcended from them into a corporate or group setting. Findings from this study are in line with what many authors say are the ingredients of truly great companies. For example, Steve Jobs built Apple out of his own vision; both those who worked for the company and its customers have a special feeling when it comes to Apple. Vision makes your values transcend beyond your immediate environment and space into people's hearts. This was seen in Masaru Ibuka and Sony, Martin Luther King Jr. and the Southern Christian Leadership Conference (SCLC), Nelson Mandela and South Africa, Mother Teresa and the Missionaries of Charity, Henry Ford and Ford Motor Company, Joseph and Israel, Helen Keller and her impact on people with disabilities, Walt Disney and the Disney Company. There is a unique sense of values, ideology, or code reflected in the lives of these extraordinary individuals; it became the bedrock for the institutions they started. Learning from these extraordinary individuals afforded me the ability to expand the underlying process, principles, and practices discussed in this book into an institutional, corporate, and organisational setting.

In previous chapters, we spent extensive time discussing about the individual "you." It was deliberate because you need to become that right "who": your true self. There first must be a rewiring of the mind's eye to see. It is not first what you do but who you truly are. Once you become the right who, the what, where, and when can easily be answered. This book is deliberately about making you become the authentic you, and the principles of vision bring you into the reality of who you are. Who you are is a revelatory, evolutionary process that hinges on opening your mind's eye to see the potential and power within you. With this revelatory experience which we call vision, we become extraordinary. It is imperative that you must first and foremost understand the principles and practices of personal vision to understand the concept of corporate vision.

> **Vision makes your values transcend beyond your immediate environment and space into people's hearts.**

In this closing chapter, we extend the focus of what we have been discussing so far into the dimension of corporate vision. By its nature, personal vision finds its full manifestation within the frames of a corporate vision. As we discussed in the previous chapters, extraordinary individuals become so because they served humanity with their gifts. And to reach even more people, to be truly expanded by your vision, requires that you operate within a group setting, where various visionaries come together and move in a similar direction or towards a shared sense of purpose. Corporate vision is essentially two or more visionaries coming together. Corporate vision is agreeing to a dominant or primary vision, out of which other visions become fulfilled. It is not just relegating one's destiny; it is finding opportunities to get one's personal vision and purpose fulfilled within the frame of a larger, bigger, far-reaching corporate setting.

> **...to reach even more people, to be truly expanded by your vision, requires that you operate within a group setting...**

As shown in Figure 22, a true corporate vision is established when two or more individuals with shared values and beliefs come together to fulfil a larger, primary vision (note that this diagram is an expansion of Figure 8, "Operating from The Core"). When there is an environment of shared belief systems, ideologies, and values, getting to work and accomplishing objectives ceases to be a chore. Individual A, B, C, and D can work towards a larger vision which, for example, is being inspired by individual A. In short, you don't need to motivate such a group to work. Each member of the unit is effective in their space, complete in their own, yet interdependent in the accomplishment of a larger vision. The process, principles, and practices that operate at the corporate level is only an expansion of what occurs at The Core. The corporation itself can be viewed as a living entity. The corporation that visionaries establish will therefore have its own unique Core (the "who" of the organisation), which gives rise to the "why" and "what" of the organisation.[126] Corporate vision as an entity, operating from the core principle, will therefore have its own purposeful work.

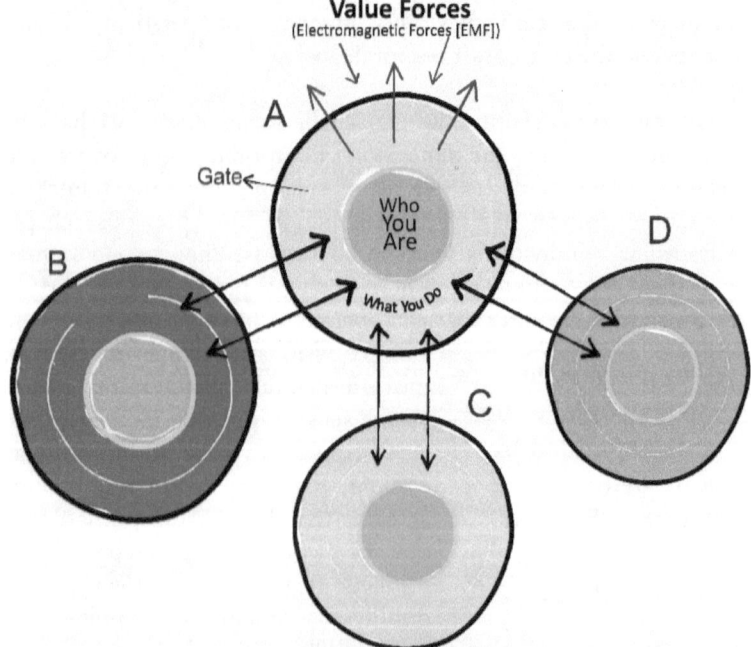

FIGURE 22: Interconnected value forces
and the concept of corporate vision

It goes without saying that corporate vision requires each party being the right who at the core. Vision allows you to not only discover your gift but also fan it into a flame for the benefit of humanity. As you become more specialised, you are not only aware of your capability, you also get to know what you cannot do. You recognise that it's more effective to cooperate, collaborate, or partner with other people. While there's always a lead visionary with the dominant vision within any corporate setting, everyone is inspired by the power of their unique vision, each being guided by the same sets of principles and practices that make ordinary people become extraordinary.

> **Vision allows you to not only discover your gift but also fan it into a flame for the benefit of humanity.**

By its nature, certain people are more likely to get attracted to a visionary than others. There is going to be a group of special people who are attracted to a visionary in such a way that they eventually share a collective sense of purpose and persuasion. These people not only understand the principles and practices of vision but more importantly share a corporate destiny with the visionary.

What, Then, Is a Corporate Destiny?

Let me use this illustration: Let's say you live in Canada and are planning a trip to Lagos, Nigeria, with someone living in France. You choose to travel via an airline that has a stopover in Europe, and the other person has a stopover in another African country. The point is that you both arrive at the same destination, Lagos. Corporate destiny is the ability for more than one person to come from different origins, possess different gifts and abilities, and navigate different divine pathways, yet see (not with mere eyes) the same destination they're heading towards. This is the basis for establishment of corporations and institutions.

One person cannot reach the whole world. One of the greatest errors of modern day is the idea that once you start to sense your personal purpose and gifts, you become autonomous, separate, and independent. The constrictionary power of vision separates you from the crowd but not from your destiny partners. Many have defined entrepreneurship based on this wrong understanding and have taken it as a license to ignore potential helpers and support systems. In order to accomplish a corporate purpose or make a larger vision come to pass, you must share your personal gift and unique vision with other people, who themselves are vision oriented. To reach more people, to allow our influence to reach a larger audience and to have a resounding impact, we need others. We need destiny helpers and co-visionaries to help us create enduring legacies.

> **Just as a car functions when all the parts of the engine work together, so also does a corporate vision require each person working together for a collective purpose.**

One person cannot reach the whole world. Just as a car functions when all the parts of the engine work together, so also does a corporate vision require each person working together for a collective purpose. Each part is unique; the piston is different from the fuel filter, which is different from the starter unit, and so on, yet each submits to one another to make the car function. The same is true for the principles of vision; personal unique visions can work together to become a corporate vision. Grand accomplishments are never done by only one person.

Derivations from the Theory of Operating from The Core

As discussed in earlier chapters, science has proven that energy radiates from the core, producing an electromagnetic field (EMF).[127] People around us can flow in the same rhythm of this EMF. This energy (power) that flows from us is transmitted to others and theirs to us. Both energies can be tuned and become rhythmic so that two or more people can flow at the same wavelength. This type of electromagnetic force can easily be decoded. It's like the aura you carry. Positive energy and power radiating from your core (external value forces) can calm the nerves of people around you. Your children fall into a joyful and peaceful mode when they feel your presence and the energy radiating from you, without you needing to say a word. Your coworkers quickly decode this and feel the grace and comfort when they're around you. This comes with the expansionary power of vision, as your character becomes more defined and people know you for who you truly are. And this EMF becomes so effective in group synergy and becomes the very root of corporate destinies.

Corporate Destiny in Your Home and Immediate Environment

Corporate vision and destiny call for important human resources and destiny helpers. I have found that your spouse is very important in the discourse of corporate vision. An extension of what I learnt from extraordinary individuals was that they had a strong culture in their immediate environment. Although I am not an expert in this area, I tell people who are considering a life partner, when the time comes, the most important thing to look for in your future partner is a shared sense of core values and corporate destiny. Ensure that the people you build a home with see the same future you do; they must have a glimpse of the destiny where you're collectively headed. To a large extent, they need to be vision oriented, disciplined in thoughts, disciplined lifestyle, and disciplined action. More than that, you must share a corporate destiny, sharing the same big picture filled with extraordinary accomplishments. It's risky to go into a long-term relationship with two separate visions. Two separate vision without a corporate destiny is the root of division. You also risk not having a BHAG, which can serve as the inspiration to keep your unit going.

> **Two separate vision without a corporate destiny is the root of division.**

Corporate Destiny in Your Organisation

As we already established, vision is a heart matter at the core. Truly great organisations are not just established on paper. Truly great companies are established by people who connect with others from the heart. If your only objective is to make money, you and your company will never become extraordinary. Martin Luther King Jr. pioneered the SCLC organisation that continues till today simply because it was built on the power of vision. Nelson Mandela's ANC continues to remain a formidable force in South Africa's geopolitical landscape (and has indeed produced most South African presidents since the end of apartheid). Joseph oversaw operations in Egypt simply because he related to hearts and the energy and focused on others.

Organisations that will thrive today must go beyond ads and even the brick and mortar that so represent them physically to touching hearts and lives in intangible ways. Instead of building loyalty, which is harder because it takes a long-term approach, many are applying what has now been called "woke washing," a phenomenon where companies make statements that show their interest in the needs of the society and other external stakeholders without any real commitment.[128] Loyalty is built by the feelings in the heart in ways that cannot be measured. As organisations build around a corporate vision, not following trends, fads and what the competition is doing, they will be able to lead their industry simply by staying within their Hedgehog Concept. It's counterintuitive and sounds strange but this is what was found with extraordinary individuals who pioneered extraordinary institutions. From Steve Job's Apple to Walt Disney's Disney Land (including the newly launched Disney +) and so on. What you find is the strong, cult-like feeling that you find with their customers and fans.

> **Organisations that will thrive today must go beyond ads…to touching hearts and lives in intangible ways.**

Corporate Destiny of Nations

Many nations today are suffering because they lack visionary leaders. Any nation that fails to define its purpose and lacks visionary leaders will continue to live the pain of its past. Citizens of a nation must understand the principles of vision and then share in a corporate vision. What makes a nation truly great are citizen who work to bring their nation to greatness through the exercise of their unique vision and gifts. I have experienced first-hand what it means to live in a developing economy, including facing the reality of everyday struggles, which is why I felt to write a note specifically to developing economies.

Chapter 30
A NOTE TO DEVELOPING ECONOMIES

Emerging economies have historically been called the Third World, which is defined as those who did not participate (or were not allowed to participate) in the Industrial Revolution. "Third World" is a phrase that can be used to describe a class of economically inferior nations. Researchers have classified the inferiority based on key economic metrics like gross domestic product (GDP), GDP growth, GDP per capita, employment growth, and unemployment rate. According to reports, inferior production and labour markets in emerging economies are usually paired with relatively low levels of education, poor infrastructure, improper sanitation, limited access to health care, and lower costs of living.

Third World countries are often among those on close watch by the International Monetary Fund (IMF) and World Bank, which seek to provide global aid with comprehensive projects that help to improve infrastructure and economic systems. Put that together with the tyranny of slavery, indentured servitude, and subjection to imperial power these nations have witnessed, they appear to only exist in the echoes of their enslaved brothers, who are allegedly free in foreign lands yet clamouring for mental freedom. Even though developing nations appear to have obtained their liberty and freedom through independence, they still struggle for survival. Today, an internet search of the word "poverty" will return back pictures of malnourished children pleading for food, with all searches leading back to one emerging nation or the other.

Yet, if we go by the first principles of personal purpose and passion, any nation can self-actualise.[129] Any nation can radically redefine itself. You can change your paradigm from being busy to being proactive. You can move from redundancy to becoming a global economic agent. Each emerging nation can become focused and effective in the areas of their core capabilities and potential. The need to change negative stereotypes and change this narrative is what this book is all about. With the power of vision, all the negative stereotypes stacked against you can be demolished.

The force of vision is one of the most powerful forces on earth. Yet it is free and available to all human beings. The ability to hope is one of humanity's greatest motivations to continue to live. Vision, an inherent human ability, provides us with the opportunity to creatively visualise the future and bring things into existence using the power of our imagination and conscience. In the midst of perverse hopelessness and dire situations, your vision can spark a ray of hope that can restore your nation to glory. This will happen not because you are dreaming of your past but because you are empowered to create a brand-new future, better than your past and present put together.

The three-dimensional power of vision affords you the special ability to view your past and present and to collect data from both in order to create a desired and more effective future. Unlike wishes and mere desires that only appear futuristic in nature, vision creates the future by equipping you with a strategy, actions steps, and motivation. Vision brings you into vivid understanding of what you had in the past and where you are coming from, acknowledges the current reality, including factoring the benefits and importance of current development, and allows you to imagine what you want the future to be for you.

Past and current realities might not have been the greatest, but you learn from them. Records show what was and what is. It is time to begin to hope for what can be and that is yet to come. Without hope, the pain of the past could be overwhelming. With an expectation of a better future, disillusionment can become a way of life. It is time to activate the dynamic power of vision to raise you out of physical, mental, and economic doldrums. What you need first and foremost is not an action plan; it's a change in perspective.

You need to defined core beliefs and values system. Your need to shift your paradigm from your first script and rewire yourself to your own true, original script. You need to believe in yourself and recognise that you have all you need to fulfil your glorious destiny. No donations or grants will create the future you desire if you don't have a core belief or value system. You must develop unwavering faith, even in the face of past and current brutal and unpleasant realities. With the right core beliefs in yourself, you develop the right value systems that allow you to focus on your potential and giftedness. Your core strength is what keeps you standing, attracts resources to you, and allows you to identify your comparative advantages among other nations.

While I primarily addressed individual vision in this book, national vision is essentially the corporate vision of a country. And corporate vision itself is an extension of individual vision, except it's a collection of two or more visions, with individuals heading in a corporate destiny.

> **You need to believe in yourself and recognise that you have all you need to fulfil your glorious destiny.**

As members of a nation, we share in our economic challenges and prosperity, and we also partake in a corporate destiny. We share in a sense of what we know is true, right, and appropriate for our nation. You must apply inner wisdom to stir the inner gift that resides in every household unit so we can arrive at the glorious destiny we envision.

To start, we need to define ourselves by having an overwhelming conviction of who we truly are and what we can do. That is the basis for national integrity. Despite the labels and definitions you've been given, you can define yourself based on a new script. We must realise that fulfilling our destiny is not done under duress, seeking the latest invention and innovation in town, but by abiding with unchanging core principles and practices that can elevate a nation to global relevance. You must dream again. Believe again. Reaffirm your conviction in a glorious destiny.

With vision, you can be sure to walk a distinct pathway for your nation, and you will fulfil your purpose. And this is what we learnt from extraordinary individuals. They not only created new trends; they powered their nations to greatness. Individually and collectively, you have resident in you what it takes to become great. Tap into it. Current generations must commit to become Level 7 leaders who commit to a new cause and are determined to bring their nation back to life.

Level 7 leaders are the only leaders who abide by the interpersonal, interdependent nature of vision. It is my hope that with firm resolve, you will realise that there is no need to copy. You will only need to activate the culture of discipline to bring to life all that is inherently yours. It is my hope that leaders who are selfless, who are committed to serving with the excellence of their gifts, and who can inspire a sense of purpose will lead the world. There is an urgent need for leaders who will not promote their personal agenda but who are guided by the principles and practices of vision and, as a result, will build the national corporate vision and birth the creative capacities of individual visions.

Third World countries are often the target of investors seeking to identify potentially high returns through growth opportunities, though risks are also high. While Third World countries are generally characterised as inferior economically, innovative and industrial breakthroughs can lead to substantial improvements in a short amount of time.

> **What we need is the conception of noble vision that can power nations out of hopelessness, helplessness, depression, destitution, disillusionment, and devastation.**

One thing that has become obvious is that each nation has its unique gifts and natural resources. It will require a national Hedgehog Concept to fully harness them for economic value. Discipline is needed at all layers in thoughts, lifestyle, and actions to lift the nation up and to eradicate the plight of poverty. If there is continuous mismanagement of resources, like foxes that pursue many ends at the same time, you will only see the complexity and not a clear solution. If nations continue to operate like foxes, they are will end up being scattered or diffused, moving on many levels.

What the developing world needs are leaders who integrate their thinking into one overall concept or unifying vision. The answer to the dilemma of nations will not come from more foreign aid, UN handouts, or loans; nor will IMF debt cancelation programs help. What we need is the conception of noble vision that can power nations out of hopelessness, helplessness, depression, destitution, disillusionment, and devastation. We need leaders to emerge who can see beyond their past accomplishments and personal pockets to capture and conceive a desired national vision.

We must learn to dream again. We must face the brutal facts of the day with unwavering faith and believe in our vision of a better future. Confronting facts with resolute faith and action can be a great combination for national progress. It's time to build ourselves individually and to gain our confidence back because the bedrock of any economic improvement is self-development. And at the core of any self-development effort is a mental big picture of a better future that supersedes current realities.

> **We must learn to dream again.**

This is how we can fully inspire people and encourage them to activate their creative abilities as they pursue their personal dreams and vision.

It is my hope and prayer that vision will propel you to greatness by igniting the passion of purpose in the lifeblood of your personal corporate, collective, national existence. May you be inspired to conceive, nurture, and fulfil the vision in your hearts and maximise the potential trapped within you, potential that was buried in the historical grave of low self-esteem and self-doubt. May your dreams inspire the dreams of many generations to come and cause them also to have visions of a better world. May your vision break through and manifest. May the world of emerging economies fulfil your destiny. May you become a model and an example for all the world to see. May your mind's eye remain perpetually open for you to see farther than your mere eyes can look.

> **It is my hope and prayer that vision will propel you to greatness by igniting the passion of purpose in the lifeblood of your personal corporate, collective, and national existence.**

APPENDICES, ENDNOTES & INDEX

APPENDIX 1: SUMMARY OF RESEARCH FINDINGS

(This table of research summary is available for download at www.thepowerofvisionbook.com/research)

Name and time period	Born with Special Ability or disability	Became known in the area, industry or field they became started with	Their Vision	Accomplishments and Legacy	Extended Accomplishments
Martin Luther King Jr. 1929-1968	No, was an average student	No, started as a clergy/pastor to civil Rights struggle	A free and equal world. Racial and economic freedom for all. That all people should be judged not "by the color of their skin, but by the content of their character." At Dexter's Sunday service, King reveals to the congregation his vision of one year earlier in which a divine voice told him to lead the bus struggle without fear.	A scholar and minister who led the civil rights movement and became the pioneer of equal rights and freedom. Won the Nobel Peace Prize in 1964	Played a pivotal role in ending the legal segregation of African-American citizens in the United States, as well as the creation of the Civil Rights Act of 1964 and the Voting Rights Act of 1965. Martin Luther King Day, new era of civil right movement, non-violent advocacy in struggles and freedom. Biblical theology and intersections with politics, race, culture and democracy

Nelson Mandela 1918–2013	No, was a school dropout	No, started as a la to freedom fighter	The ideal of a democratic and free society in which all persons live together in harmony and with equal opportunities.	Fought against apartheid and segregation and to become first black president of South Africa, elected after time in prison for his anti-apartheid work. He won the Nobel Peace Prize in 1993	His ability to unite two opposing group has been regarded as almost a saint-like attribute. Established the roots and foundation for democracy in South Africa.
 Mother Teresa 1910–1997	No, a nun, didn't have any special attributes	No, starting as a teacher to helping the slums of Calcutta aiding poor	To work in the slums of Calcutta aiding the city's poorest and sickest people	Pioneer of a charitable cause and altruism. One of the 20th Century's greatest humanitarians. Awarded Nobel Peace Prize 1979	Challenged entrenched notion of cast and gender roles, worked closely with lepers and others people who are marginalized and dispossessed. By 1986 Operated 517 in more than 100 countries.
Henry Ford 1863–1947	No, self-taught fixing wrist watches. Farm boy with less than a sixth grade.	No, started as a farm boy to becoming an industrialist	To democratize the automobile	Revolutionized the automobile industry, revolutionized assembly line production for the automobile, making the Model T one of America's greatest inventions	Ford was responsible for accelerating the transition from the agrarian era to industrial era not only measured by how many people now use automobiles through his work but also through the establishment of automobile plants that revolutionised not only car manufacturing but manufacturing as a whole.

	Background	Education	Vision/Mission	Contribution	Legacy
Walt Disney 1901–1966	No, a farm boy who dabbled into many things and was a below average student who often fell asleep in class. Developed colouring and drawing abilities	No, worked as a mail boy, a scrambling young businessman to pioneering artist and, finally, to entrepreneur on a grand scale. He pioneered American Motion picture and entertainment	"To bring happiness to millions" and to celebrate, nurture, and promulgate "wholesome American values."	Pioneer of American Motion picture and entertainment. Created many memorable characters and influential films. His impressive record of 22 Academy Awards is one that has yet to be beaten.	Popularized the word "imagineering" and "imagineers". The disneyland, Space Mountain and many other ideas of Walt Disney remain world renowned attraction till date.
Masaru Ibuka 1908–1997	No, was a Photochemist	No, graduated in engineering to Photo chemistry to electronics.	He had no specific product idea but Ibuka spoke about it's purpose in Sony's 1946 Prospectus as follows: • To experience the sheer joy that comes from the advancement, application, and innovation of technology that benefits the general public • To elevate the Japanese	His development of the tape recorder, transistor radio, and many other products put Sony at the forefront of technological innovation for more than three decades and made it the world's most successful and recognized electronics company.	Pioneer of the electrical electronics industry. Propelled Japan into international trade.

 **Helen Keller** 1880 – 1968	No. Was blind and deaf at the same time from age 19 months	No, learnt to read braille and to make sign languages then started out writing and later became a lecturer	culture and national status • Being a pioneer—not following others, but doing the impossible • Respecting and encouraging each individual's ability and creativity	None in specific	Having developed skills never approached by any similarly disabled person, Keller began to write. She wrote many books that vision being a process of seeing with the mind's eye as opposed to seeing with our physical eyes.	Her education and training represent an extraordinary accomplishment in the education of persons with these disabilities. Cofounded the American Civil Liberties Union in 1920. Prompted the organization of commissions for the blind in 30 states by 1937
Steve Jobs 1955–2011	None, dropped out of college	No, started as an orphan who was directionless but picked up interests in electronics and gadgets		"Building tools that amplify a human ability"	Revolutionalised six industries: personal computers, animated movies, music, phones, tablet computing, and digital publishing. He pioneered a series of revolutionary technologies, including the iPhone and iPad. Propelled a company from zero	Pioneered a new era of marketing, business and management approaches. His counterintuitive approach to design which many often argue against have consistently proven to be market winner. The foundation he laid made Apple

Joseph
1600 – 1800BC	Was a farm boy who dreams and interprets dreams.	No, started as a farm boy to house servant to Prime Minister	Wear the coat of many colours and leading people older than him	to the top a multiple times.	Prime Minister who saved Egypt (a foreign land) in charge of the most important affair of a critical time of famine.	officially the first America company to reach a market cap of $1 trillion Fed his brothers and saved a whole generation from hunger and starvation

APPENDIX 2: COMPOSITE 3D AND PHASAL NATURE OF VISION

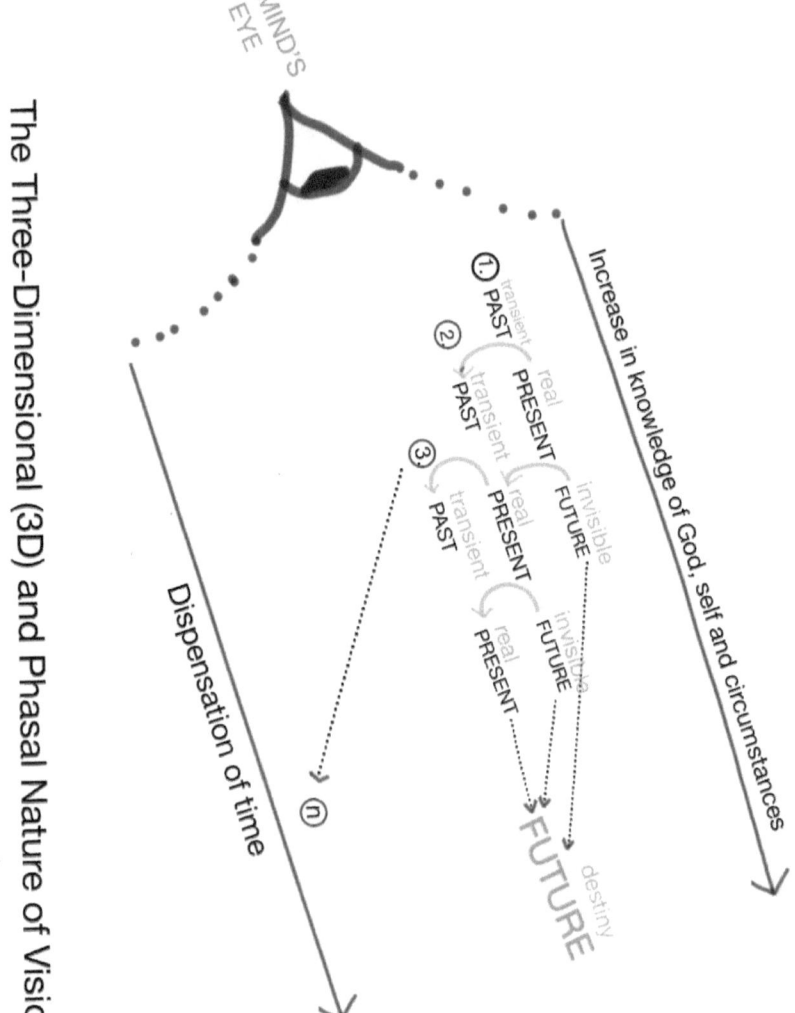

The Three-Dimensional (3D) and Phasal Nature of Vision

APPENDIX 3: THE UPWARD SPIRAL: EVOLUTION OF THE VISION FLYWHEEL

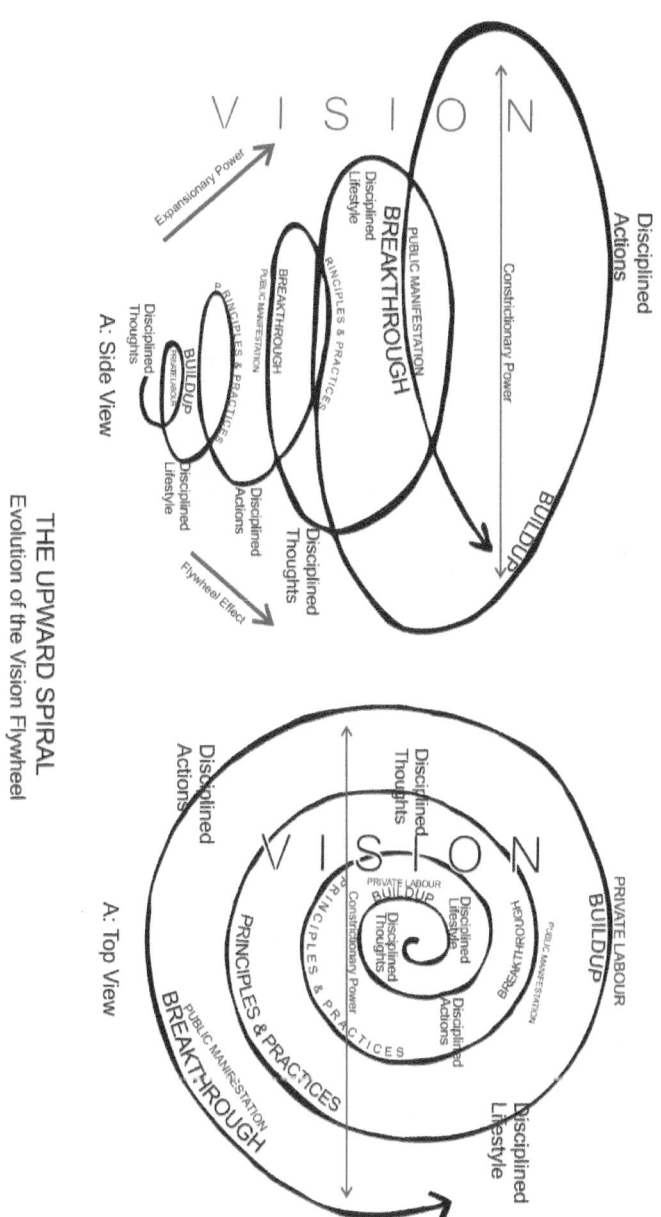

Bonus Materials & Resources

(Visit www.thepowerofvisionbook.com for details and access)

Dig deeper into the power of vision research. Learn the 7 Habits from nine extraordinary individuals powered by vision that will make you become extraordinary too.

Separate the truths from the false narratives about vision and better prepare yourself for enduring greatness.

Twelve Myths about Vision demystified so that you can be inspired to bring your visions and dreams to life.

Principles and practices to help your institution become extraordinary.

 While there is no one defined way to conceptualize and articulate your vision, this guide provides a frame to capture and document components of what forms your vision

 A Report on Five Common Internal and External Obstacles in Accomplishing Your Vision and how to overcome them.

 The Power of Vision Study Guide and Workbook – A companion for group study and putting the principles and practices to work

 Turning the Vision flywheel: An Accompanying Monograph to The Power of Vision

ENDNOTES

CHAPTER 1

[1] In the 2016 book, *The Code of the Extraordinary Mind,* author Vishen Lakhiani, talked extensively about Culturescape (and possibly the one that introduced the word). He described it as "the world we live in with all its messy and conflicting ideas, beliefs, and patterns that we've invented in an attempt to keep humanity safe and under control." In other words, culturescape is the environment around you which is made up of human ideas, cultures, mythologies, beliefs and practices. It is what is acceptable Yet, they form rules that tell us how to exist and which when challenged brings us to a new level of revelation or paradigm shift.

[2] The school system works in a very interesting way. You get to make two choices on the application form but for some reasons you get picked for an option that doesn't primarily include your choices. I am yet to understand why that is the case or if that has changed as of yet.

[3] There were many positive key findings in the 10-15 year MTO data for adults including improved mental and physical health. A negative, rather surprising, outcome was that MTO had little to no effect on economic self-sufficiency. For youth, MTO had little to no measured effect on physical health, and no detectable effects on math and reading achievement. More information on MTO is here: http://www2.nber.org/mtopublic/ and an overview of the moving to opportunity experiment: a random assignment housing mobility study in five u.s. cities is available here: https://www.nber.org/programs-projects/projects-and-centers/moving-opportunity?page=1&perPage=50

[4] Raj Chetty, Nathaniel Hendren, and Lawrence F. Katz, "The Effects of Exposure to Better Neighborhoods on Children: New Evidence from the Moving to Opportunity Experiment." American Economic Review, 106 (4) (2016): 855–902.

[5] J. D. Bremner, "Traumatic Stress: Effects on the Brain." *Dialogues Clin Neurosci.* 2006;8(4):445–61.

[6] Out of the 177 self-made millionaires, 105 (59 percent) came from middle-class households and 72 (41 percent) came from poor households. The Business Insider article is here: https://www.businessinsider.com/3-ways-to-build-wealth-2018-7 Corley research study background and methodology are explained here: https://richhabits.net/rich-habits-study-background-and-methodology/

[7] Covid-19: US registers record one-day toll of 2,129; total crosses 25,000 https://economictimes.indiatimes.com/news/international/world-news/covid-19-us-registers-record-one-day-toll-of-2129-total-crosses-25000/articleshow/75150979.cms?from=mdr

[8] Leaders reveal the 'most severe' impacts of COVID-19 https://www.hcamag.com/ca/specialization/financial-wellness/leaders-reveal-the-most-severe-impacts-of-covid-19/219603

[9] Extract from the Founding Prospectus provided by Sony and available here: https://www.sony.net/SonyInfo/CorporateInfo/History/prospectus.html Since it was originally written in Japanese, various English translation including this one uploaded by Sony may contain various words and transliterations but they provide the exact same meaning and context

CHAPTER 2

[10] See full table of research summary in Appendix 1. A more comprehensive summary of research table is available at www.thepowerofvisionbook.com/flywheel

[11] Many had often thought Mandela was in prison for only 27years. He was actually imprisoned for more than that. Evidences shows that his imprisonment started since November 7th 1962 at the Pretoria Local Prison before being transferred to various prison including Robben Island where he stayed the longest for 18years from June 1964 to March 1982. More details here: https://www.nelsonmandela.org/content/page/trials-and-prison-chronology

[12] The creative engine, which is a conglomerate of up 140 different disciplines, implementing creative ideas into practical form; https://disneyimaginations.com/about-imaginations/about-imagineering/

[13] Michael Barrier (2007), The Animated Man: A Life of Walt Disney, Berkeley: University of California Press, pp18-19. Indeed this book was a good read that shows the life of Walt Disney as human

CHAPTER 3

[14] See Appendix 3 for a graphic description of this upward spiral evolutionary process.

[15] You can download a printable version of this Vision Flywheel at: thepowerofvisionbook.com/flywheel

[16] Mind the Workplace – Mental Health America (MHA) Workplace Health Survey 2017 https://www.mhanational.org/sites/default/files/Mind%20the%20Workplace%20-%20MHA%20Workplace%20Health%20Survey%202017%20FINAL.pdf

[17] The report went ahead to discuss the implication for businesses spending on labor. Payroll costs typically represent 15% to 30% of gross revenue so actively disengagement at work warrants attention. The report is available here: https://www.gallup.com/file/workplace/238079/State%20of%20the%20Global%20Workplace_Gallup%20Report.pdf

CHAPTER 4

[18] Simon Sinek says to start with your "why" in his popular book but I believe starting with your "who" is more appropriate. Both appear to be equally important. This will be a good topic to further research: Your "Who" or Your "Why", which one should you start with?

CHAPTER 5

[19] There is an ongoing argument that empirical research only have to include quantitative methods but that has long been debunked. Qualitative research is empirical research. There are numerous scientific evidences to support this. Raul Pacheco-Vega, PhD provided a background here http://www.raulpacheco.org/2018/09/qualitative-research-is-empirical-research-stop-equating-empirical-with-quantitative/ including a large body of other evidences in the article

[20] Tilda Gaskell (2000) The process of empirical research: a learning experience?, Research in Post-Compulsory Education, 5:3, 349-360, DOI: 10.1080/13596740000200084

[21] https://www.guide2research.com/research/what-is-empirical-research

[22] Powner, L. (2015). Empirical Research and Writing: A Political Science Student's Practical Guide. Thousand Oaks, CA: Sage, 1-19. https://dx.doi.org/10.4135/9781483395906

[23] The table contains the following information on these individuals: Name and time period; Born with special ability or disability; Became known in which area, industry, or field; Their vision; Accomplishments and legacy.

[24] Amal Makarem, who witnessed the two-stage evacuation in Beirut as reported in Fady Noun, "Mother Teresa, the War in Lebanon and the Rescue of 100 Orphans and Children with Disabilities." AsiaNews.it LEBANON. February 9, 2016. http://www.asianews.it/news-en/Mother-Teresa,-the-war-in-Lebanon-and-the-rescue-of-100-orphans-and-children-with-disabilities-38470.html

[25] I coined the word *constrictionary* from the root word *constrict*, which appears to be an appropriate word to capture the phenomenon of vision creating a mental boundary that allows the vision to build and gain strength. Vision does not contract you; it constricts you.

[26] Cobb, James G. (December 24, 1999). "This Just In: Model T Gets Award". New York Times. Available here: https://www.nytimes.com/1999/12/24/automobiles/this-just-in-model-t-gets-award.html A jury of 126 auto experts from 32 countries, under the auspices of an entity called the Global Automotive Elections Foundation, gave 742 points to the Model T, compared with 617 for the runner-up, the Mini of Britain. The rest of the top five: the Citroen DS, 567 points; the Volkswagen Beetle, 521; and the Porsche 911, 303

[27] FBI Records: The Vault, Steven Paul Jobs https://vault.fbi.gov/steve-jobs. His GPA record is found on Page 79 of this file

CHAPTER 6

[28] This report also finds that a little more than half of workers (52 percent) have a perpetual case of the Mondays—they're present, but not particularly excited about their job. And even perks don't help. See here: https://www.today.com/money/americans-hate-their-jobs-even-perks-dont-help-6C10423977 and here: https://www.nydailynews.com/news/national/70-u-s-workers-hate-job-poll-article-1.1381297

[29] Daniel Vassallo - Only Intrinsic Motivation Lasts - Why I Quit a $500K Job at Amazon to Work for Myself https://danielvassallo.com/only-intrinsic-motivation-lasts/

CHAPTER 9

[30] To arrive at the definition of vision was not an easy task. To an extent I tried to define it based on what I found in the data but I also reviewed a number of books on vision including George Barna's *The Power of Vision* (2018 paperback edition) and Dr. Mysles Munroe's *The Principles and Power of Vision*

[31] Ron Carucci·TEDxSnoIsleLibraries - How to be more powerful than powerless https://www.ted.com/talks/ron_carucci_how_to_be_more_powerful_than_powerless

CHAPTER 10

[32] These illustrations were adapted from *The 7 Habits of Highly Effective People* by Stephen R. Covey but are not new to the book. In fact they date as far back as 1888. American cartoonist William Ely Hill (1887–1962) published it in an American humour magazine, on 6 November 1915. However, the oldest known form of this image was in 1888 Germany and was first seen publicly on a postcard for the "Anchor Buggy Co". In 1930 Edwin Boring introduced the figure to psychologists in a paper titled "A new ambiguous figure", and it has since appeared in textbooks and experimental studies.

[33] In the book, *Conversations With Myself* (Anchor Canada, 2011, pp 233-234), in the section titled "From A Letter to Winnie Mandela, Dated 9 December 1979," Mandela reflected ruefully on the contradictions in people's lives, and what it is to be human and fallible. The book itself is an unhindered insight into the human side of Mandela himself.

CHAPTER 11

[34] This was discussed extensively in Bench, S. W., Schlegel, R. J., Davis, W. E., & Vess, M. (2015). Thinking about change in the self and others: The role of self-discovery metaphors and the true self. *Social Cognition*, 33(3), 169–185.

[35] As Daniel Goleman reports in *Emotional Intelligence*, psychologists have referred to Self-awareness using a rather ponderous term called *metacognition* to refer to an awareness of thought process, and *metamood* to mean awareness of one's own emotions.

[36] A slew of scientific research have elaborated on what the Wise Advocate is but Dr. Jeffrey Shwartz work appear to provide more precise description as found in his book, *The Wise Advocate: The Inner Voice of Strategic Leadership*, and a number of his work which are available online including this which speaks specifically on the topic: https://youtu.be/UN06weU0anc

[37] These examples are provided by John Mayer and Peter Salovey and present in page 47 of Daniel Goleman's book, *Emotional Intelligence*

[38] Some psychologists have used both self-awareness and mindfulness to mean the same thing. Daniel Coleman, Ph.D. author of the popular book *Emotional Intelligence*, refers to it as self-reflexive, introspective attention to one's own experience.

[39] John D. Mayer and Alexander Stevens, *An Emerging Understanding of the reflective (meta) Experience of Mood,"* unpublished manuscript (1993)

[40] The practice of Conscious Engineering has been widely discussed by Vishen Lakhiani in the book, *The Code of The Extraordinary Mind*, pp 41-42 as well as other authors.

[41] The art of being yourself by Caroline McHugh | TEDx Talks Milton Keynes Women https://youtu.be/veEQQ-N9xWU

[42] Quantum information theoretic approach to the mind–brain problem, Danko D. Georgiev, Progress in Biophysics and Molecular Biology 158:16-32 (2020)

[43] ibid

[44] Science of the Heart, Exploring the Role of the Heart in Human Performance https://www.heartmath.org/research/science-of-the-heart/

[45] Disney popularized the word Imagineering from imagination and engineering and the movement continues till date https://dsnynewscast.com/2018/07/disneyland-will-never-be-complete-re-imagining-the-disney-parks-in-plain-view/

⁴⁶ AP News August 21 1987 report
https://apnews.com/8eaa2f0e5442a4dd298b5dea8015a706
⁴⁷ As indicated in Sony's 1946 Prospectus which was originally written in Japanese but translated to English and available here:
https://www.sony.net/SonyInfo/CorporateInfo/History/prospectus.html
⁴⁸ This 1980 vintage footage of Steve Jobs is one of those rare documentation where he declared Apples core purpose and vision of "Amplifying the Human Ability" https://youtu.be/GfxxRKBgos8 (curtesy of Computer History Museum (CHM) and gift to CHM by Regis McKenna). Fun fact is that he was only 25 in this video.

CHAPTER 12

⁴⁹ Whether you look at it from a pure scientific point of view or from a spiritual or religious lens, man has evolved a brain fitted to be used as a vehicle for experiencing this physical reality. Man can do deductive and inductive logic, which no other species can do (as far as we know). Man has imagination, which is the creative force in the universe (consciousness). We stand out.

⁵⁰ Eric R. Kandel (2007), *In Search of Memory: The Emergence of a New Science of Mind*, W. W. Norton & Company, page xi

⁵¹ Jeffrey Schwartz and Rebecca Gladding (2011), *You Are Not Your Brain*, (The Penguin Group: New York), pp. 5

⁵² Strohminger N., Newman, G., and Knobe, J. (2017). The True Self: A psychological concept distinct from the self. Perspectives on Psychological Science

⁵³ Couture, M., Desrosiers, J., Leclerc, G. (2007). Self-actualization and poststroke rehabilitation. International Journal of Rehabilitation Research, 30(2), 111-117. doi:10.1097/MRR.0b013e32813a2ea5

⁵⁴ *You Are Not Your Brain* pp. 7

⁵⁵ This image was adapted from *You're Not Your Brain*, by Dr. Jeffrey Schwartz and Dr. Rebecca Gladding

⁵⁶ This diagram can be found on page 64 of *Your Are Not Your Brain* by Jeffrey Schwartz MD and Rebecca Gladding MD (paperback edition 2012), Avery

⁵⁷ These two research papers provide more insight on the mind-brian-physics nexus: Quantum propensities and the brain-mind connection, Henry P. Stapp, Foundations of Physics 21 (12):1451-77 (1991) and Quantum no-go theorems and consciousness Danko Georgiev Axiomathes 23 (4):683-695 (2013)

⁵⁸ Their work was published in this paper: Schwartz, Jeffrey M., et al. "Quantum Physics in Neuroscience and Psychology: A Neurophysical Model of Mind-Brain Interaction." Philosophical Transactions: Biological Sciences, vol. 360, no. 1458, 2005, pp. 1309–1327. JSTOR, www.jstor.org/stable/30041344.

⁵⁹ Derived from the theory of Attention Density, *Your Are Not Your Brain* by Jeffrey Schwartz MD and Rebecca Gladding MD (paperback edition 2012), Avery, page 67

⁶⁰ This diagram is a slight modification of "unhelpful aspects of the self-referencing center in charge" found on page 89 of *Your Are Not Your Brain* by Jeffrey Schwartz MD and Rebecca Gladding MD (paperback edition 2012), Avery

CHAPTER 13

⁶¹ James C. Collins and Jerry I. Porras (2002), Built to Last: Successful Habits of Visionary Companies, Harper Business

⁶² Daniel J. Boorstin, *The Americans: The Democratic Experience* (New York: Vintage Books, 1974), pp548.

⁶³ Robert Lacey, *Ford: The Neb and the Machine* (New York: Ballantine Books, 1986), pp89–100.

⁶⁴ Ibid

⁶⁵ *Genryu: Sony Challenge* 1946–1968, Special Collection of Sony Management Newsletters, 40th anniversary edition (Tokyo: Sony, 1986), pp131.

⁶⁶ Akio Morita, *Made in Japan* (New York: Dutton, 1986), pp74.

⁶⁷ ibid, 66–69

⁶⁸ Ibid., 74

⁶⁹ *Genryu—Sony Challenge* 1946–1968, Special Collection of Sony Management Newsletters, 40th anniversary edition (Tokyo: Sony, 1986), pp. 98

⁷⁰ Ibuka had a way of creating market for products people never anticipate
https://www.sony.net/SonyInfo/CorporateInfo/History/capsule/21/

⁷¹ It has been arguments if Henry Ford actually quoted this as there seem to be no source of attribution. Patrick Vlaskovits in a Harvard Business School publication in 2011 provided couldn't validate the source either as reported here: https://hbr.org/2011/08/henry-ford-never-said-the-fast But Patrick provided an important point which underscores the message being passed across here which is this: "An innovator should have understanding of one's customers and their problems via empirical, observational, anecdotal methods or even intuition. They should also feel free to ignore customers' inputs."

[72] The Verge, Sony's Electric Car Is The Best Surprise Of CES: A real working car stuffed full of Sony tech https://www.theverge.com/2020/1/8/21056404/sony-vision-s-electric-concept-prototype-first-look-ces-2020

[73] The impressive performance of Sony PS5 has been lauded by many reporters. In just two weeks, the PlayStation 5 outsold the PlayStation 4. That's impressive considering the impressive debut the PS4 had at the time. It shows the power of BHAG. See for example here about the record breaking release: https://www.gamesindustry.biz/articles/2020-11-25-ps5-is-biggest-console-launch-in-history

[74] Sony will be launching a new brand of TV called Bravia featuring OLED, HDMI 2.1, Android TV as the operating system, new new Bravia Core streaming platform, new XR processor, better sound quality and more. The report is here: https://www.de24.news/en/2021/01/sony-introduces-the-new-bravia-xr-oled-for-2021-with-hdmi-2-1-and-google-tv.html

[75] Shanghai Disneyland Reopens With Strict Safety Procedures, New York Times: https://www.nytimes.com/2020/05/11/business/shanghai-disneyland-reopens.html

[76] My friend Paul Donkor reflecting on the life and legacy of his Father, Dr. Samuel Donkor, a man who we all love and respect and whose impact is transgenerational

CHAPTER 14

[77] Gravitational potential energy is the energy stored in an object as the result of its vertical position or height. The energy is stored as the result of the gravitational attraction of the Earth for the object. https://www.physicsclassroom.com/class/energy/Lesson-1/Potential-Energy. For the nerds reading, the formula is GPE=m*g*h where GPE is gravitational potential energy, m is mass and h is height.

[78] Carol S. Dweck, Mindset: The New Psychology of Success (updated Edition), Random House: New York, pp 142

[79] This is a conversation that I will build on in a sequel to this book but in the meantime, Dr. Craig Wright, Professor Emeritus of Music at Yale University has done a lot of work on talents, IQ and the secrets of greatness and his book *The Hidden Habits of Genius* (2020) is a suggested read on arguments relating to schools and education as it pertains to greatness.

[80] AP News: Trump wants federal hiring to focus on skills over degrees https://apnews.com/c3f85aaa9048c245dd534f508c11a56d?ncid=APPLENEWS00001

[81] CNBC: Google, Apple and 12 other companies that no longer require employees to have a college degree https://www.cnbc.com/2018/08/16/15-companies-that-no-longer-require-employees-to-have-a-college-degree.html

[82] AP News: Trump wants federal hiring to focus on skills over degrees https://apnews.com/c3f85aaa9048c245dd534f508c11a56d?ncid=APPLENEWS00001

[83] USA News https://usa-newnews.com/uncategorized/elon-musk-said-a-college-degree-isnt-required-for-a-job-at-tesla-and-apple-google-and-netflix-dont-require-employees-to-have-4-year-degrees-either/

[84] Myles Munroe (2003), The Principles and Power of Vision: Keys to Achieving Personal and Corporate Destiny, Whitaker House, pp. 33

[85] See Jim Collins (2001), *Good to Great: Why Some Companies Make The Leap and Others Don't*, Harper Business, pp 90 – 91 for more about the Hedgehog Concept

[86] Jim Collins Drucker Day Keynote is available on YouTube here: https://www.youtube.com/watch?v=7qZP4kaYcXU But someone at 100xreturn.wordpress.com did a great job doing the transcript and uploaded it here: https://100xreturn.files.wordpress.com/2009/12/jim-collins-transcript.pdf

CHAPTER 15

[87] The video and transcript is available here at Stanford University News website: https://news.stanford.edu/2005/06/14/jobs-061505/

[88] ibid

[89] About Steve Jobs at Reed College where he learnt Typography and some of Steve Job's proprietary fonts: http://www.wondersandmarvels.com/2011/12/steve-jobs-and-typography.html Steve's Contribution to Caligraphy is detailed here: https://www.cnn.com/2011/10/05/opinion/garfield-steve-jobs-fonts/index.html

[90] Jack Canfield on Aligning Goals with Your Purpose https://www.jackcanfield.com/blog/aligning-goals-with-your-purpose/

[91] The phasal nature of vision is annotated in Appendix 2

[92] To bring these process to life, various other resources from this research will help. The 7 Habits of Extraordinary Individuals Powered by Vision documents the various habits that glue the process and the value adding framework together. There are also various Power of Vision workshops and seminars to help in applying these principles.

CHAPTER 16
[93] Lockhart, K. L., Chang, B.,& Story, T. (2002). Young children's beliefs about the stability of traits: Protective optimism? *Child Development*, 73(5), 1408–1430. And Molouki, S., & Bartels, D. M. (2017). Personal change and the continuity of identity. *Cognitive Psychology*.
[94] Daniel H. Pink (2009), Drive: The Surprising Truth About What Motivates Us, Riverhead Books
[95] *Atomic Habits* by James Clear (Avery, 2018) page 15

CHAPTER 17
[96] Vishen Lakhiani (2016), *The Code of the Extraordinary Mind*, Rodale, pp 3-9
[97] Genesis 37:9
[98] Genesis 42:6
[99] See Appendix 3 for vivid details of the evolution of the Vision Flywheel process
[100] Napoleon Hill, Think and Grow Rich p. 137
https://www.successlearned.com/napoleon-hill-think-grow-rich/files/basic-html/page136.html (accessed January 10, 2020)
[101] Walter Isaacson, *Steve Jobs* (Simon & Schuster, 2011), pp.117-120
[102] ibid
[103] ibid
[104] ibid., pp. 124
[105] Read more about Henry Ford's formal apology for anti-semitism
https://www.thehenryford.org/collections-and-research/digital-resources/popular-topics/henry-ford-and-anti-semitism-a-complex-story

CHAPTER 18
[106] *Japan Electronics Almanac* (Dempa Publications, 1988), 282 (Original from the University of California, Digitized 19 Jul 2011, accessed 12 Dec 2019)
[107] The Flywheel Effect is another adaptation from *Good to Great* by Jim Collins (2001, HarperBusiness). But unlike in Jim, I have focused this on individuals rather than institutions. You will find the original model on Page 174-178 of *Good to Great*

CHAPTER 20
[108] See Appendix 2 for a conceptual presentation of the phasal nature of vision
[109] Franklin D. Roosevelt Presidential Library and Museum sources
https://www.fdrlibrary.org/eleanor-roosevelt

CHAPTER 23

[110] In a CNN Money article titled *20 That Made History*, a section titled "1914: Ford offers $5 a day." This 1914 announcement hit America like a thunder clap and made headlines in Newspapers like the Wall Street Journal. The CNN Money article is available here: https://money.cnn.com/magazines/fortune/fortune_archive/2005/06/27/8263412/index.htm

[111] An extract what appeared to have been published in Wall Street Journal is here: http://www.waratuman.com/2011/01/09/ford/ Ford would go ahead to be remembered as a great man for this decision. It helped the middle class rebound and became one of the pillars of 20th century economic wisdom as described here: https://www.nytimes.com/2006/04/04/business/worldbusiness/a-century-after-henry-ford-middle-class-does-less-to.html

[112] The Middle Class Took Off 100 Years Ago … Thanks To Henry Ford? https://www.npr.org/2014/01/27/267145552/the-middle-class-took-off-100-years-ago-thanks-to-henry-ford

[113] The Stockdale Paradox is better explain in Jim Collins (2001), Good to Great: Why Some Companies Make The Leap and Others Don't, Harper Business, pp 83 -87

CHAPTER 24

[114] Glattfelder J.B. (2019) The Consciousness of Reality. In: Information—Consciousness—Reality. The Frontiers Collection. Springer, Cham. https://doi.org/10.1007/978-3-030-03633-1_14

[115] But serving and solving unique problems is definitely part of the call

[116] In the book *7 Habits of Highly Effective People*, Stephen R. Covey spoke about 7 habits. Habit 4: Think Win/Win discussed about the dimensions of character. See page 215-246 of the 25th Anniversary Paperback Edition

[117] See Appendix 3 for a graphic description of this upward spiral evolutionary process

CHAPTER 28

[118] See the full six-level Purpose-Driven Model of Leadership here at Harvard Business School Working Knowledge: https://hbswk.hbs.edu/item/are-you-a-level-six-leader

[119] Jim Collins Level 5 Leadership framework is fully explained in Jim Collins (2001), Good to Great: Why Some Companies Make The Leap and Others Don't, Harper Business, pp 17-40

[120] I recommend you read Jim's book, *Good to Great,* and Maidique's article, *Are You a Level-Six Leader?* in *Harvard Business School's Business Research for Business Leaders,* to learn more about their leadership models

[121] Did CEO Dunlap save Scott Paper-or just pretty it up? https://www.bloomberg.com/news/articles/1996-01-14/the-shredder

[122] Albert J. Dunlap with Bob Andelman, *Mean Business: How I Save Bad Companies and Make Good Companies Great* (New York: Fireside, 1997), 132.

[123] A group now referred to as the Big 10 - https://www.washingtonpost.com/lifestyle/style/in-march-on-washington-white-activists-were-largely-overlooked-but-strategically-essential/2013/08/25/f2738c2a-eb27-11e2-8023-b7f07811d98e_story.html

[124] Nelson Mandela and the Power of Forgiveness: https://blog.nationalgeographic.org/2013/12/06/nelson-mandela-and-the-power-of-forgiveness/ From the Archives: Nelson Mandela: Anti-apartheid icon reconciled a nation: https://www.latimes.com/local/obituaries/la-me-nelson-mandela-20131205-story.html

[125] Mandela's Roots in Methodist Faith was discussed extensively including by Dion Forster in *Mandela and the Methodists: Faith, fallacy and fact* available here: http://www.scielo.org.za/scielo.php?script=sci_arttext&pid=S1017-04992014000200007, and in this 2013 South Africa's Mail and Guardian article titled: *Mandela and the confessions of a closet Christian* available here: https://mg.co.za/article/2013-12-12-mandela-and-the-confessions-of-a-closet-christian/. Mandela himself already made this clear in his book *Long Walk to Freedom: The Autobiography of Nelson Mandela, 1st Paperback Ed (Back Bay Books, 1995)* page 13-38

CHAPTER 29

[126] Simon Sinek explored this in his book, *Start with Why*

[127] Science of the Heart, Exploring the Role of the Heart in Human Performance https://www.heartmath.org/research/science-of-the-heart/

[128] As many corporate entities are beginning to launch their brand with new statements that show them in good light, journalists and observers were quick to identify what is now referred to as "woke-washing" Read more in these two reports: Davies, Rob (June 19, 2019), "Unilever Boss Says Brands Using 'woke-washing' Destroy Trust." *The Guardian* https://www.theguardian.com/media/2019/jun/19/unilever-boss-says-brands-using-woke-washing-destroy-trust

Jones, Owen (23 May 2019), "Woke-Washing: How Brands Are Cashing in on the Culture Wars." The Guardian, www.theguardian.com/media/2019/may/23/woke-washing-brands-cashing-in-on-culture-wars-owen-jones.

CHAPTER 30

[129] We can essentially extrapolate a national self-actualisation idea from Maslow's self-actualisation theory. This is an intuitive idea after all. Read Maslow, A.H. (1970). *Motivation and Personality*. New York: Harper & Row. Maslow, A.H. (1943). A theory of human motivation. *Psychological Review* 50(1), 370-396. doi:10.1037/h0054346

INDEX

A

Action, towards vision, 178
Africa, 12, 16, 35

B

Balanced Life, 101, 102
Be, Do, Have, 5, 177, 206, 207, 208
Biased Perception, 72, 75
Big Hairy Audacious Goals (BHAGS), 49, 104, 106, 107, 108, 109, 110, 111, 113, 114, 115, 116, 117, 118, 119, 130, 150, 155, 156, 157, 175, 176, 180, 182, 201, 207, 226
Brag (Braggadocious), 40, 111, 117

C

Character, 177, 192, 194, 195, 196
Charisma, 34, 144, 177, 192, 193
Charity, 51, 78, 136, 137, 221
Cognitive, 29, 95, 171
Competition, 38, 45, 115, 120, 125, 140, 227
Coronavirus/COVID, 8, 9, 79, 115, 127, 191
Corporate Destiny, 157, 221, 224, 226, 227
Corporate Vision, 221
Culturescape, 5, 159

D

Data (information for vision), 33
Developing Economies, 228
Disciplined Thinking, 81
Disney, Walt, 16, 33, 38, 45, 92, 114, 116, 117, 192, 193, 203, 221
Distressed life, 102
doom loop, 22, 124, 165, 172, 173, 197
Doom Loop, 170, 174

E

Effective Interdependence, 195, 196
External Value Forces
 Negative External Value Force (NEVF), 89, 198
Extraordinary, 1, 3, 18, 19, 21, 33, 47, 90, 91, 120, 134, 138, 139, 145, 162, 166, 167, 170, 177, 183, 194, 213, 217
Extrinsic, 43, 44

F

Flywheel of Vision, IX, 1, 19, 20, 21, 22, 23, 24, 34, 62, 65, 139, 143, 146, 147, 150, 155, 157, 159, 161, 168, 170, 171, 172, 173, 174, 175, 176, 179, 183, 186, 189, 196, 197, 198, 201, 202, 220, 221
Fox, 133
Future-focused, 57

G

Genius, VIII, 2, 17, 124, 177, 187, 190, 249
Gravity, of Potential, 123

H

Habit, 39, 151, 163, 192
Hedgehog, 133, 134, 135, 136, 137, 141, 142, 159, 162, 179, 184
Hedgehog Concept, 21, 133, 134, 135, 137, 138, 139, 140, 142, 144, 145, 146, 147, 156, 157, 161, 163, 165, 176, 178, 181, 193, 221, 227
Helen Keller, 15, 33, 36, 45, 135, 140, 142, 169, 221
Humility, 4, 13, 34, 40, 67, 68, 85, 116, 117, 157, 162, 209, 210, 213, 214, 218

I

Ill-Conceived Vision
  Adolf Hitler, 64, 65, 70, 209
Institution, 211, 215
Interdependence, 195, 196
Intrinsic, 43
iPhone, 39, 46, 134

J

Japan, 10, 11, 15, 38, 110, 112, 113, 115, 169, 170, 203
Jim Collins, 106, 133, 138, 189, 191, 209, 210, 212, 214
Job, 25, 42, 43, 48, 94, 104, 123, 124, 126, 127, 128, 129, 137, 147, 160, 184, 188, 198, 211
Joseph, 169, 217

L

Legends, 15, 33, 34
  Legends, 15, 33, 34
Level 7 Leader, 68, 144, 162, 209, 210, 214, 215, 217, 218, 219, 220, 230

M

Martin Luther King Jr, 15, 17, 22, 26, 29, 33, 35, 45, 69, 77, 78, 88, 89, 92, 104, 105, 106, 114, 132, 142, 202, 216, 217, 220, 221, 226
Metacognition, 82
Model T, 15, 37, 38, 51, 132, 187
Mother Teresa, 15, 26, 33, 35, 45, 50, 51, 69, 78, 92, 106, 134, 136, 137, 140, 142, 143, 144, 156, 169, 172, 176, 178, 192, 193, 217, 220, 221
Moving to Opportunity (MTO) Research, 6, 75

N

Nelson Mandela, 11, 16, 33, 35, 45, 69, 78, 88, 184, 217, 220, 221, 226
Neuroplasticity, 93, 99, 100, 101

P

Paradigm Shift, 19, 80

Passion, 42, 144, 185, 186
Patience, 3, 4, 71, 126, 144, 152, 161, 168, 170, 183, 184, 185, 194, 199
Perception, 1, 70, 74, 75, 76, 77, 79, 160, 168
Persistence, 177, 185
Personal Management, 149, 150
Perspectives, 77
Phasal, Nature of Vision, VII, 66, 179, 201
Planning, 178, 179
Potential Energy, 169
Poverty, 6, 7, 25, 59, 75, 228, 231
Power of focus, 100
power of solitude, 82, 84, 112, 175
Pradigm Shift, 1, 4, 19, 22, 86, 98, 101, 106, 129, 176, 198
Principled Life, 101, 170
Principles and Practices, VI
Private Labour, VI, 21, 22, 28, 41, 65, 66, 67, 125, 152, 158, 168, 183, 185
Prosperity, 203, 204
Provision
  Pro-vision, 177, 201, 203, 204

Q

Quantum Mechanics, 99
Quantum Physics, 88, 89, 99
Quantum Theory, 88
Quantum Zeno Effect (QZE), 98

R

Reality Distortion Field, 62
Research(Data), IX, 1, 3, 15, 17, 33, 34, 57, 112, 214, 229
Rewiring Your Mind, 83, 84, 94, 95, 96

S

Significance, 4
Sixth Sense, 90
Sony, 11, 15, 29, 38, 46, 92, 106, 110, 111, 113, 118, 169, 170, 171, 221
South Africa, 12, 16, 35, 78, 184, 217, 221, 226
Steve Jobs, 16, 33, 39, 45, 78, 88, 92,

107, 112, 115, 117, 134, 140, 142, 156, 162, 164, 165, 186, 193, 203, 221
Stockdale Paradox, 189, 190, 191
Sustainable Growth, 43, 149, 151, 152, 153, 154, 166, 171, 196

World War II, 10, 15, 64, 110

T

The power of focus, 100
The Three Circles, 111, 123, 138, 139, 144, 145, 147, 163, 175, 178, 193, 200
The Vision Process, VI, 19, 167, 168
Three Circles, VI, 111, 138, 200
True Self, IX, 5, 20, 25, 50, 52, 71, 79, 82, 84, 85, 87, 91, 94, 95, 96, 98, 99, 103, 120, 143, 149, 155, 193, 194, 207, 222

V

Vision
    Attention Density (VAD), 20, 65, 98, 99, 103, 106, 114, 131, 175, 186, 200
    Defined, 56
    Mountaintop Analogy, 61
    Overcoming Crisis, 8
    Simplifies, 53
    versus Dreams, 12, 17, 18, 21, 119, 180, 199, 202, 241
    3D of, VII, 58, 59, 60, 155, 178
    Constrictionary Power of, 37, 50, 53, 65, 66, 67, 125, 158, 196, 199, 221, 224
    Exoansionary Power of, 27, 37, 53, 65, 67, 68, 107, 119, 156, 178, 196, 200, 201, 204, 221, 225

W

Wise Advocate, 56, 65, 82, 84, 88, 90, 95, 96, 100, 155
Work, 1, 2, 4, 10, 12, 15, 24, 26, 29, 30, 131, 135, 136, 137, 139, 142, 146, 147, 151, 154, 158, 159, 160, 165, 166, 171, 172, 175, 181, 182, 183, 184, 187, 188, 194, 200, 202, 204, 206, 207, 210, 213, 216, 219, 223, 225, 227